# MORE THAN LOVE

## AN INTIMATE PORTRAIT
## OF MY MOTHER,
## NATALIE WOOD

### NATASHA GREGSON WAGNER

SCRIBNER

New York   London   Toronto   Sydney   New Delhi

Scribner

An Imprint of Simon & Schuster, Inc.

1230 Avenue of the Americas

New York, NY 10020

First Scribner hardcover edition May 2020

SCRIBNER and design are registered trademarks of The Gale Group, Inc.,
used under license by Simon & Schuster, Inc., the publisher of this work.

For information about special discounts for bulk purchases,
please contact Simon & Schuster Special Sales at 1-866-506-1949
or business@simonandschuster.com.

The Simon & Schuster Speakers Bureau can bring authors to your live event.
For more information or to book an event, contact the Simon & Schuster Speakers Bureau
at 1-866-248-3049 or visit our website at www.simonspeakers.com.

Manufactured in the United States of America

1   3   5   7   9   10   8   6   4   2

Library of Congress Cataloging-in-Publication Data has been applied for.

ISBN 978-1-9821-1118-2
ISBN 978-1-9821-1120-5 (ebook)

*For Delia, who believed I had my own story to tell.*

*For Courtney, my intrepid sister, my comrade-in-arms.*

*For Clover, the golden glue, my dearest one.*

*For we think back through our mothers if we are women.*
— Virginia Woolf

*The world is violent and mercurial—it will have its way with you. We are saved only by love—love for each other and the love that we pour into the art we feel compelled to share: being a parent; being a writer; being a painter; being a friend. We live in a perpetually burning building, and what we must save from it, all the time, is love.*
— Tennessee Williams

# Prologue

## November 29, 1981

The voice from the clock radio is tinny and muffled.

"The body of actress Natalie Wood has been found off the coast of Catalina Island."

It is Sunday morning, and I'm sleeping over at my best friend Tracey's house. I am eleven years old.

The man on the radio repeats the words "body" and "Natalie Wood."

I am no longer asleep, but not yet awake; on the brink of awareness. If I keep my eyes shut, I think, the voice might be part of a dream, which means that if I open my eyes it might be real.

Now the man on the radio is saying "accident" and "drowned" and my eyes are open so this can't be a dream. But there has to be some horrible mistake. My mom and stepfather, Robert Wagner, whom I call Daddy, are out on their boat, safe and sound. My dad is the ship's captain, and my mom is the first mate. They spend weekends on the *Splendour* all the time.

I am snuggled in Tracey's spare single bed, the one her mom put in her room especially for me because I am such a frequent guest. Tracey's house, in the Bird Streets neighborhood of the Hollywood Hills, is my home away from home. Janis, Tracey's mother, is my mom away from my mom. How could anything bad happen to me here? Tracey has a brand-new wood-paneled clock radio. It must have gone off at seven by mistake because this isn't a school day.

I sit up. I need to call my mom. I go to the living room, but when I get there, the receiver is off the hook and I can't get a dial tone. I go

1

to find Janis and tell her I need her help. Together we try to call my mom on the boat, but we can't get through. I decide to call the house. Liz Applegate, my mom's assistant, picks up.

"Liz, what are you doing at my house on Sunday?"

"I'm just working today, lovey," she says in her familiar British accent.

Before I can ask her another question, I turn around and my nanny, Kilky, and my dad's driver, Stanley, have arrived to pick me up. I look at my sweet Kilky for answers, but her face seems frozen, like someone in a fairy tale turned to stone. I immediately know that something is very wrong. Outside, the ground feels cold and damp beneath my bare feet, wet from rain the night before. Why am I allowed to go outside without my shoes on? Wasn't I supposed to stay at Tracey's all weekend? I don't ask these questions. Instead, I climb into the back seat of my mom's cream-colored Mercedes. Stanley gets into the front seat. He never drives my mom's car, only my dad's. What is going on?

On the way home, thick blankets of clouds hang low in the sky. The world is dim and charcoal gray; everything is blurred around the edges, like a picture postcard submerged in a puddle. After the engine rumbles to silence, the car door opens. We go through the front gate. In the yard, the leaves from our birch tree are scattered on the ground.

The familiar wooden front door of our house clicks shut behind me, but I don't feel the usual safety and comfort of returning home. There are too many people here for a Sunday morning, especially since my parents are away. Liz is there. One of my godmothers, Delphine Mann. Our family friends the Benjamins.

Suddenly, Tracey's mom, Janis, is here too.

"What's going on?" I ask Liz and Janis.

"We don't know, lovey," Liz says. "We're not sure." They are grown-ups. Aren't they supposed to have the answers?

My dad is going to be home soon. Janis and I go upstairs and crawl into my mom's bed together to wait for him. The sheets and blankets smell of my mom's gardenia perfume, of my mother and her warm hugs and soft kisses. As I wrap myself in the familiar scent, Janis strokes my hair, comforting me. I have known and loved her since I was in kindergarten. She's the physical opposite of my brunette mother, with bleached blond hair, tan skin, and a low, soothing voice. We wonder aloud what happened, why the man on the radio made that awful announcement, saying those words that could not be true.

"Maybe she isn't dead. Maybe she just broke her leg," I say, trying to convince myself.

Janis agrees. Her voice is warm and gravelly. I snuggle into her embrace and pray to God that Mommie is okay.

How long do I spend upstairs with Janis? It might be thirty minutes or three hours. Then I hear the front door open and close quietly. I know it is my dad.

Down the carpeted stairs I step without a sound, still in my nightgown. I'm expecting to see my dad's familiar face, always smiling, with blue eyes that sparkle when he greets me or my mom or my sisters. But the man at the bottom of the stairs isn't smiling; his face is ashen and his eyes look pale, haunted, devoid of any light. He doesn't speak when he sees me and I know in a sudden horrifying flash that it's all true.

The floor seems to fall away beneath me. I drop into his arms and we cry together. My seven-year-old sister, Courtney, shuffles down the stairs in her nightie, sleepy-eyed and confused. He pulls her into our embrace.

"You're not going to see Mommy anymore," he says. "But I want you to know that I'm never going to leave you. We're still a family."

I close my eyes. This can't be real, I tell myself. Even as I hear myself weeping and crying out, "It's not fair!" I still can't believe it.

Minutes or hours pass, I can't tell. I open my eyes and the house is full of people. Outside the window, reporters, photographers, and TV cameramen perch at our front gate like a roost of crows.

She's gone. She's never coming home again. What's going to happen to me? To all of us?

I have no clear memory of the rest of the day. I'm sure I must have eaten and slept, but I don't know what I ate and I don't remember going to bed. I just remember that everything seemed different. Our house felt different. It smelled different. There was no safe place for me. I needed a hug from my mom. I needed to hear her voice, but she wasn't there.

A few weeks later, once the autopsy is complete, the coroner and the Los Angeles County Sheriff's Department conclude that my mother's death was a terrible accident, without any evidence of foul play. That she had gone down to the dinghy attached to our boat and then likely missed a step, slipping and falling into the water, her water-logged parka weighing her down so she couldn't hoist herself out. The case was closed.

Losing my mother was the defining moment of my life. No other event would ever again so sharply etch its mark upon my soul, or so completely color the way I navigate the world, or leave my heart quite as broken. We had shared only a little over a decade together, yet I missed her with such intensity that she remained on the cusp of my every thought, the echoes of her face reverberating back to me each time I looked in the mirror.

The following year, we moved out of the house in Beverly Hills. It was too sad to stay there any longer without her. My mom had decorated our home to the brim with carved wooden furniture and paintings, knickknacks, photos in silver frames. Everywhere I looked there was another object that led me back to her: the forest-green upright piano she practiced on when she was a little girl; the set of sterling-silver goblets that Spencer Tracy had given to her for her first wedding. After she died, all her belongings were boxed up and taken away, put in storage. My dad let Courtney and me pick out whatever we wanted to take with us to our new house in Brentwood. I chose a few framed photographs and pieces of her jewelry and art, precious mementoes that I would carry with me wherever I went in the world: away to college, to my first apartment, to each place I called home.

In the years after her death, I learned to protect myself from her memory, afraid I might be subsumed by it. Even with my therapist, whose office I sat in each week after my mom died, I feared that if I examined my mother's story too closely, it would overwhelm me. Would my rose-tinted view of her be shattered by some ugly truth she had hidden from me? Or would I simply be reminded of how perfectly wonderful she was, generating a fresh wave of devastation over losing her? The joy of loving and being loved by her had ended so abruptly and with such finality that even my happiest recollections of her were difficult for me to think about.

My mother was famous, which meant I also had to protect myself from other people's perceptions of her. Whenever a new biography or article came out about Natalie Wood, I ignored it. If authors sent me copies of their books about her, I mailed them right back. I was not interested in what a complete stranger thought about my mother's life; I only wanted to talk to people who actually knew my mom, her closest friends and confidants. People like my godfather, Mart Crowley, who kept every letter she wrote to him. "Darling, no one was stronger than your mother; she was the strongest of us all," he often reminds me. My mom's close friend Delphine told me that when my mother ordered her chopped salads at La Scala she always asked for "no garbanzo beans!" or if she was out to dinner and wanted to touch up her lipstick, she used a knife for a mirror. When you have famous parents there's so much noise, so many people trying to tell you who your parents *really* were, that you have to shut yourself off from the chatter. You block it out, relying on the close circle of people you trust and your own memories, of course.

If I stumbled on an article in a magazine about "The Tragic Life and Death of Natalie Wood" at the doctor's office, I would scan the piece to see if perhaps they had managed to get something right. Usually there was more that was wrong. The people who wrote the articles seemed to only want to portray my mother as someone who was

5

troubled and deeply depressed at times. Who was my mother? Was it possible I didn't really know her? Did she put on a cheerful act for her children and live a secret life of despair behind closed doors? The same tabloids have long been fixated on the night of her death and the so-called unsolved mystery of how she drowned. They continue to repeat the same stories, that my mother was allegedly having an affair with the actor Christopher Walken, who was also on the boat, that my dad was jealous, that she had fought with my father on the night she died, that somehow her death was the result of foul play.

Over the years, when I was asked to comment on my mother's life, I usually declined. I didn't want to speak to the press or give interviews about her. I knew people would only want to dwell on the negative or more sensational aspects of my mother's life and on her death. I didn't want to join the circus of speculation. I wanted to keep the mother I knew to myself.

It was only when I became a mom myself, at the age of forty-one, that I began to think about my mother's legacy in a new way. Might I play some part in telling her story? Soon after my daughter's birth, I agreed to help put together a book of photographs celebrating my mother. This meant I had to track down as many images of her as possible to fill the book's pages. It also meant having to pay a visit to her belongings, still boxed away safely in a storage unit in Glendale, California.

The skies over Los Angeles are impenetrable and white, wrapping the city in sticky heat as I drive over to the storage facility where my mother's possessions are housed. For decades, I've avoided coming to this place, reluctant to spend time rummaging around in the past. The only other time I've been here was in 1991, as a twenty-year-old, when I visited with my sister, Courtney, selecting a few pieces to keep for myself before fleeing, not wanting to be reminded of the pleasures of my childhood and the pain of my mother's absence.

This time around, I've decided to approach my trip to the storage unit as a job that needs to be done. I'm here to find photos. I park my car in the lot and make my way toward the building. The storage unit is a large, square, unremarkable concrete block. I walk up the ramp and check in at the front desk. The owner leads me along a corridor and to my mother's unit. He's known our family for years, as my mom's things have been kept here since the early 1980s. He's kindly, familiar, fatherly in his button-down oxford and khakis. He pushes the mechanism on the front of the giant door and it swings open, like one of those massive doors on a Hollywood soundstage. Appropriate, I think.

Inside, the temperature dips dramatically. The rooms here are kept chilled, to better preserve their contents. I look around me. I'm in a space about the size of a small bedroom, its walls lined with wooden shelves filled with boxes and books. My mother's publicity stills and movie posters are strewn across the walls in frames. The scent of old paper and cardboard boxes, of basements and attics, hangs in the air.

The owner anticipates that I might feel cold so he brings in a small space heater. Then he leaves, closing the giant door behind him. It clicks shut and the outside world is gone.

I'm here to do a job, I tell myself again. I'm looking for photos. I start pulling out scrapbooks and large leather albums from the shelves. Some of the albums have images inside them but others are filled with all the letters my mother kept, each one pasted carefully in place. My mom was a collector by nature. She saved every letter and card—and our family received many. In the days before texting, email, and social media, everyone mailed letters and thank-you notes. My parents sent vacation photos and postcards when they traveled, and had telegrams, flowers, and presents delivered on special occasions. Here are albums that contain every one of my report cards and birthday cards. I soon find the scrapbooks my grandmother put together, chronicling my mother's movie career. Inside are yellowed newspaper articles, color-saturated pages from long-lost publications like *Screenland* and *Movie Mirror*, transporting me back to the 1940s, when my mother's career as an actor began.

Both my parents loved making family memories and recording them, either in writing or with a camera. At home, photos and home movies filled albums, shelves, and boxes. The same is true of the storage unit. On one of the wooden shelves here I see the large velvet photo albums that I remember from my childhood. I open a page in the middle of the book. Here's a picture of Mommie and me bending down to pet a black goat. I have a knitted cap on my head. My mother crouches over me with a look of wonder and glee on her face, as if she too is seeing a goat for the first time. I remember this about her. Her childlike excitement in step with mine. Her hair is long and chestnut brown, parted in the middle, shining in the sun.

I flip to another page. We are on the cover of a magazine called *Lady's Circle*. The year is 1979. My mom wears a turquoise top and my dad's turquoise-and-silver necklace. She looks straight into the camera. Professional, poised. I stand behind her, my arm draped casually around her, my smile as big as can be. I look proud, safe, loved.

I make my way to the end of the book. My mother is standing in the garden of our home on Canon Drive. Her hair is curly, framing her most lovely face. She smiles; she's happy. I stand next to her with my arm around her waist. I wear a green-and-white-striped T-shirt. My hair is long and blondish brown—the same color hers was when she was my age. I am older here, probably ten. There is certainty in the smile on my face. The certainty that all is well.

I stay for hours, exploring the unit, forgetting my duties as a photo researcher. On the ground are stacks of silvery canisters filled with reels of film. Later I learn that many of these are filled with Super 8 movies of my childhood, the early years of her career, outtakes from the films in which she starred. A filing cabinet contains her datebooks starting in 1964 all the way to 1981, the year she died. Here are her bound movie scripts from films like *Rebel Without a Cause*, the movie she made with James Dean; *Gypsy*, in which she starred as Gypsy Rose Lee, with Rosalind Russell playing the ultimate stage mother Mama Rose; and *Love with the Proper Stranger*, her romantic comedy-drama with Steve McQueen. On the top shelves are her awards: her Golden Globes, her international film festival awards. In one corner, I discover a bronze bust of her friend James Dean, whom she always called Jimmy. At the back of the unit I find clear plastic containers filled with her hairpieces from her many movie roles—the small, chocolate-brown ponytail she wore in the movie adaptation of the Tennessee Williams play *This Property Is Condemned*; the gray, curly wig from the scene in the comedy caper *Penelope* when her character dresses up as an old lady to rob a bank; the pageboy wig from *Inside Daisy Clover*, one of my favorite movies of hers, in which she plays a tomboy misfit who makes it big in Hollywood—all her hairpieces yet none of her hair.

It's getting late. I really should leave. But as I'm getting ready to go, I notice a battered cardboard carton that looks like it's about to be thrown away. I open it, sifting through the unrelated papers and objects. I pull out a notebook and open it. I realize I am holding one of her journals in my hands. On the first page is a handwritten note, taped in place, that reads: "Two lonely stars with no place in the sun, found their orbit—each other, and then they were one." Underneath, my mother explained that this was the note that she had given to Robert Wagner, my stepfather, on the first anniversary of their falling in love, the same day they became engaged.

"I didn't dream it," I remember thinking to myself. "This was real. My mom, her love for my dad and for me, our house, our happiness, it all existed."

After that first visit, I made countless trips back to the storage unit. A regular pilgrimage of sorts. I entered the space, and, for a few hours, time stopped moving forward. My mother's belongings were so distinctly hers, radiating everything that I loved and missed about her. In some strange way, I felt as if she had been patiently waiting all those years, like Sleeping Beauty, for someone to come and awaken her memory. Had she been hoping for me to come and rediscover her?

During those hours in the unit, memories long ago pushed away surged to the front of my mind. There were moments when I found myself overcome by a sadness so all-consuming that I wondered if I had made a mistake ever coming here. Leaving the building, I would put on dark glasses to mask the hot tears brimming in my eyes. My car was usually parked close by. I knew as soon as I opened the door and slid into the driver's seat, I could let go and cry. What a relief that was. Glendale is about forty-five minutes from my home in Venice. Those emotional drives were part of my journey—my journey back to her.

I began to arrange the pieces of my mother's life, the stories of my childhood, the photos of our family, our home movies, the letters she saved, the datebooks where she recorded the details of our days. I made a gallery wall of sorts in my mind. These are the pieces that make me the person that I am.

# PART 1

# With

# Chapter 1

Natalie and Natasha at home
on North Bentley Avenue, 1971.

My first memory is an awareness of comfort and love, a feeling of being held in the cocoon of my mother's embrace. All is right with the world. I can see her face above me, her velvet brown eyes, doe-like, smiling down at me. Her dark hair falls in my face in soft waves as she bends down to kiss me. The unmistakable scent of her gardenia perfume. Her sweetly musical voice she uses just for me, "Hello, my little Natooshie, I love you," the sound of it sighing slightly upward. These are my earliest sensations.

My mother loved to sing, and I loved to listen. At night, when she tucked me into bed—or anytime I was tired or upset—she sang a lilting Russian lullaby called "Bayushki Bayu." Later, I learned the song was about a wolf that comes in the night and drags little babies out of their beds and into the forest. My mom's parents were Russian immigrants and she had grown up hearing the language all around her. She could speak it a little, although not fluently, but when she sang to me, the sounds seemed to come to her naturally. Other times, when we were driving in the car, she sang "Frère Jacques" or "My Favorite Things" or a silly song called "Fried Ham."

When I picture my mother during the days of my childhood, she isn't dressed up for a party or working on a movie set. She's at home, in her favorite white cotton nightgown with the pink or blue rosettes, or wearing soft, gauzy dresses in Indian printed fabrics, or down by the pool with a caftan thrown over her bikini. Her skin is tawny and lightly freckled. Her hair is tied back. She rarely wore much makeup, maybe a dab of gloss on her lips. If people came over, she would do her eyes, but even then, makeup wasn't a form of armor, just a natural extension of her routine, like brushing her teeth or putting on her perfume.

Her hands were pale and slender, with long, delicate fingers that always glinted with a fresh French-tip manicure. Mommie not only spoke with her hands, fluttering them like butterflies to express her meaning and mood, but she was forever touching me with a loving caress. If we were in the same room, her smooth hands would be stroking my forehead, playing with my hair, brushing gently against my face. Ruby and sapphire rings adorned her fingers like Christmas tree lights, her gold bangles and charm bracelets tinkling as she moved.

On her left wrist she wore a larger gold or silver bracelet, more like a cuff, to camouflage an injury she'd gotten as a child while working on the film *The Green Promise*. I knew that my mom had been working as an actress since she was a little girl and that in one of her movies, she had to run across a wooden footbridge that was supposed to collapse when she got to the other side. Instead, the bridge caved in too early, while my mom was still on it, and she broke her wrist. The bone had never been set properly and so she wore the cuff on that arm. "I have this horrible bump on my wrist and I like to keep it covered," she used to say. I never thought the bump was that terrible. I liked it. It was part of her.

My mother named me Natasha. Before Hollywood renamed her Natalie Wood, she had been Natasha Gurdin. She was Big Natasha, and I was Little Natasha. *We* were Natasha. She was Mommie and I was her "Natooshie." She also called me "Natashinka," or her pet name for me, her "petunia."

For as long as I can remember, people told me I took after her.

"You look just like your mother when she was a little girl," friends and even strangers said.

"Natasha, you're just like me," my mom repeated, taking my face in her hands, smiling.

We did closely resemble each other, especially as children. Aside from a few slight differences—her eyes were larger, while mine were more almond-shaped—we were both petite, elfin brunettes with the same turned-up nose, tall forehead (although mine was taller than hers), and high cheekbones.

The first time I saw my mother in a movie was a TV broadcast of *Miracle on 34th Street* one Christmas. I was about four or five. I remember sitting cross-legged in front of the screen while my mom stood behind me buzzing with proud excitement, watching me watching her on TV. In the film, she played Susan Walker, a little girl who doesn't believe in Santa Claus, even when she meets him. After each scene, my grown-up mom looked at me expectantly, to see how I was reacting. Was I smiling? Was I laughing? Was I scared? "That's me when I was your age," she told me. "See how much you look like me?" This little black-and-white girl shooting skeptical looks at Santa Claus *did* resemble me. I remember getting up and walking behind the television set to see how she managed to get in there. Was the girl on the TV me or was she my mother? Once Mommie explained it to me, I tried to hold these strange slivers of conflicting information together in my mind. *This is Mommie when she was little, thirty years ago. She looks more like me than Mommie, but it's not me. It's her.*

Besides our looks, we mirrored each other in temperament. We were both readers who loved to curl up with a book. My mother had gotten hooked on books as a child when she was working on movie sets. For her, reading was a way to refresh herself in between scenes and setups. As soon as I learned to read, books became my reset button as well. If a lot of people were at our house or a play-date had lasted too long, I took myself up to my room and crawled into bed with my book. Other times, Mommie would read to me as I sat in her lap: Russian fairy tales, Caldecott's fairy tales, *Winnie-the-Pooh*, *The Wizard of Oz*, stories by Dr. Seuss, or one of my favorites, *Rapunzel*, the tale of the beautiful princess locked in a high tower. She once gave me a copy of her favorite book, *The Little Prince*, by Antoine de Saint-Exupéry, inscribing it with a beloved, often quoted line from the book: "Dear Natasha, remember: 'It is only with the heart that one can see rightly. What is essential is invisible to the eye.'"

We both loved to bathe, the feeling of the water and bubbles on our skin, the wrapping up of ourselves in soft towels afterward. I was always welcome to come into her bathroom when she was in the tub, to ask her a question or try to make her laugh. Mommie would be lying there, bubbles up to her neck, as she read a book or talked on the phone, the long, curly telephone cord resting on the frothy soap-suds. She loved telephones and we had one in almost every room. The phones seemed to like my mother too because they were always ringing, and she was forever talking and laughing into a receiver. She had the most delightfully uninhibited mix of a giggle and a guffaw that could be heard throughout the house, impossible to avoid and completely infectious.

We were both fond of order, tidiness, structure. As a child, I actually enjoyed straightening up my room. I would observe my mother fussing with the heights of books in our bookshelves, repositioning them so they stood more aligned, and then I would imitate her in my bedroom, lining up all my stuffed animals and porcelain dolls in a row on my bed and bookshelves, arranging them from highest to lowest.

We looked so much alike and had so much in common. Where did the mother end and the child begin? We were so completely connected—and she was so sharp and perceptive—that I sometimes believed she could see right into my mind. She could anticipate my needs, those times when I was on the verge of a tantrum or melt-down, and would take me for a rest or sing me a song. Sometimes all it took was a hug from her and I would feel calm again.

I was born at Cedars of Lebanon in Hollywood on September 29, 1970. It was a Tuesday. That day, my mother wrote in her small spiral-bound datebook, where she recorded all the details of her daily life: "Natasha born 9:11 p.m. 6lb. 8 ounces." It was an easy labor. Only six hours, then one push and out I came. Later she wrote in a letter to my godmother, the actress Norma Crane, that I had my father Richard Gregson's legs and dimple, and a combination of both of their noses: "A small, tender toughie." In a photo of my mother leaving the hospital a couple days after my birth, she is a vision of beauty—beaming, her famously expressive eyes painted to perfection, holding me in her lap in the front seat of my British dad's brown Mercedes. No car seat or seat belt back then to keep me safe, just my mother's loving arms. My father once told me that during the first few months of my life, my mother hardly ever put me down. "You two adored each other," he recalled. "She was like a panther, ready to spring if anyone said anything about you which she didn't like."

I know about these early months of my life because my mother captured every detail in my baby book, which was bound with the same smooth ivory cover and embossed with the same gold lettering as the binding on her film scripts. She called it *Natasha's Book*. My baby book reports that my first distinct words were "ha ha." After that, I began adding new words to my vocabulary: "Mama" and "good girl."

My parents separated when I was eleven months old. I don't have any memories from the time they were together, and perhaps as a result, I have always had a hard time picturing them as a couple. My father was an Englishman, reserved and levelheaded. My mother was the complete opposite, all feeling and passion. In hindsight, their separation seems inevitable. At the time, it must have been devastating for both of them.

My parents met in LA in the mid-1960s, at a dinner party given by a PR company. My mother was at the height of her fame, having already starred in some of her most iconic adult roles, as Deanie Loomis in *Splendor in the Grass*, Maria in the movie version of the musical *West Side Story*, and Gypsy Rose Lee in *Gypsy*. She had three Academy Award nominations to her name. She was a sharp conversationalist, and she could be a little intimidating. My dad was "an English top dog," as he put it, a well-dressed, elegant man with almond-shaped hazel eyes and prematurely gray hair. Born in India and raised in England, he was evacuated during the war and sent to boarding school in Canada. He began his career in London, working for a literary agency in the film and TV rights department and later established himself as a Hollywood agent. I'm sure my mother was drawn to his intelligence and charm, as well as his confidence. He was interested but didn't fawn over her. That evening, she was smoking a menthol cigarette through a long, black plastic holder. "A woman of your beauty and style and distinction should have a jade holder," he said. "I'll buy you one." And that's how it started.

Soon they were spending all their time together, going to parties and to the Daisy nightclub in Beverly Hills. He repeatedly said, "Let's get married," and she repeatedly said, "No." She was reluctant to rush into a commitment. My father had already been married once and had three children, Sarah, Charlotte, and Hugo, with his first wife, Sally. My mother was drawn to all three of his kids, relishing the potential role of stepmother. Finally, she went to visit him on the set of the movie *Downhill Racer* in Wengen, Switzerland. Richard was producing the film for his client and friend Robert Redford, who was shooting his scenes on the slopes. On a day off from filming, my parents went skiing and my mother had a fall, fracturing a bone in her leg. She was back at the hotel, elevating her plaster-encased leg and resting in bed, when she said she wanted to have a talk with my dad. Something (other than a cracked bone) must have shifted for her.

"How come you never ask me to marry you anymore?" she said.

"Because you always say no," he replied.

"Ask me again and I'll say yes."

They got married at the Holy Virgin Mary Russian Orthodox Cathedral in Los Angeles on May 30, 1969. Robert Redford was best man. Edith Head designed my mother's white-and-pale-yellow silk gown, basing it on a dress worn by an eighteenth-century Russian princess. My mother wore a white-and-yellow flower-decorated tiara with ribbons flowing in her hair. At the time, she was more than ready to settle down and become a parent. Her movie *Bob & Carol & Ted & Alice* had become one of the highest-grossing films of 1969. She had points in the movie (in other words, she got a percentage of the film's gross income), and had made a lot of money as a result. The following year it was nominated for four Academy Awards. She was in a good place to put her career on hold and focus on starting a family.

According to my father, I was conceived in the Oscar Wilde Suite at L'Hotel in Paris on New Year's Eve 1969–70. Who knows if that is true, but soon after, my mom discovered she was pregnant and the Gregsons settled down in a white brick house my mother owned on North Bentley Avenue in Bel-Air. My dad would tell me she repeatedly stated during her pregnancy, "I'm having a girl and her name is Natasha," even though there was no sonogram or ultrasound technology in those days. Somehow she knew. She didn't give me a middle name. I later asked her why. She told me, "I thought Natasha was such a beautiful name, it stood on its own."

After I was born, right away, my parents clashed over their differing styles of parenting. My dad's wealthy British mother had been remote and non-maternal, the polar opposite of how my mother had been raised. Her Russian mother—my grandmother Maria—loved

19

her daughter with a passionate sense of eternal devotion, and Mommie lavished me with the exact same degree of focus and attention. My mother had gone through a difficult transition to adulthood. She had been a working actor since the age of six, cosseted and accompanied everywhere by her mother, who also served as her manager. Growing up in a world of Hollywood fantasy and illusion, where she was adored, not just by her overprotective mom, but by the millions of Americans who were her fans, it was hard for my mother to figure out who she wanted to be. Everyone has to figure out their identity as they shift from childhood into the adult years, but my mother had to do it while watched by gossip magazines, studio heads, her adoring fans, and her parents, who monitored her every move.

In her early twenties, she started seeing a therapist and began her long journey to discovering who she was, independent of the image she projected on the movie screen. It wasn't easy. My father later confessed to me that, early in their marriage, he didn't understand my mom's moods, those times when rages and nameless fears would apparently consume her. He also derided her dependence on psychoanalysis. "At that time, the English thought LA brain scrapers were a joke," he explained. By the time I knew her, my mother had benefited from a lot more therapy and from a stable marriage. To me, she never seemed anything less than wholly secure, a woman who knew who she was and what she wanted.

But it was different in those early days of my life. Even during the pregnancy, her love for me had bordered on obsessive, and she shut out her husband so much that he later joked, "It was as if the Immaculate Conception had come to Hollywood." Every ounce of the dedication she had previously reserved for her acting career she now aimed at the life growing inside of her. My dad felt pushed aside and irrelevant. Once I was born, I took over completely as the main object of her affection. My father dealt with feeling neglected by starting an affair with my mother's secretary. My dad was by nature a stable, family-oriented kind of guy. If my parents hadn't gotten married at the height of the sexual revolution—when having a fling was all the rage—I find it difficult to imagine that he would have cheated on my mother so blatantly. But that's exactly what he did. My mom was apoplectic when she found out. She kicked my dad out of the Bentley house, then she called her beloved older sister, Olga, and her best friend Mart Crowley and asked them both to come with us to Europe. We left on the SS *Raffaello* ocean liner. Mart recalls the trip as "a nightmare." He says my mother was painfully thin. She was so distraught she wasn't eating enough, and he was concerned for her health. They docked in Naples and flew to the island of Sardinia. Here, she spent a lot of time resting and recovering, while Mart and Olga took care of me.

After we returned home to America, my mother and I went to live in the house on North Bentley Avenue in Bel Air. Only one week after we returned from Sardinia, she threw my first birthday party in the backyard. In her datebook, she scribbled the names of the five little friends who attended my party from noon to 3:30 p.m. Daddy visited me at 4 p.m. For the first several months after she left my father, she allowed him brief visits but kept him on the outskirts of our world. She even kept her parents at a distance. She was my only caretaker for a while, and she had no intention of sharing me.

That soon changed. Robert John Wagner (always known to my mom as R.J.) came into my life when I was a little more than a year old and stayed there. By seventeen months, my baby book states, my favorite new word was "R.J." He was also my favorite new person. Apparently I was constantly saying "R.J." and kissing his photograph. I don't remember this. As far as I recall, I have always called him Daddy. Considering how close my mother and I were, I could have easily resented him as an intruder in our world, and yet I never felt that for an instant. His presence made my mom so happy.

To me, he was this sun-kissed man who seemed to radiate warmth. I remember he wore a gold chain around his neck and a gold ID bracelet on his wrist. When he held me, I jingled his chains, and he laughed. In photographs from that time, he's dressed in denim shirts, silk ascots, flared slacks, or a denim shirt and shorts, and always the gold chains. In 1973, my mom told a reporter about our relationship: "That little girl and that man adore each other so that if I didn't love them both so much, I think I'd be jealous!" R.J. became a real father to me, treating me just like his own daughter. I soon began to take it for granted that I had not one but two loving dads and I even came up with names for each of them. Daddy Gregson, who had moved back to England, and Daddy Wagner, who lived with us in California and was the constant caring presence in my daily life. It would be some years before I realized that not everyone had the luxury of two fathers.

When I was still a toddler, we moved to Palm Springs, where R.J. owned a stone-covered house in the Mesa neighborhood up in the foothills. I was still so young, but I have the impression of wide-open spaces, mountain views, and palm trees swaying above me. My mother brought her two Australian shepherd dogs along with us. Their names were Penny and Cricket and they were large shaggy creatures with light eyes; they looked like stuffed animals come to life. As a little girl, I couldn't get enough of them.

She also brought her parents, my grandparents, Maria and Nick Gurdin. My mother had nicknames for everyone she loved and so she called them Mud and Fahd, short for "Muddah" and "Faddah." To me, my grandmother was always "Baba," short for Babushka, and my grandfather "Deda," short for Dedushka, the Russian words for grandmother and grandfather.

Baba and Deda were often at our house, my grandmother taking care of me when my mom was working or out with my dad. I didn't like it when Mommie was away from me. I wanted to always be close to her. During this time, she took a role in the TV movie *The Affair* alongside my dad. Whenever she was away on set, there was my grandmother in the long purple dresses she always wore, making me food, tucking me into bed, attending to my every need. I remember once my grandmother switched on the TV because my parents were appearing on a talk show together. When I saw them there, tiny and trapped in a box, I was so upset, I became inconsolable. I couldn't understand how they had gotten in there. Baba had to turn off the television set so I would finally calm down.

In one of my earliest memories of my grandmother, I must have been around three years old, and we are in the sun-drenched kitchen of our Palm Springs house. She is making something. She pulls bottles out of the fridge, empties them into a bowl, and with a sharp twist of the whisk, froths the liquid, then pours it into glasses for the two of us. The drink is slightly sour with a hint of sweetness. I sort of like it, but I want to like it more because I want to like what she likes. Later my mom chastises my grandma for giving me beer.

"But, Natalie, I mix with milk," my grandmother protests in her strong Russian accent. "Makes Natasha's bones grow strong. You drank when you were little!"

There were always these squabbles, with me caught in the middle. In Palm Springs, I remember we had a swimming pool in the backyard. My mother loved hanging out by the pool. She was not a strong swimmer, and she wanted her daughter to be comfortable and confident in the water. I soon grew to love splashing around in the shallow end, and even holding my breath and sinking to the bottom to fetch my plastic Pokey horse. One day, my grandfather Deda decided to teach me how to swim.

"Come to Deda, Natashinka," he told me. "I want to give you a hug." I jumped in his arms. Next, I remember the fleeting feeling of security as he held me, and then, without warning, he dropped me in the deep end. I was plunged underwater and terrified. I think perhaps this was his old-world Russian way of toughening me up. He meant no harm. But Mommie was furious. She jumped in after me, carrying me to safety and calming my fears. As soon as I was on dry land, my mom flashed those intense brown eyes at her father.

"How dare you throw my baby in the pool," she said. "Get out of my house."

Before long Deda was forgiven, and my grandparents were invited back again, Baba always staying with me if my parents needed to go out for the evening.

When I turned three and a half, it was decided that I was ready for preschool. Each morning my mother dropped me at the door of the Leisure Loft, a small local nursery school. After she left, I missed her desperately. *Why can't Mommie stay with me?* I wondered. "Natasha started preschool," my mom wrote in my baby book. "She wants mother there ALL THE TIME!" It wasn't only at preschool that I missed her. At night I didn't want to sleep in my own bedroom. I'd often tiptoe through to my parents' room so I could snuggle under the covers with them. My mother had to slowly train me to stay in my own bed.

Oftentimes, when she was out during the day, I'd wait for her, longing to hear our front door creak open, followed by her sweet, familiar voice rising up through the rafters. Her tone lifted an octave when she called out, "Natooshie, Mommie's home! Where are you?"

I dropped whatever I was doing and raced down the stairs to meet her, her arms and her fragrance enveloping me as I hugged her, clinging so tightly that she used to laugh and say, "You're trying to kill me!" I just could never get enough of her. To me, our whole house lit up when Mommie walked inside.

My mother was my mirror. When I saw myself reflected in her, it was a self that was bigger and better and brighter. If I ever doubted myself, she was there to fill me with confidence. *I am just like her, and she's okay. So I must be okay.*

It also worked the other way around. I knew that I was my mom's mirror too. If I was okay, then *she* was okay. Any uncomfortable feelings of my own created discomfort in my mom and I knew that.

In one of my earliest memories, I'm with my godfather, Mart, who is feeding me noodles. My mother is in another room. Somehow, I understand that my mom is feeling sad, which is why she can't feed me herself. I am spitting the noodles out, enjoying the way they slip through my front teeth. Mart is trying to be patient but I hear the frustration in his voice. I am caught between enjoying the feeling of the slippy noodles and the awareness that someone I like is showing signs of becoming exasperated with me. Where is my mother? I want her to come back in the room. She will not find my noodle-slurping game to be irritating. She will laugh and talk to me in her adoring "just for Natooshie, my little petunia" tone.

But I don't cry. I know I need to be a happy girl so my mom can be happy too. My success ensures her success. We are like the sweet peas tangled on a fence in the backyard, entwined.

# Chapter 2

R.J. and Natalie, with baby Natasha,
on the *Ramblin' Rose*, on their second
wedding day, July 16, 1972.

In the early spring of 1974, life was blooming anew. Roses and gardenias were budding in our Palm Springs backyard, our dog Penny gave
birth to a litter of puppies, and my mom went away to the hospital
and emerged with a baby.

There's a home movie of me kissing her pregnant belly, so I'm sure
my mom must have explained her pregnancy to me, but I was too
young to understand and I don't have any memories of that time.

What I do vividly recall is the shock of suddenly seeing my mom arrive at our house in Palm Springs in an ambulance.

I was allowed to climb up into the ambulance to see her. She was resting on a stretcher and clutching a tiny swaddled bundle close to her chest.

"Natooshie, this is your new sister, Courtney, and she's brought you a present," my mother announced. I liked presents, but I was suspicious. What was the catch? I unwrapped the package tied up with a ribbon. Inside was a pretty new doll.

"Would you like to hold Courtney?" Mommie asked in a lullaby voice. "She looks so much like you!"

I peeked into the fuzzy blanketed bundle and saw a little sleeping face that looked more like Daddy Wagner to me. *Who is this person in my mother's arms? I'm supposed to be the only one in my mother's arms!*

I hoped we could work out a bargain. Could I keep my doll but send the baby back?

It soon dawned on me that, unlike Penny's puppies—which we gave away to good homes—Courtney was here to stay.

Now that my parents had two children, they decided to move back to town and settle down in Beverly Hills. We rented a house there while my mom shot the comedy *Peeper* with Michael Caine, and then a place in Malibu, before moving into a house on North Canon Drive. My stepsister Katie—Daddy Wagner's daughter from his prior marriage who was six years older than me—lived nearby with her mother and so could easily come to visit us.

Our new white Cape Cod–style two-story house was in the heart of Beverly Hills. Designed by the architect Gerard Colcord, it had dark blue shutters framing the windows and a tall sycamore tree shading the wide, flat front yard with its low picket fence. In the back was an oval pool with turquoise tile. Boughs of bright pink bougainvillea dangled over potted pansies, geraniums, and hibiscus flowers. In the fall, the lemons would ripen from green to yellow on our lemon tree. Bees, butterflies, and hummingbirds hovered year-round.

The house itself was large but not showy. My mom was very

involved in the decor. Decorating was not just her favorite hobby; she even ran her own freelance interior design business for a few years—Natalie Wood Interiors—decorating houses for her clients, who were mainly her friends. My mother loved to make statements with bold patterns and colors, particularly her favorite, blue. There was floral-patterned wallpaper covering nearly every wall: blue laurel wallpaper in my parents' bedroom, a pink-and-green rose pattern in my bedroom, and a motif of red, green, orange, and purple lilies in the hallway. It was as if she wanted to bring her favorite season, spring, inside. She loved when everything was blooming in the garden, and would often be outside, cutting roses and her favorite fragrant white gardenias to arrange in silver vases around the house.

I remember fireplaces in almost every room, with a picturesque, hand-carved marble fireplace in my parents' bedroom. Heavy dark wood pieces sat alongside wicker furniture and big, upholstered chairs and sofas. Photos of family and friends in silver frames dotted shelves and long tables; on the walls hung framed Chinese needlepoint and works of art. Everything had a connection to someone famous or admired, or to a relative or friend. A Marcel Vertès painting of a ballerina hung in the living room, given to my parents by Jack Warner, my mom's boss back in her Warner Bros. contract days. Our long travertine coffee table had once been owned by Marion Davies. She had been a famous movie star my dad remembered fondly from his childhood. The word that comes to mind when I think of this time is "bountiful."

For my mother, having children was a do-over, a chance to raise us in a way she wished she had been raised, to give her daughters the childhood that she had missed. My mother had been working as a professional actress since she was six. She was a wunderkind, balancing her acting work with public appearances, school, ballet, piano lessons, Girl Scouts, and horseback riding. She was also the breadwinner for her family, supporting her parents and her sisters from a very young age. She didn't stop working her entire childhood. She couldn't. The prosperity of her family depended on it.

"I never got to have a real childhood," she used to say, her voice sounding a little sad. "I grew up on studio soundstages." Or, "I learned how to decorate my home from the sets on my movies." She used to say she could concentrate on schoolwork only when someone was banging a hammer because she was so accustomed to studying on noisy, bustling movie sets.

The childhood she created for us at the house on Canon Drive was very different. Our home was alive with animals and close friends and family, yet our bedtimes were enforced, we went to regular school, and we kept regular hours. Dinner was on the table at six, and no ifs, ands, or buts, we took showers every night. Above all, we were given time to play and to simply be young, roaming the gardens, lost in our games.

As well as dogs, we had cats, guinea pigs, mice, and birds we kept in shiny cages in the small kitchen adjacent to our playroom. The animals were always having babies, and so then there would be puppies, kittens, and baby guinea pigs as well as tiny mice that appeared one morning in the mouse cage after the mommy mouse escaped and somehow located a daddy mouse. My mother was a true animal lover. She often favored the ugly ones, like the small black Labrador–Jack Russell mix with rotten teeth and bad breath that she adopted from Dr. Shipp's Animal Hospital. We called him "Siggy," but his full name was Sigmund, after Freud himself. "I'm naming him Sigmund Freud," my mom joked, "because everybody needs a good shrink in the house."

She had a special way of communing with animals. When one of our cats, Maggie or Louise, would saunter by, I would grab at them, holding them awkwardly. They would inevitably wriggle out of my arms, leaving a small scratch or two as they pulled away from my grasp. My mother seemed to know how to pick them up so they were soothed and still, rocking them like babies and talking to them in her most delicate voice. The cats would relax immediately, folding themselves into her embrace, purring contentedly. "How does she *do* that?" I asked myself.

One day she was in the playroom holding Courtney's white cockatiel on her finger. I had friends over and we were sitting quietly on the floor, marveling at how the bird stayed there, perched on her extended finger as if drawn to her magnetically. "Hello, beautiful bird," she cooed in a voice as light as air, stroking the bird gently as we all watched, enraptured. Out of nowhere, our black-and-white cat, Maggie, swooped into the room, leaped toward my mom's hand, and ate the cockatiel in one swallow! A few white feathers in the air were all that remained. We were completely stunned. My mom's expression was a cross between wonder, shock, and respect for Maggie's feline abilities. "R.J.!" she called. "Maggie the cat just ate Courtney's bird!" My friends and I sat openmouthed, not knowing whether to cry or laugh.

My mother was stricter than people might imagine a movie-star parent would be with her daughters. Our home atmosphere was casual, but always within the parameters of certain expectations. We knew we had to be polite at all times, be respectful, be well turned out, and stick to the schedule. At home we were not allowed to eat sugary cereals for breakfast or to play when we had homework to do. Our TV watching was monitored. We were taught to always say "please" and "thank you," and to send thank-you notes for every gift we received. Back then I thought my mother was overly bossy. There was one recurring verbal exchange we had more than any other.

"How come I always have to do what you tell me?"

"Well, I'm the mommy," she would say. "When you're the mommy, you can make the rules, but I'm the mommy now, so I get to make the rules."

That always put an end to the conversation.

Being well groomed and looking our best was also considered important. On special occasions, Courtney and I would be taken to buy velvet or lace dresses from a children's boutique in Beverly Hills, and Mommie curled our hair with her hot rollers. I remember standing in her bathroom as she put the big, heavy plastic rollers in our straight, baby-fine hair, expertly securing them with long, silver pins. Once we had five or six rollers in our hair we were free to play for ten or fifteen minutes. Inevitably, one or two would slide out and we'd return to my mom's bathroom so she could put the roller back on the warming stick and redo the curl.

During these early years of my childhood, my mother worked very little as an actress and mostly stayed home with us. By the time she became pregnant with me, she was thirty-two years old and had been working steadily as an actress for twenty-six years, paying her dues and making her eligible for her pension. Although she took on a couple of projects after I was born, she made a conscious choice to spend time simply raising her family.

In the hot summer months we splashed in the pool, playing Marco Polo, having swim races, and diving for objects at the bottom, my dad shirtless in his swim trunks, golden chains dangling around his neck, my mom wearing a block-printed Indian dress over her bathing suit, her hair in two pigtails, usually held together with colorful elastic pom-poms. She'd sit on a lounge chair and watch my dad and Katie dive off the diving board or do backflips into the pool. Or she'd be in and out of the shallow end with me and Courtney, water wings firmly wrapped around our skinny arms, guiding and encouraging us through the water. At lunchtime, the kids ate grilled cheese sandwiches or bowls of Campbell's cream of celery soup sitting on the warm redbrick ground while our parents and their friends lunched nearby under the shady sycamores.

Soon after Courtney was born, my parents hired a woman named Willie Mae Worthen to cook for us. Mommie and Daddy Wagner were great at many things, but cooking was not one of them. Their idea of food preparation was snacking on shredded wheat or All-Bran cereal with raw sugar and half-and-half on top, making BLT sandwiches, or heating up their favorite canned soups. My dad's specialty was something called "Salisbury corn skillet," which was basically beef patties with canned corn on top. Willie Mae was from Atlanta, Georgia, and she made us succotash, chicken potpie, sweet potatoes, and green beans. When my British dad came to visit, he taught her how to make my favorite shepherd's pie; she made it her own by adding corn and Worcestershire sauce. Willie Mae was tall and lean, with the softest skin and biggest laugh—rivaling even my mom's. We fell for her so completely that my mom asked her to be our nanny and she soon became a beloved fixture in our family. When my Russian grandmother first met Willie Mae, she unwittingly rechristened her by mispronouncing her name "Vilka Maka" with her thick Russian accent. Katie, who was nine at the time, morphed her Russian pronunciation into "Kilky," and somehow it stuck. To Courtney, Katie, my parents, and me, Willie Mae was known as Kilky.

Even though we had Kilky to help take care of us, my mother was the one who drove me to my new preschool, the Sunshine Nursery School, in Brentwood. I was almost four by then, but once again, I hated being away from my mom; I missed her so acutely, with such a sharp pang, that I could barely make it through a minute before the tears would well up and I'd start crying. My mother consulted her therapist, who told her to give me something of hers so I could hold on to it while she was away. She decided to give me her Cartier Panthère watch, if you can believe it. When it was time for her to leave, she put the beautiful watch in my hand, looked me straight in the eye, and told me, "Natasha, I promise I will be back to pick you up when the big hand is on the twelve and the little hand is on the twelve." Her voice was strong and direct and let me know that we were in this thing together. I held on to her watch for a week or so before I was ready to spend those few hours at preschool without her.

Another time, she made a deal with me. "If you can stay at school the whole day without crying once, I'll buy you a present."

She asked what I wanted.

"I want a blue talking dog," was my response. She couldn't quite make this happen, but she came awfully close, buying me a stuffed dog that talked when I pulled its string to reward my next tear-free school day.

Once, I fell off the jungle gym at preschool and cut a gash just above my eyelid. I remember hitting the ground—boom—my mouth full of dirt, then warm liquid trailing down my face that tasted like metal. When I saw the adults around me looking nervous, I started to cry. The school called my parents, who rushed me to a doctor. My next memory is of both my parents standing over me in a doctor's office, each holding one arm. I see my dad looking at me and then looking at my mom. His gaze is steady and his eyes are telling her, "Stay calm, Natalie, Natasha needs you to keep it together, Natasha is going to be fine, keep it together, Nat." She keeps it together while the doctor takes the gleaming needle out and sews up the skin above my eyelid, pulling the thread through and through. I am awake but sort of lulled; my mom is awake but not at all calm. If she cries, I cry, if she panics, I panic. I remember receiving a clear message: my happiness is her happiness. If I'm sad, she's sad. The world is dangerous, especially if Mommie isn't there. If she's here, I'm safe.

At age five, I started kindergarten at the Curtis School. Both my mom and I were worried about how this separation would go. Luckily I locked eyes with another skinny little five-year-old named Tracey, and we soon became inseparable. She was my surrogate safety blanket when my mom left. Just a glimpse of her blond curls and grin let me know I was going to be okay.

Meanwhile, my sister Courtney was quickly growing from a swaddled baby into a small blond bulldozer. When she was three, she wore a T-shirt with "Here Comes Trouble" printed across the chest. I felt this was an accurate description. Later we became incredibly close, but in those days, she seemed hell-bent on destroying everything that was mine. If I were quietly playing with Barbie dolls in my bedroom, she barged in without knocking, breaking all the furniture in Barbie's DreamHouse before rolling out again. Though she was more than three years younger than me, she was the bully and I was her victim. I lived in fear of her. Her favorite means of domination was hair pulling. Her fingers were like the jaws of a pit bull. "Oooow! Mommie! Kilky! Courtney's pulling my hair!"

At the sound of my cries, Kilky came running. She was physically stronger than my mom, so it was usually her job to pry Courtney's hand open. In my sister's palm would be a clump of my hair. "Courtney," Kilky would say in a serious tone of voice, "you leave Tasha alone." Sometimes my mom would gently intervene. "Courtney, sweet pea, come with me. I want to show you something in my bedroom. . . ."

It got to the point where, whenever I saw my sister coming, I'd yell, "Get out of my room! Get out now or I'm going to tell!" Before Mommie or Kilky could get there, Courtney had already bitten the nose off my beloved stuffed snoopy, Jennifer, or kicked my wooden dollhouse to the floor.

My stepsister Katie posed a different kind of problem. With her strawberry-blond hair cut into a shag and freckles across her fair skin, Katie seemed exotic, untouchable to me. She was older and lived with her mom and two brothers in an apartment and dressed like a boy in rock T-shirts and bell-bottoms, while I was always in dresses. To her, I was a mama's girl, a Goody Two-shoes, something of a Beverly Hills princess. As with Courtney, I would later grow to love her completely. But back then, I think I saw Katie as more Courtney's sister than mine. They shared the same father by birth, whereas Katie and I were not technically blood relatives. While I stuck close to my mom, Katie stuck close to her father and Courtney. She took it upon herself to act as Courtney's protector, always siding with her in arguments and making me feel outnumbered. My mother took her role as stepmother to Katie very seriously. She went with Katie to her very first appointment with the gynecologist, they shopped together to pick out furniture for her room at our house, she let Katie drive her little Mercedes when Katie first got her driver's license. Despite our different biological mothers and fathers, my mother made sure her three daughters knew that we were a family.

• • •

My parents had this saying, "I love you more than love." To me it meant they loved each other more than any other parents loved each other. But I think what they meant by it was that the way they felt about each other was bigger than any word they could come up with. They had started saying it when they first started seeing each other, and they continued to say it for the rest of their time together. They engraved the words on silver frames, gold jewelry, just about anything they gave to each other.

When my dad wasn't calling her "darling," he called my mom "Nat" or sometimes "Nathan." He loved to make her laugh with his impressions of Cary Grant, James Cagney, and other classic movie stars. My mom also made him laugh—sometimes with her sharp wit, sometimes because she had her not-so-sharp moments. We used to have this crazy dog named Winnie who once chewed up all the grass in one section of our yard. My dad called the landscaping company and hired them to lay down new grass, then we all went out of town for the weekend, but not before he had sequestered Winnie so he couldn't get near it. When we got home, we went in the backyard and saw that Winnie had been on the rampage again.

"That goddamn dog," my dad shouted. "He broke loose and tore up the new grass!"

"But, R.J., this is a really smart dog," my mom said, a note of wonder in her voice. "Look. He chewed the grass in perfect squares."

"No, Natalie," Daddy pointed out. "The gardeners laid the grass in squares!"

Whenever he had to patiently explain an obvious fact to her, he called her "Natalie."

If I wanted a favor from my mom, I had a unique method that usually worked. I would take a whole grapefruit (her favorite) and stick a toothpick in it with a piece of paper attached that would read something like, "Can my friend Jessica spend the night, please? You are beautiful." Or "You are the best actress in the world." I would wait upstairs for her to come into the entryway, then I would roll the grapefruit down the stairs, where it would land with a thud at her feet.

"What's this?"

Jessica and I would watch from the top of the stairs as she picked up the grapefruit and read the message aloud. Then she and my dad, consummate actors that they were, would pretend to deliberate.

"Can Jessica spend the night? Well, I don't know. R.J., what do you think?"

"I don't know," my dad would muse. "Jessica, do you really *want* to spend the night?"

"Yes, I do!" Jessica would say earnestly.

Finally, my mom would give in. "Okay. Let me talk to Jessica's mom."

One year, our nanny Kilky gave Courtney and me two fuzzy little ducklings as an Easter present and our parents let us keep them. Once the baby ducks started growing, one of them became a very mean drake we had inappropriately named Sunshine. Sunshine was quarantined off to the side of our garden, where an abandoned wooden playhouse stood next to a small pond. Meanwhile, the other duck started flying around our neighborhood, making the rounds like it owned the place. My mom would get phone calls from surrounding houses. "Um, Mrs. Wagner, your duck is in our pool." She'd hang up the phone and shout, "R.J., the duck is in the neighbor's pool again! What are we going to do?" Then she and my dad would crack up laughing. They thought it was hilarious that there was this duck flapping around in fancy people's yards and pooping in their pools, all those Beverly Hills housewives opening their drapes in the morning and screaming, "There's the Wagners' duck again!"

Finally, my mom called a family meeting.

"Girls, we're going to have to get rid of the ducks."

Courtney and I screamed, "Nooooo!"

"Well, they can't just fly into other people's pools!"

My dad piped up with, "Well, why can't they?"

My mom pondered this for a moment, and then echoed my dad. "Well, why can't they?"

So we kept the ducks for a little longer until they wore out their welcome for good. One morning, Courtney and I decided to revisit our old playhouse by the duck pond. But this was Sunshine's turf now, and he did not welcome our visit. He cornered Courtney, hissing at her in a loud, scary screech. Courtney let out a series of bloodcurdling screams as I ran to get help. My mom, who had been applying a facial mask in her bathroom, heard the kerfuffle and raced down the stairs like a flash of lightning, her face slathered with bright blue clay. I shot into the house toward my mom so fast that we collided with each other like Laurel and Hardy. My mother, Kilky, and I stumbled over one another to get to the playhouse, slipping in the mud from a recent rainfall. Kilky and my mom rescued Courtney from Sunshine, getting covered with brown muck in the process. It was sheer mayhem. "That is *it*!" my mom decided with finality. "We are getting rid of these ducks!" Sunshine and his sister were swiftly donated to the Malibu wetlands that same afternoon.

After we moved to Canon Drive, Daddy Gregson, who had been living in England, rented an apartment in Malibu where he would stay when he was in town. I loved when he came over to visit or to take me out, greeting me with his posh British accent—"Hello, dahling, it's so good to see you!"—and grinning widely, with his silver hair and eyes that crinkled like raisins. He and my mom sat at the bar chatting, trading stories about the business, updating each other on common friends, discussing my progress, my schedule, my life. They respected and liked each other. My American dad and my British dad always seemed genuinely happy to see each other as well. There was an ease to their conversations and a respect for their differences as well as a shared understanding that they had both loved the same woman and they both loved the same child.

Most times, Daddy Gregson took me to Hamburger Hamlet on Sunset and Doheny, where I ordered the number eleven (a bacon cheeseburger) and a strawberry milkshake. Sometimes he took me to backyard barbecues or family parties given by his friends. Other times he bought me a present. There was a toy store a few blocks from our house, but my excitement over his suggestion "Let's go to the toy shop" was always dampened by his insistence that we walk there. Walk? On foot? "No one walks," I explained to him with a sigh. "Why can't we drive?" Being English, he never understood why we couldn't walk there, and being American, I never understood why we couldn't go by car.

As a child, I thought the story of how my mom met and married my two dads was perfectly unremarkable. Only later did I realize how extraordinary it was that my mom had met and married my Daddy Wagner, divorced him, *then* met my Daddy Gregson and had me, and then happily *remarried* Daddy Wagner.

Robert John Wagner, aka R.J., had been my mother's childhood movie crush. My mother loved to tell the story of the first time she saw him. It was 1948, and she was ten years old and under contract at 20th Century-Fox. She was walking down a hallway with my grandmother when she saw R.J. walking toward her. He had dark brown hair, bright blue eyes, and golden skin. He was eighteen years old and under contract at Fox as well. As he brushed by her in the studio hallway, he didn't look back, but my mom did. In that instant, my mother turned to her mother and whispered, "When I grow up, I'm going to marry that man." For the next seven years, when she saw Robert Wagner, it was only in movies. Then, when she was seventeen and he was twenty-four, they met again at a fashion show at the Beverly Wilshire Hotel, where a photographer snapped pictures of them together. A few weeks later, R.J. called and asked for a date. On July 20, 1956, my mom's eighteenth birthday, he took her to a screening of his movie *The Mountain* with Spencer Tracy. In the morning, he sent my mother yellow roses and a note promising to see her again. She found him handsome and kindhearted, with a great sense of humor. They kept their relationship secret from the press at first, meeting at quiet restaurants, off the beaten track. Their romance was youthful and tender. "R came over with a pair of yellow pajamas as a gift for me because I had been in bed all day sick with the flu," my mother wrote in her journal from the time, "what a dear heart."

R.J. was older than my mother, seemingly secure in himself. He'd learned his self-assurance the hard way. R.J.'s father, a Detroit steel executive, disapproved of him becoming an actor, wanting him to follow him into the family business. But R.J. had been determined, carving out a career for himself in Hollywood. He first came to public attention in the 1952 movie *With a Song in My Heart*, in which he played a shell-shocked soldier, and after that, he began to win leading-man roles. In 1954, he appeared in *Prince Valiant*, the adventure film that made him a star. Like Natalie, he understood what it meant to live with the glare of flashbulbs wherever you went. When they met, they realized they both felt lonely and isolated in their families—and by life in the spotlight. Now that they were together, the loneliness disappeared. They both wanted the same things in life, to have a family and to give their children the kind of pure, unconditional love that they hadn't always received from their own families.

In October 1957, my mother went upstate to shoot scenes for her movie *Marjorie Morningstar*, alongside Gene Kelly. R.J. went with her, staying for the three-week shoot. Both my grandparents adored R.J.; they thought he was kind, handsome, and talented and approved of the relationship.

After my parents returned in December, R.J. took my mother out for a champagne supper. My mother spotted something shining at the bottom of the champagne glass. It was a diamond-and-pearl ring. The inscription on it read: "Marry me." She said yes. In order to escape the press, my parents ran away to Scottsdale, Arizona, to get married, and invited only their closest friends. The wedding date was December 28, 1957. They traveled by train and checked into their hotel under fake names. The night before the wedding, my dad wrote my mom a note.

"Darling, I miss you. Are you going to be busy around 1 p.m. tomorrow? Love you, Harold."

My mom wrote back: "I won't be busy. How about getting married? All my love, Lucille."

On their wedding day, my mother wore a white cocktail dress

with a lace hood instead of a veil and long white gloves, a bouquet of calla lilies in her hands. My dad wore a dark suit, a sprig of lilies of the valley in his lapel. In a home movie of the events, my parents can be seen walking past a building, posing for pictures, and getting on a train to leave for their honeymoon.

My mother was not yet twenty years old. Her new husband was twenty-eight. They agreed to put their plans to start a family on hold for a couple of years, realizing they weren't old enough for that responsibility just yet. R.J. not only loved my mother but respected her enough to support her career—something not many men did for their wives in the 1950s. Immediately after they married, she refused to take a part in the film *The Devil's Disciple* with Burt Lancaster. Under the studio contract system, she simply had to show up for work. It didn't matter if the part, the director, or the script was to her liking. Her contract stated that she had to do it anyway. But after fifteen years in the business, she'd had enough. After she said no to the Lancaster film, Warner Bros., her studio, placed her on suspension. My grandmother pleaded with her to go back to work. But R.J. bolstered my mother's confidence and encouraged her to stand up for herself. With his support, she remained on strike at Warner Bros. for eighteen months—and it worked. In February 1959, Warner announced a new agreement between the studio and Natalie Wood. Not only had she been given a raise, but she would also be allowed to make one film a year of her own choosing, outside of the studio.

By then my parents had bought their own place, on North Beverly Drive, and my mom set about renovating it. It was going to be opulent, with marble flooring, crystal chandeliers, and a giant marble bathtub upstairs adjacent to their bedroom. While work on the house continued, my parents costarred in their first film together, the drama *All the Fine Young Cannibals*, in which R.J. played a jazz trumpeter in a tortured relationship with the character played by my mother. But the film was not a critical or box office success, and after the failure, both my parents were looking for a hit.

My mother found it in the form of Elia Kazan's *Splendor in the*

*Grass*, a powerful 1961 drama in which she starred as Deanie Loomis, a young woman from a middle-class Midwestern family. Warren Beatty played her boyfriend, Bud, in his first leading film role. The part required my mother's character to undergo an emotional breakdown, culminating in a suicide attempt, with Deanie trying to drown herself in a reservoir. My mom was working on one of the most professionally fulfilling projects of her career. At the same time, R.J.'s career experienced a downslide. Fox decided not to renew his contract, and he was out of work.

In the chaos, they fought. They had been married barely three years. At night my mother couldn't sleep. She was anxious. Their arguments left her feeling lost. At home the ceiling under the floor that held the giant marble bathtub started to show large and dangerous cracks, dust falling onto the furniture below. My mom told my dad she wanted to go into psychoanalysis. My dad felt they should be able to work out their problems without the help of a stranger.

After finishing work on *Splendor*, my mom went straight to the set of *West Side Story*, in which she starred as Maria. She had no time to give to their shaky marriage. The ceiling under the bathtub could be reinforced; the problems in their relationship were not so easily fixed. Not knowing what else to do, they decided to separate. The failure of their relationship shattered them both. My mom later wrote that she jumped straight from childhood into matrimony without ever discovering who she really was and what made her tick. She had never stood alone on her own two feet.

In the months after they split, my mother missed R.J. terribly. She moved out of the half-renovated home they had shared together, renting a house by the beach where she tried to recover. R.J. missed her just as much, escaping to Europe, where he hoped to revive his career. He still loved her but had no idea how to restore what had been broken between them.

*Splendor* and *West Side Story* opened in October 1961 and were instantly successful. My mom earned her second Oscar nomination for *Splendor*. She had become an A-list actress, highly regarded by her peers. By now she had also begun working on a new movie, *Gypsy*, based on the Broadway musical. Professionally, this was one of the most exciting times in her career. She became totally immersed in the work. She started dating Warren Beatty, but it was not a happy relationship. She later observed that after her divorce she was looking for the "Rock of Gibraltar" and she discovered "Mount Vesuvius" instead.

My mother's next film was called *Love with the Proper Stranger*, with Steve McQueen. When she wrapped that movie, she bought herself a home of her own on North Bentley Avenue in Bel-Air. The house was more modest than the one she had shared with R.J., and finally put her on a more stable footing. R.J. had returned from Europe and found success in the movie *Harper*, alongside Paul Newman. He had also met and married Marion Donen. My mother later wrote that when she learned R.J. had had a baby daughter—Katie—with his new wife, she wept for what might have been and for his newfound happiness.

My mother made two more great movies during the 1960s, *Inside Daisy Clover* and *This Property Is Condemned*, both alongside Robert Redford. At the time, Redford was a little-known actor, but my mom saw his promise and told the director of *Inside Daisy Clover*, Robert Mulligan, "I want him." Redford was hired, and it helped to launch his career. My mom insisted he be cast in her next film, *This Property Is Condemned*, as well. (It was while *This Property Is Condemned* was still in production that she was invited to the dinner party where she met Richard Gregson, the man who became my father.)

I enjoyed hearing stories about my mother's dating life in those years—after her second divorce, she dated Steve McQueen briefly, among others—but my favorite was the one about how R.J. and my mom reconnected. One day, R.J. asked if he could come and visit my mom and me. I was still only a little older than a year. By now R.J. had divorced his wife Marion. He arrived at the North Bentley Avenue house with his mother, Chattie. Later he told me about the first time we met. "You had a shock of solid black hair—so much so that we could have turned you upside down and swept the floor with you," he recalled. When it was time for me to take a nap, I didn't want to go. My mom was singing my lullaby, "Bayushki," to me, patting my back and walking me around the room, rocking me. I refused to go to sleep. When R.J. turned around, Chattie had slid from her chair. She had fallen asleep to the sound of my mother's singing.

The next day, R.J. sent my mother flowers. In her datebook at the top of one of the pages, she has an entry that says, "R.J. called!"

It was clear to both of them they had never stopped loving each other. Life had knocked them around, they had each married again and divorced, each had a child. They had matured beyond many of the problems that troubled their first marriage and were ready to try again.

According to a story my parents both told over the years, my mother and R.J. had first run into each other again when they were still married to their other spouses, at a party given by their mutual friends John and Linda Foreman in June 1970. My mom had come to the party without my British dad, as he was in London. At the time, R.J. was separating from his wife Marion and was also at the party alone. My mother was six months pregnant with me. The two of them struck up a friendly conversation. When the party ended, he gave her a ride home. After she was safely inside, he pulled his car over and had a good cry; my mother walked into the front door of our house on North Bentley Avenue and burst into tears. They both realized that the love they had was real, and it was as strong as ever. As my mom was still with my dad, neither one did anything about it.

Now that they were reunited and so happy, my parents decided to get married again. Their wedding took place at sea, on July 16, 1972, just off the coast of Catalina Island. Their friend Frank Sinatra arranged for them to be married on a boat called the *Ramblin' Rose*. His classic song "The Second Time Around" played over the loudspeakers. I don't remember the wedding, but to commemorate it, they had a series of portraits taken in the summer of 1972. In one they are seated outdoors, Daddy Wagner leaning in close as Mommie holds a stark-naked me in her lap, my tiny toes dangling above the long skirt of her ivory-and-lavender-checked peasant wedding dress. When I look at it, I'm floored by the sheer joy that they radiate, the Southern California sun bathing their faces. How many people get a second chance at love? My parents did and they seized it.

It's no coincidence that my parents were married at sea. During their first marriage, my dad had a boat called *My Lady* and my parents spent many happy times together on it. My dad taught my mom how to fish on that boat: how to use the radio and the mooring, how to work the radar and drive the dinghy. She enjoyed becoming one of the crew. After their second marriage, around the same time they bought the Canon Drive house, my parents purchased a sixty-foot yacht my mother christened the *Splendour*, after the line "splendour in the grass," from the William Wordsworth poem that had inspired the title of her film. On weekends we'd take trips to Catalina, an island about twenty-five miles off the California coast.

My parents were different on the boat—more peaceful. We all were. Even Courtney and I got along better on those weekends away. Our deckhand was a sandy-haired man from Florida named Dennis Davern who had worked on the boat even before we owned it, and took care of it year-round. Weekends on the boat, my dad and Courtney and I would be out on the deck, fishing, or my mom would be sitting next to my dad as he steered the ship. Other times, all of us would hang out together inside, playing cards or reading, or talking with the many friends that joined us on those weekends. When we docked, we would go to the arcade, where we kids could play games, then go out to a casual dinner on the island. For Courtney and me, Catalina was like an unspoiled island in a storybook, with its bright blue sea and lush, tropical foliage. From our boat, we could see the wild bison roaming on the hillsides, and dolphins and giant fish swimming around us in the waves.

Other times Daddy took us out in the motorized dinghy, and we'd spin through the craggy reefs and caves along the coast looking for garibaldi, a bright orange fish native to Southern California. Once, I remember my dad diving for abalone, and showing Courtney and me how to pound the mollusks flat with a special hammer so that we could flash fry them and eat them hot from the pan. My dad was an excellent fisherman. He taught Courtney and me how to hook the bait on the fishing line, cast our rod with a flick of our wrist, and patiently wait for the hoped-for tug. He explained how to reel the catch in *slowly*, using what strength we had, speeding it up as the hooked fish got closer to the top of the water. I held the record for catching the largest fish on board the *Splendour*: a forty-two-pound halibut, almost as big as I was at the age of ten. Reeling that salty sucker in required the manpower of all the grown-ups on the boat that day. Another favorite pastime of Courtney's and mine was watching our guests find their sea legs. Most of them were not used to being out on the water, and soon they'd be throwing up over the side of the boat. For some reason, Courtney and I found their seasickness deliriously entertaining.

Our swimming spot of choice was Emerald Bay, off the northeast tip of Catalina, where the water is shallow, turquoise, and clear. Although my mom loved being out on the water and swimming in the heated pool at home, in general, she didn't enjoy the colder temperatures of the ocean or "when I can't see the bottom." Emerald Bay was the only place where she felt comfortable swimming because she could see the sand on the ocean floor below.

Sometimes I wonder if life was ever really this sweet.

# Chapter 3

Natasha with her grandmother Baba (center)
and Natalie on Christmas Day, 1974.

My maternal grandparents, Baba and Deda, were fixtures of my childhood. When I watch old home movies from that time, they are almost always there, either in the background or part of the action itself. I loved being around them. They spoke with funny accents, and they were always kissing and hugging me and talking to me in their make-believe-sounding language: "Natashinka, *moya princessa, lyu blu.*"

My grandmother had raven-black hair cut in bangs and dark blue eyes, like a grown-up Snow White. She always wore long ornate gowns of crushed velvet in shades of deep emerald or purple often embellished with shimmering metallic appliqués or gold brocade. When I visited my grandparents at their home, my grandmother would be chattering away, standing over the stove making strange brews. My grandpa was much quieter, more docile, and altogether less dramatic than my grandmother. He had dark hair and an impish smile, eyes that looked straight into the depths of yours. He played with me, carrying me on his shoulders, pushing me in my swing, letting me bury him under my stuffed animals. He played an instrument that looked like a guitar but had a silly name—balalaika—and sang to me in Russian. According to my parents, Deda wanted to go back to Russia, his homeland, but felt it was no longer his, and so he drank too much.

To visit my grandparents was to follow the White Rabbit down the rabbit hole. Wherever we lived, whether it was in Palm Springs or Los Angeles, they always had a house close by. Any and all childlike possibilities existed at their place. My grandma let me have sugary treats whenever my heart desired, something that was closely monitored in my mother's house. Their home smelled of sautéed onions and garlic, and the warm, lumpy stew that Baba brought to me in small bowls always tasted delicious. Whenever I visited, there was a new toy for me, a little handmade doll or a stuffed animal. The dolls were so different from the ones you could buy from the toy store. They wore makeup and jewelry and had colorful ribbons tied in their hair. Even when Baba gave me a store-bought doll, she made sure to enhance her by adding fancy clothes, rhinestones, and a tiara or crown. An ordinary doll wouldn't have been special enough.

Like the dolls she made for me, Baba was always bejeweled. For special occasions, she wore real jewelry of gold and precious or semiprecious stones. On an average day at home, she adorned herself with costume necklaces, bracelets, and earrings. She loved to wear her birthstone, amethyst—purple, the color of royalty. If we were going out for dinner, Baba made up her face, and when she did, her lipstick and eyeliner were usually painted a little askew, as if she had applied them in a bathroom by candlelight. When I snuggled in my grandmother's arms, I remember the heavy fabrics she wore emitting a musty odor, mingling with the powdery notes of her White

Shoulders perfume. After she sat on the sofa in our home, the pillows smelled like her for days. Baba's birthday was February 8 (the same day as James Dean's). I remember my parents buying her birthday jewelry sparkling with little purple amethysts and taking her to dinner at a restaurant she loved, the Hawaiian-themed Luau in Beverly Hills, where she was treated to her favorite dessert, lychee nuts on ice.

But the thing that defined Baba most of all was the intensity of her love for me and my mom. Her passionate affection for us was fierce, unwavering, even overwhelming. When I was with her, she didn't leave my side, just as she had never left my mom's side when *she* was a little girl. Baba hovered, she exclaimed excitedly at my every word, she was my biggest and most adoring fan.

When I was about six, my hair was light golden brown, much lighter than my mom's, and was cut in a feathered pageboy. I remember one afternoon, Baba coming to visit. She had been to the beauty salon, where she had instructed the hairdresser to lighten, cut, and style her hair exactly like mine.

"Look, Natashinka," she said, grinning broadly, "we have the same hair now!"

Baba had gone from having black hair like Snow White to having light brown hair like mine. As a child, I didn't think Baba's new hairdo seemed strange. I considered Baba my grown-up child friend, and so in some way, her matching haircut just made sense. Looking back, however, it seems quite bizarre that an adult woman would want to look like a little girl. But that was Baba. For her, love meant fusing with the object of your adoration so completely that you even looked exactly the same.

Deeply religious, my grandmother filled each of her apartments with golden, glimmering icons, placed reverently in the corners of each room. Almost every time Baba came to our house, she brought a tiny bag of Russian holy flowers and a vial of holy water. I knew the drill. After hugging me, Baba opened the golden oval-shaped locket with a cross on it that I always wore around my neck. My mother had given the locket to me when I was a baby. Inside were the dried flowers Baba had put in there last time. She would switch them out for new ones, before flicking holy water on my face and saying a prayer over my head. The flowers and the water were meant to ward off evil spirits. As long as I had the locket with holy flowers around my neck, Baba told me, nothing bad could happen to me.

My mom grew especially exasperated with my grandmother when she performed her rituals on me. "Mud," she'd say—or "Mother," if she was really annoyed—"please don't fill Natasha's head with Russian nonsense."

Baba knew my parents didn't approve of her superstitions, but instead of stopping, she chanted her prayers in a low whisper. When my parents weren't watching, she and I hid in the linen closet, switched off the lights, and sat down on the floor cross-legged. Then Baba sang a Russian prayer and flicked more holy water in my face. Of course, Baba approached these secret ceremonies like a child would—a little too loudly, a little too brazenly—and my parents usually found out what we had been up to and got irritated with her.

It was from Baba that I learned to worry about the world. Whenever we were together, she warned me of things I should be fearful of. People I should watch out for. Doorways I should avoid. Rituals to keep me safe.

She had all kinds of superstitions. She knocked on wood, spit over her shoulder three times, and threw salt here and there. Every time my parents left on a trip, Baba wouldn't let anyone put away anything they had used before they left—a bottle of juice left out of the fridge, a plate on the counter—until my mother called to say that they had arrived at their destination. If you even put so much as a knife or fork away, that was considered bad luck. Once Baba knew my parents were there safely, she'd spend the next hour or so frantically tidying up the house.

Baba never got mad at me, but she was often in a bad mood with other people. If she was mad at someone—her daughter Lana, my grandfather, Daddy Gregson, someone who didn't smile at her when she smiled at them—she sewed a voodoo doll out of fabric, stuffing it with cotton balls, using sequins for eyes, and drawing red lips on with a marker. Then she'd stick needles in it or submerge it in water or put it in a dark closet. The little dolls fascinated me and confused me at the same time, but I was never worried Baba would make a doll of me—I knew she loved me too much for that. Other times if someone made her angry, she wrote the person's name on a piece of paper and put it in cold water in a coffee cup in the freezer. I could tell if she was mad at someone because when she walked by the fridge, she made a face. At the time, I think I knew her behavior was unusual, but I loved her completely and so accepted her quirks.

When I was very little, I remember being in the backyard with Baba and pointing to a spider a few feet away.

"Look at the spider!" I said innocently.

Baba leaped to my rescue. She positioned her body between me and the dangerous insect.

"Oh! Did it bite you, Natashinka?"

She knelt down in front of me, examining my arms and legs for any signs of attack. "Are you all right?"

The spider was minding its own business and had come nowhere near me. I was fine. Her reaction frightened me more than any insect.

Baba was also extremely wary of people she didn't know, especially men. Throughout my childhood, she was convinced that intruders were about to enter our house to take me away. Once, when I was woozy with jet lag after a trip to England with my mom and Daddy Wagner, my grandma accused my parents of drugging me. My parents were furious. But she couldn't help it. She saw danger everywhere.

My parents were in a near-constant state of exasperation about Baba. Whenever she came to visit, I could see Daddy Wagner barely concealing his sighs and frowns. He tried to be nice, but I knew he felt resentful of my grandparents. He felt they tried to control their daughter. It annoyed him that my mother continued to support them financially, as she had done since she became a star at six years old. My mom still felt responsible for her parents, she loved them and was loyal to them, but they were exhausting. My mom joined my dad in forming a silent, invisible barrier between my grandmother and me. Baba was always close by, but as I got older, my mother tried to keep her at arm's length—inviting her for holidays and festivities but no longer asking her to babysit when they went out or away on a trip.

The problem was, I was drawn to Baba. I found her magical. Make-believe was her comfort zone, and for a child, that was intoxicating. My grandmother took me on her lap and fed me her fairy stories, which were just as delicious as her bowls of beef stroganoff or broth with dumplings.

"Natashinka," she cooed, "we are special. There is nobody like us. We come from a long line of Russian princesses. I am a princess, your *mamatchka* is a princess, and you are a princess too."

She made me think we were fragile, delicate, unique, like Fabergé eggs. The fact that Baba, Mommie, and I were physically small seemed to prove that we were to be treated with extra care, in case we might break.

In my grandmother's version of her life story, she was born a princess, related to the Romanovs, Russia's last doomed royal family. Years later I found out that in fact she was born Maria Stepanovna Zudilov, the youngest daughter of Stepan Zudilov, a well-to-do businessman who had made his money in soap and candle factories. Zudilov was considered landed gentry, not royalty. Her mother, Maria Kuleva, may or may not have had distant Romanov connections—no one knows for certain—but in some ways, it doesn't matter. Baba believed her story with such fierce commitment that it became her truth. When Baba made her claims about us being princesses, my mother would shrug her shoulders, saying, "Maybe we are!" Meanwhile, I drank in every word of it. Why would I doubt my grandmother? In her burgundy and purple embellished gowns, she looked like royalty to me.

What I do know is that my grandmother was born in 1912 and spent her early childhood in Siberia during the final years of the reign of Nicholas II, the last czar of Russia. She had two half brothers and two half sisters from her father's first marriage, and a sister and two more brothers from his second marriage to her mother. According to Baba, her parents were White Russians, wealthy beyond measure, with glittering jewels they kept in a vault in the family's vast estate in the countryside surrounding the southern Siberian city of Barnaul. Growing up, my grandmother was waited on by servants and cooks. She was taught at home by a governess and spent little time with her own mother, from whom she yearned for maternal affection. Despite the lavish setting of her upbringing, the adults around her were cold and forbidding. "When I was bad," she told me, "my governess would punish me by making me kneel in the corner with uncooked peas beneath my knees." As a child, my grandmother promised herself that when she grew up and had her own children, she would shower them with the love and attention she herself had never received.

When the Russian Revolution broke out in 1917, little Maria was five years old. Her father supported the czar, and as a landowner, he was considered an enemy of the Bolsheviks. After the czar and his family were executed by the Red Guards in July 1918, Maria and her family prepared to flee their home. They gathered their money and jewelry, concealing it in the peasant clothes they wore as a disguise, and ran to a prepared hiding place on their estate.

Maria's older half brother Mikhail happened to be out of the house that day. As the rest of the family hid on the estate, they had no way of warning him that the Red Guard soldiers were close by. After the soldiers left, the family emerged from hiding to see something hanging from a tree. As they came closer, they realized it was Mikhail. Little Maria was so traumatized by the sight of her murdered brother she broke down in convulsions. The memory of that moment must have haunted her for the rest of her life, but my grandmother never told me about her brother or his murder. I only learned about Mikhail many years later from talking to my aunt Olga and her family and, later, from reading Gavin Lambert's biography of my mother, one of the most reliable sources of information about my family ancestry.

Instead, Baba told me about her family treasures. The family knew the soldiers were likely to return, so they wrapped their jewels in silk scarves, burying them deep in the ground, so they could come back and find them someday. She explained that the jewels belonged to us, but they were trapped in Russia and one day she would go back and claim them. Anytime she saw a photograph of some particularly dazzling piece of Russian jewelry, she showed it to me and explained that it was ours. Anything sparkling and gorgeous had been part of those untold riches that had been left behind but belonged to us.

Six-year-old Maria and her family boarded a train in deepest winter, escaping for their lives. After traveling almost three thousand miles, a journey that took many weeks in freezing conditions, they arrived in Harbin, China, a city with a large exiled Russian community. Maria and her parents were now just another immigrant family, one of hundreds of thousands. They were able to bring enough money with them to survive, but my grandmother was no longer being taught at home by governesses. Baba once shared a memory with me about her mother giving her a baked potato before she walked to school in the mornings, and how she would put it in her pocket. "I held on to it as I walked through the snow to keep my hands warm, then when I reached school I would eat the potato," she said. It wasn't an uncommon sight in Harbin to see formerly wealthy Russian families begging for change just to survive. No wonder little Maria learned to be superstitious, to see catastrophe around every corner.

Despite the fact that my grandmother spent her teenage years in relative poverty, she never forgot the vanished opulence of her childhood. Whenever she told her story, she was always a princess with many admirers. Sometimes it felt to me as if Baba were the movie star, not my mother. In her version of events, everyone loved her and never stopped talking about her stunning looks, and all the handsome young Russian military captains in Harbin wanted to marry her.

It was in China that she met a gypsy fortune-teller who predicted that one day Baba would have a daughter who would be a great beauty. The woman also warned my grandmother that her daughter would die by "dark water." As a result of this prediction, my mom didn't like to be out of her depth, where the water was very dark or deep, even though she loved to swim in our pool and spend time on our boat.

When my grandmother was about eighteen, she met a Russian-Armenian officer who was stationed in one of Harbin's military units. His name was Alex Tatulov, and he was dark-haired with dark eyes just like my grandmother. Alex had dreams of finding his fortune in America and my grandmother was irresistibly attracted to him. She married him in secret, because she knew her father wouldn't approve. In 1929, Alex left for the US, to seek his fortune in San Francisco, promising to send for Maria as soon as he got himself settled. By now my grandmother was pregnant and unable to hide her secret union from her parents. When the baby was born, she named her Olga.

In November 1930, Maria learned that she had been granted an American visa and said goodbye to her family. The voyage across the Pacific Ocean took many weeks and she traveled alone with her baby daughter, a testament to my grandmother's courage and her ability to dream of a future for herself independent of anyone else's expectations.

Alex met her quayside in San Francisco. While they had been separated, he had met another woman. What's more, although he was working at a shipyard, he was a long way from finding his fortune, having arrived on American shores right as the Great Depression began.

Maria had no choice but to stay with Alex in the rooming house where he lived with other workers from the shipyard; from there the couple moved from apartment to apartment, trying to find a foothold. Alex continued to see his lover, often leaving my grandmother alone with a baby to take care of, in a foreign country where she didn't speak the language and in the midst of the greatest economic slump in American history. But Baba soon discovered a way to help her forget her troubles: she started going to the movies. The talkies had just arrived, and the screens were filled with singing and dancing in glorious black and white. Fred Astaire and Ginger Rogers danced cheek to cheek, Nelson Eddy and Jeanette MacDonald sang their hearts out, and Shirley Temple tapped and curtsied her way to child stardom. Baba and little Olga went to see romantic dramas, comedies, and musicals, the images on-screen feeding my grandmother's hopes and daydreams.

Down at the docks, Alex befriended another Russian exile named Nikolai Stephanovich Zakharenko, who had shortened his name to Nick Gurdin. This was my grandfather. Nick was dark-haired, strong, and good-looking. Maria loved when he played his balalaika and sang soulful Russian folk songs. Before long, my grandmother left Alex, moving into Nick's apartment with Olga. Not long after, she finalized her divorce, and in October 1937, Nick asked Maria to marry him.

Like my grandmother, my grandfather was a child refugee who had fled Russia during the war. He was born and grew up near the port of Vladivostok, in Far Eastern Siberia, one of three sons. His father was a worker at a chocolate factory, but he supported the czar and quickly joined the White Army in their fight. Before he left for the front he told his son, "When I come home, Nikolai, I will bring you a *kaska*." In Russian *kaska* means helmet. But little Nikolai thought he meant *skazka*, which is Russian for fairy tale. He waited for months for his father to return with a special story for him, but his father was killed in the fighting and never came home. After that his mother fled by train with her family to Shanghai. Somehow, she managed to get herself aboard a boat bound for Vancouver. Nikolai was eight and spent the rest of his childhood in Canada. At the age of eighteen, he started working, slowly making his way down the West Coast by taking manual jobs, finally landing in San Francisco, where he met my grandmother, two Siberian exiles by way of China. They were married in 1938.

By then Baba was already pregnant again. When my mother was born, on July 20, 1938, my grandparents named her Natalia Nikolaevna Zakharenko, but everyone called her Natasha. "Was most beautiful baby in the whole world," Baba wrote in Natasha's pale pink

baby book. "Everyone stopped me in the street and admire her. My princess!" Baba's baby had a special spark, with her big brown eyes and button nose. From the moment she was born, all Baba's hopes for recovering the prosperity and happiness she had lost as a child revolved around tiny Natasha.

"You are a princess, Natasha!" I can just hear Baba whispering that to my mother in her cradle. In Natasha, Maria had found someone to shape into the kind of screen idol she worshipped, a partner to play with in her world of make-believe. My mother was literally nursed on movies. Baba would bring her newborn baby to matinees, breastfeeding her and rocking her to sleep right there in the darkened theater. As a preschool-age child, my mother's favorite game was called "Movie Star." Each morning, she checked into the "studio" (the garage) as Vivien Leigh or Bette Davis, pretending to act in their movies, then checked out again for lunch. My grandmother helped prepare my mother for fame by teaching her to sing and dance, and to always smile, talk to people, tell them stories, and sing songs.

Little Natasha cried often when she was a baby and a doctor had told the family it was because the San Francisco dampness made her joints ache. And so, by the time America entered World War II in 1941, the Gurdins had moved to Santa Rosa, a little town sixty miles north of San Francisco, and bought a small starter home. (My grandfather's dream had been to buy a farm in Oregon and bring his children up there, but my grandmother wasn't interested in a farmer's life.) In Santa Rosa, Deda worked in construction as a day laborer. Theirs was not the happiest marriage. Deda liked to drink, he was constantly shifting between jobs, and the couple often fought.

What they were able to give to their daughters was an appreciation for the imaginary. With her father reading her stories like *The Little Mermaid*, *Bambi*, *Snow White*, and *Grimms' Fairy Tales*, my mother grew up believing in magic, elves, fairies, saints, and angels. Baba used to take my mom for walks in Santa Rosa, and as they walked along, my mother would often find coins and even toys on the sidewalk.

"Look, Mama," she'd say to Baba. "Is this magic?"

"Yes," Baba replied. "There is magic even on the street. But you must look for it. And if you want your heart's desire, you must work hard. And you must always do as you are told."

Eventually, my mother figured out that it was Baba—and not magic—scattering the coins and toys on the sidewalk for her daughter to find there. It was the first of many times my mother would become aware of my grandmother's propensity for illusion.

Baba continued to follow the movies. In 1943, a Santa Rosa schoolgirl named Edna May Wonacott appeared on-screen in Alfred Hitchcock's *Shadow of a Doubt*. Hitchcock had discovered the nine-year-old while she was waiting at a bus stop. Now she had a Hollywood contract. My grandmother took note. When the director Irving Pichel came to town to shoot a movie, my grandmother seized her chance. Pichel was looking for a young girl to play a bit part in his movie *Happy Land*. It was early July, just a few weeks before my mother's fifth birthday. My grandmother dressed my mother in her best pinafore, rolled her straight, brown hair into Shirley Temple curls, and pushed through the crowd of hopefuls toward Mr. Pichel.

Baba whispered to Natasha, "Smile at that man." And my mother did.

Mr. Pichel asked little Natasha to sit on his lap. She put her arms around him and sang a little song.

"Would you like to act?" he asked her.

My mother looked at Baba and then nodded.

Mr. Pichel told this little girl to walk down the street with an ice-cream cone, then to drop it and burst into tears.

After my mother was given the cone, she told the grown-ups, "I don't want to drop it, it tastes good."

Mr. Pichel looked at Baba. Baba looked at Natasha. Natasha dropped the cone.

The director told my mother to cry; she told him she didn't feel like crying.

So Baba told her daughter a story about a butterfly who burned its wings. My mother loved butterflies, but even this wasn't enough

to make her cry. Then Baba reminded her about her beloved puppy who had been killed in a car accident. After that the tears came and my mother couldn't stop crying. When she was interviewed about it she always said that was the beginning of her career: "I dropped an ice-cream cone and Hollywood taught me to cry."

Pichel saw potential in her and promised her a bigger role in his next production. Before long, he invited my mother to go to Hollywood to audition for a new part. My grandfather was against the whole idea. He wanted his daughter to have a normal childhood. He fought furiously with my grandmother about going. My grandmother remained calm. She pointed out the audition would probably come to nothing and that his daughter would never forgive him if he didn't give her this chance. "Don't do it for me, do it for Natasha," she reasoned.

Natasha won the part in the film. It was *Tomorrow Is Forever*, a World War II drama starring Orson Welles and Claudette Colbert. She played an orphan, a part that required her to learn some German, speak with a German accent, and cry on demand. Welles himself later described her performance as "almost terrifyingly professional." The film was released in February 1946 and was my mother's major motion-picture debut. She was seven. The Gurdins never did return to Santa Rosa.

By then the powerful men of Hollywood had decided my mother's name sounded too Russian—this was Cold War–era America, and anything seemingly related to Russia or Communism carried a stigma—so they changed it to Natalie. The producer William Goetz informed my mother that her last name was going to be Wood, in honor of his friend the director Sam Wood. "Couldn't it at least be Woods with an *s*?" my mother asked. "Don't worry," Mr. Goetz said, "Wood will look good on a marquee." My mom really didn't like "Wood," but she made her peace with it because it made her think of the forest and all the magical creatures that lived in it. She always missed her first name—this was why she eventually named me Natasha.

My mother had a new life now. She no longer went to school.

Instead she had a revolving set of private teachers and chaperones who taught her on set. When she wasn't acting or studying, she took ballet and piano lessons. There was no time to play imaginary games in her make-believe "studio" anymore. She was too busy working for a real studio. Her big sister, Olga, would help her learn her lines and pronounce words correctly.

The biographies of my mother will tell you that my grandmother pushed my mom into the movies at a very young age and exploited her talent. In the simplified version of my mother's life, Baba is usually cast as the wicked queen, abusive and controlling. But I have a hard time seeing her that way. She was an immigrant who spoke very little English and a refugee of war. She came to America and somehow managed to steer my mother's career in Hollywood, a notoriously tough business. And my mother was no passive victim. She had a talent for acting that couldn't be forced and that my grandmother nurtured. Young Natalie's brown eyes were not just beautiful, they radiated an intelligence that was uncommon for child actresses. She was able to make you fall in love with her and want to take care of her, while letting you know not to mess with her as she was probably smarter than you. She may have missed having a "normal" childhood, but she loved acting in the movies. She soaked up the attention, thrived on being around movie stars, and was a born performer. I often wonder if my mother's childhood career gave her a sanctuary, a movie set of make-believe to turn to when her home life failed her.

After *Tomorrow Is Forever*, my mother's next role was as Barbara Stanwyck's daughter in the comedy *The Bride Wore Boots*, also directed by Pichel and released in 1946. My mom often worked with actors who were much older than she was, many of them Hollywood legends. By all accounts, they adored her. When she played alongside Stanwyck, who was in her late thirties by then, my mother took a liking to Barbara's gardenia perfume. After the production wrapped, Stanwyck sent her a bottle of it, which made a lasting impression. As soon as she was old enough to wear it, my mom adopted the scent—Jungle Gardenia—as her signature perfume.

Natalie kept working. In her third film, released in 1947, she played the daughter of Gene Tierney in *The Ghost and Mrs. Muir*, directed by Joseph L. Mankiewicz. Next she appeared in *Miracle on 34th Street*, playing Susan Walker, the daughter of Maureen O'Hara. At home Natalie was encouraged by Baba to keep her head in the clouds of fairy-tale fantasy, but that didn't stop her from throwing herself into the role of Walker, the little girl who doesn't believe in Santa Claus. In the movie, she's a sharp and analytical kid, a skeptic with her feet firmly planted in reality. The film was released in July 1947, and it was such a success that Maria was able to negotiate a two-picture contract with Fox, including jobs for my grandfather as a studio carpenter and for herself as the person managing Natalie's fan mail.

The movies were quickly becoming the Gurdin family's lifeblood and, increasingly, their main source of income. Maria managed every aspect of my mother's career, down to the smallest detail. After my mother's sister Svetlana was born in 1946, Baba was determined this new daughter would have a career in Hollywood as well and so she gave her a Russian name that could be conveniently shortened to match the first name of her favorite screen star, Lana Turner. As soon as Lana Gurdin was old enough, she began auditioning for roles, and in 1956, when she was ten years old, she would make her screen debut playing Natalie's childhood self in the movie *The Searchers*, directed by John Ford. Like Natalie, Lana changed her last name to Wood.

When my mother was twelve, my grandpa suffered the first of several heart attacks and couldn't work. My mom became the sole provider for her family while also attending junior high school. Suddenly, winning acting roles became a source of great worry. Every time a casting director told her no, she felt rejected personally and heartbroken—she knew her family's financial stability was at risk.

My mother continued to work consistently into her teens, but as she grew into a young woman, she found herself increasingly stifled by my grandmother's grip. Everywhere she turned, there was Baba: at home, at work, even chaperoning when my mom was old enough to date. Baba and Deda believed they could control not only my mom's career but her entire life. She began to rebel. When her parents wanted her to stay home, she went out. If they wanted her to dress a certain way, she dressed the way she wanted to dress. She was tired of always being told what to do and where to go.

My grandparents forbade my sixteen-year-old mom to even audition for *Rebel Without a Cause* because they did not like the way the parents were portrayed in the film as old-fashioned and insensitive, but she insisted on going up for it anyway. The movie was directed by Nicholas Ray and it told the story of three suburban teenagers rebelling against their families. My mother was determined to win the part of Judy, the heroine who bonds with her boyfriend, Jim Stark (played by James Dean), over their shared loneliness and frustration. Until this time, my mother had gone for parts because she had to, or to win her parents' approval. The part of Judy was different. She wanted it because it was meaningful to her. She auditioned three times and won the role.

My mom had first met Dean in 1954, at a rehearsal for a televised adaptation of Sherwood Anderson's story "I'm a Fool." He arrived on his motorcycle, hair in the wind and a safety pin keeping his pants up. During the filming of *Rebel Without a Cause*, they became close friends, my mom often riding behind him on his Triumph motorcycle. Dean had trained as a Method actor with the legendary teacher Lee Strasberg. Although my mother worked with a voice coach on *Rebel Without a Cause*, she had never taken an acting class. This was the first time she ever improvised on set, the first time she was asked for her opinion, to think about acting as a craft. She often said that it was the beginning of her ambition to become a serious actress.

James Dean died in a car accident only a few weeks before *Rebel Without a Cause* was released. His death was the first big tragedy of my mother's life, the first time someone close to her had died. She never forgot it. She always spoke of her friend with such fondness: about his kindness and vulnerability, as if he needed protection in the world.

The following year, at the age of seventeen, my mother was nominated for a Best Supporting Actress Oscar for her role as Judy. The more successful Natalie Wood became, the harder Maria tried to control her life. Professionally, my grandmother still negotiated the deals with the studios. At home she would sneak into her daughter's bedroom and rifle through her belongings while Nick barged in, looking for photos of friends he didn't approve of and ripping them to shreds. Natalie's name and face began to appear all over the gossip columns and fan magazines, romantically linked to all kinds of young men, even (briefly) Elvis Presley. Some of these dates were arranged by the studio for publicity purposes, but nevertheless, they sent Baba into a frenzy of suspicion. When my mother returned home from evenings out, my grandmother held her dress up to the light to see if there were wrinkles or creases in unfamiliar places. My grandparents had devoted their lives to Natalie. It seems what they wanted in return was complete domination. But now that she was older, my mother knew more about the business than they did and started making her own decisions. No longer totally in control, Baba became more willful, neurotic, upset. It was an exhausting tug-of-war.

In the end, Natalie held the position of power in the Gurdin household and everyone knew it. My dad, Robert Wagner, remembers that when the family lived on Valley Vista Boulevard in Sherman Oaks in the mid-1950s, my mother occupied the master bedroom and bathroom suite, Lana had the smaller bedroom, and Maria and Nick slept on a roll-away bed in the living room. By now Olga had left home and was married, but my teenage mom supported every other member of her family financially. If she wanted to stay out late or date a man they didn't approve of, Maria could forbid it, Nick could put his foot down and threaten punishment, but ultimately, what could they do? Natalie was in charge.

One of the reasons my mother married my dad at nineteen was to escape her controlling parents. For a time, Maria shifted her attention to Lana, hoping her younger daughter could fill the gap Natalie had left behind her. But Lana seemed to be the kind of actress who directors and studio heads could imagine only in supporting roles. My grandmother would become furious with my mother for not doing more to help Lana's career. But it wasn't her fault. Lana was a good enough actress but she simply didn't become a star.

In my grandparents' Brentwood apartment, my grandmother had a painting hanging on the wall in the living room right next to the sofa. The painting was of my mother in her twenties, posed with her arms crossed, wearing a black dress with thin black straps over her bare shoulders, her neck and arms elongated, her eyes wider than in real life. The painting was by Margaret Keane, wife of Walter Keane, who later became famous as the authentic artist behind her husband's signature portraits of children and women, their eyes dramatically large.

The Keane painting of my mother is from 1961, the same year that *West Side Story* came out. After it was completed, Baba claimed the painting. Although my grandmother coveted the portrait because it was of her beloved daughter, she wasn't completely satisfied with it. Keane hadn't included the bracelet my mother always wore on her left wrist. Baba considered herself to be the expert on all things Natalie Wood and so she decided to paint a bracelet herself, using oil paints to add on a golden cuff. My grandmother was very proud of this addition, even though she had essentially desecrated a renowned artist's work without anyone's consent.

No wonder that as a grown woman my mother tried to establish some boundaries. It didn't always work. Once, when I was very young, my parents took a trip, and while they were away, Baba decided to change the locks on their house without telling them. When my parents returned home from the airport, they couldn't get inside their own home. "I didn't want strangers getting near Natashinka!" Baba explained. My parents were furious. Another rift followed. Eventually, my mom softened up and let Baba back into our lives. This push-and-pull pattern with Mud and Fahd would continue for the rest of my mother's life.

My mother didn't want Baba controlling me the way Baba had tried to control her. She had spent years on the therapist's couch trying to untangle fantasy from reality. That's why, as I grew older, she began limiting my time with Baba, in an attempt to save me from a similar fate. But it was too late. I was already adopting Baba's rituals and beliefs as my own.

As a child, I used the locket around my neck filled with holy flowers like a talisman. When panicky feelings would creep in and I became terrified that something bad was going to happen to my mother—my whole world—I closed my eyes, touched the locket, and said a silent prayer that everything would be okay.

# Chapter 4

Natasha, Natalie, and Courtney at the house
on North Canon Drive, 1977.

My mother was a great actress, but she would have been an amazing producer. Looking at her datebooks from the 1970s, I can see how seamlessly she arranged our lives: the pages are a swirl of plans and organization—everything from my dad's shooting schedules to our after-school activities. Dates and times of ballet and piano lessons, gym classes, math tutoring, class trips, doctors' appointments, as well as social events she wanted to attend, black-tie affairs, galas, film premieres. They read like notes for a movie: *Life*, produced by Natalie Wood.

My mother had grown up on movie sets, always surrounded by a cast of characters and crew, with a mother who followed her everywhere. Even now that she was a grown woman, she wasn't comfortable being alone. She was someone who needed to be surrounded by people and a bustling household most of the time.

When we first lived all together on Canon Drive in the mid-1970s, my dad was working on a TV series called *Switch*, an action-adventure detective show. As the lead, he had to work twelve- to fourteen-hour days, but he called regularly from whatever set he was on, and the two of them were always making plans.

"R.J.," my mom would say, cradling the receiver, "we're having dinner with the Pecks tonight. What time do you think you'll be wrapped?"

Then she would nod and say, "Okay . . . amazing . . . incredible . . . I love it!"

She'd laugh her musical laugh and hang up.

A constant stream of lunch and dinner dates, parties, phone calls, visitors, and house guests vied with me for my mom's attention. Oftentimes it felt like I had to share her not just with my dad and my extended family, but also with the world.

Although I wasn't happy when my parents went out to parties or for dinners, I loved it when they stayed home to entertain. I always knew when my parents' friends were coming over because my mom did her eyes. I'd watch as she got ready, sitting with her at the vanity in the dressing room area that led to her white-and-green bathroom. My mother had a large three-way mirror that was the kind you'd find in a movie star's dressing room. The story goes that she pinched it from an MGM soundstage while she was filming her 1966 movie *Penelope*. I can still picture my mother in front of that mirror with five or six hot rollers framing her face, doing her eyes.

To start, she dipped a long, thin brush in water, then into the palette of black pressed powder to form a liquid eyeliner, which she used to paint a fine outline around each eye. With a smaller brush, she coated her eyelid in brown eye shadow and blended it with an upward motion. Next she curled her lashes with a mysterious metal contraption before stroking a wand of mascara over them. Once the eyes were done, pale pink lipstick and a swab of gloss were the finishing touches. She could talk to me or Daddy Wagner or a friend on the phone throughout her makeup routine and never make a mistake.

As my mom got ready, she'd often walk around in a nude bra and undies, curlers in her hair, one eye painted, buzzing the kitchen to ask Kilky what time the guests were arriving, how long the wine had been chilling, what Courtney and I were having for dinner. Or she would waltz into my dad's office next door to their bedroom and carry on a conversation in various stages of undress. Then she'd pick up something to wear from her enormous walk-in closet shimmering with dresses, blouses, pantsuits, hats, shoes, and fur coats. A spritz of her gardenia perfume, the same kind given to her by Barbara Stanwyck when she was a little girl, and she was ready to be the hostess.

For the most part, when we had company, everyone gathered downstairs in the den. There was a large, hand-carved walnut bar on one side of the room; my dad would stand behind it, serving drinks, and my mom would perch on a bar stool opposite him. Silver bowls filled with nuts, usually cashews, sat on the bar next to matching silver cups that held dark brown More cigarettes. Most of the guests who came over smoked in those days, until an interior designer friend accidentally burned my eyelid with his cigarette, and my mom laid down a no-smoking rule in the house.

Though bedtimes were strictly enforced, Courtney and I were allowed to join the parties early in the evening. Mommie and Daddy wanted us there to meet and greet their guests, to talk, and to enjoy the festivities. We'd wander in, fresh from bath time, wearing our nighties, our hair still wet. I would scoop a handful of cashews from one of the silver bowls and eat them while my parents and their friends drank wine and told each other funny stories, clouds of cigarette smoke wafting to the ceiling. *This is what it's like to be a grown-up*, I thought. *You make each other laugh, you wear makeup and look pretty, and you can have as many nuts and cigarettes as you want.*

Like my mother, I had an instinct for performance from a young age. I was keen to shine in social settings as long as I felt surrounded by people I trusted. I loved making my parents and their friends laugh. I could do an impersonation of a monkey that my mom had taught me, just like the one she'd done in *Miracle on 34th Street*. Or I would tell a knock-knock joke. If I didn't have a joke to tell, I'd scoop up one of our dogs or cats and wander around with them. I passed through wafts of perfume mixed with cigarette smoke, the sounds of laughter and storytelling in my ears, the beautiful ladies saying hello, asking for a hug, the silks and satins of their clothing smooth against my freshly washed arms.

My parents' circle of friends was wide, but at the nucleus were my mom's best friends Mart Crowley and Howard Jeffrey. My parents called Mart "The Little Prince" or "Martino" and Howard was "Aitchey," for the initial of his first name. For a long time, Mart lived in the pool house out back on Canon Drive and Howard lived in the guest house above our garage with his two cats.

Mart was tiny and lithe. Always dressed impeccably in purple shirts and yellow cashmere sweaters, he would stride into our house with a story. "Oh, Natalie, you just aren't going to *believe* who I ran into today. Just you wait till I tell you this!"

My mom and Mart had first met when he was hired as a set production assistant on *Splendor in the Grass*. He was assigned to pick my mother up in the mornings and drive her home in the evenings. She began confiding in Mart about the troubles in her first marriage to R.J., and by the time the movie wrapped, they had become inseparable. A few years later Mart wrote his iconic play, *Boys in the Band*, which went on to become the very first major American theater production to feature male characters who were openly gay. My mother supported and encouraged Mart in his writing, hiring him to be her assistant on her next movie, *West Side Story*, so he would have enough money to write. It was on this set that they met Howard, who was a choreographer on the film under Jerome Robbins.

Howard was tiny too with a halo of brown curls and a nasal laugh.

Silk shirt unbuttoned to reveal little chest hair tendrils and a gold chain with a gleaming Fabergé-style egg hanging from it that was a gift from my parents. Not only did Mart and Howard live with us at various times, they also traveled with us, drove Courtney and me to meet my parents at the airport when they had been away on a long trip, and always, always celebrated the holidays with us.

Mart and Howard had been with my mother during the rocky periods after her first marriage to R.J. and her breakup with my British father. They bonded over the painful things in life, difficult parents, relationship troubles, career setbacks. They all possessed that wonderful ability to laugh at themselves and their own neuroses. Mart and Howard were my uncles, my friends, my godfathers, my parents' most trusted cohorts. In my parents' will, if my mom and dad died at the same time, we were to be raised by Howard and Mart, who were not a couple but were bound by so much more than many couples are.

When it came to their wider circle of friends, my parents had a talent for picking people they loved and respected who loved and respected them too. Tom Mankiewicz was a good friend of both my parents, as well as being the son of Joseph L. Mankiewicz, who had directed my mother at age eight in *The Ghost and Mrs. Muir*. We called him "Mank" and he called me "Beano." Roddy McDowall was another. He too had been a child actor who had successfully transitioned to an adult career. The actress Mia Farrow sometimes came over with her children. The director Gil Cates was always around, as was the director John Irvin and his wife, Sophie, British friends from my mother's second marriage. Delphine Mann was also an import from the UK. With cropped blond hair and a crisp English accent, Del had no idea who my mom was when they met. Instead, they bonded over having children the same age.

Then there were my parents' "team," the people who looked after them in their careers, who came to the parties and were trusted friends: the entertainment lawyer Paul Ziffren and his wife, Mickey, who were like surrogate parents to my parents and guided their business and work lives; George Kirvay, their publicist and dear friend, who came to all the parties and on all our trips; and then later Alan Nierob, who took over from George after he passed away.

Both my parents had grown up in the studio system, and their careers spanned many generations of actors and filmmakers. As a result, guest lists for my parents' parties included a mix of the not famous at all, the so-so famous, and the very famous. Celebrities I remember seeing at our house were Bette Davis, George Segal, Gene Kelly—who lived down the street—and Gregory Peck and his wife Veronique. I was too young to appreciate that these people were legends. I just knew I enjoyed it if they were nice and paid attention to me.

I remember dancing legend Fred Astaire was always immaculately dressed in vests, ties, and cashmere blazers. He had a wide, clean face and, usually, a yellow silk scarf around his neck, and he always smelled clean, like a fresh bar of soap. My Daddy Wagner had attended the Black-Foxe Military Academy in Hollywood with Fred's son. Before my dad had any idea who Fred was, he was being picked up by him at school and staying at the Astaires' house on the weekends. Later, my dad cast Fred as his father in the TV series *It Takes a Thief*, which came out in the late 1960s. Fred was always so friendly to me. "What's your doll's name?" he asked, or "What are you learning in school?" On party nights at our house, Fred would be at the bar, telling a story, drink in his hand. Sometimes he played our baby grand.

The director Elia Kazan was another frequent guest. My mom had given one of the greatest performances of her career for him in *Splendor in the Grass*, earning her second Academy Award nomination for it. She was in awe of his talent as a director. This was the man who had made *A Streetcar Named Desire* and *On the Waterfront* with Marlon Brando, and *East of Eden* with James Dean. She always considered *Splendor* her best film and Kazan one of her greatest champions.

Everybody called Kazan "Gadge," a nickname he earned from his love of fiddling with gadgets. Around our house, Gadge wore shorts and could often be found poolside, soaking up the sun on a chaise lounge. To me he looked a little like Elmer Fudd. With rumpled gray hair, he sort of shuffled from side to side when he walked. I figured he must be very funny because my parents were constantly laughing when they were with him.

My mother had a handful of older women who were important to her. She had spent so much time around adults when she was a child that many of her friends were her senior by many years. There was Rosalind Russell, who had played her mother in *Gypsy*; the author, activist, and philanthropist Mickey Ziffren; the grand dame of Hollywood Edie Goetz (daughter of Louis B. Mayer); and the actress and writer Ruth Gordon. My mother loved and admired these fancy ladies, and so naturally I loved them too. Once, I remember being sick with a cold, lying drowsily in my mom's bed on Canon Drive, overhearing Mommie on the phone with Edie Goetz. "Oh, she would love that, Edie. No, I don't think she has ever seen a nosegay. Oh, how perfect, how divine! You are the best, Edie. Thank you." This was how I learned Edie was sending me a nosegay.

My mom was especially close to Ruth Gordon. A look of excitement and glee always passed her face as she prepped for Ruth's arrival. Ruth was my godmother, a role she had taken on after my first godmother—my mom's best friend the actress Norma Crane—died of breast cancer when I was three years old. Ruth was a brilliant performer and writer of screenplays with her husband Garson Kanin. She and my mom ran in the same social circles, and my mom was a fan of Ruth's work. They first became close after my mother handpicked Ruth to play her mother in *Inside Daisy Clover* in 1965. In the movie, my mom plays a young star growing up in Hollywood with a difficult mother whom she calls "Old Chap." To say my mother related would be an understatement. A few years later, when Ruth won the Academy Award for Best Supporting Actress as Mia Farrow's nosy neighbor in *Rosemary's Baby*, she made the audience roar with laughter by saying, "I can't tell you how encouraging a thing like this is." She was seventy-two years old. Not long after that, she played Maude, a seventy-nine-year-old woman with a much younger lover in the cult classic *Harold and Maude*.

Ruth always arrived at our house in a chauffeured limousine with her husband Garson, whom she called Gar. My mom still called her "Old Chap," and sometimes my mom called me "Old Chap" too. Ruth was a miniature person, a Thumbelina with a dramatically deep stage actress's voice and a splash of a New York accent.

"Natasha, dahling, how is my beautiful gawd-dawter?" she'd exclaim. "Gahrson and I are *so* deliiiii-ted to see you."

Ruth dressed with drama too, wrapped in swaths of silk, with huge freshwater pearl earrings clinging to her ears and perfectly round pearl necklaces at her throat, all shimmery and white. The pearls bounced light onto the tiny features sitting happily on her tiny face, which was wrinkled, a bit like papier-mâché. She wore a red lip and her brown hair pulled back and tied with a silk scarf— the color of it usually matching her dress. And she always brought presents and hugs with her. One time, she gave me a pair of cabochon ruby stud earrings from Cartier, another time, a beautiful dress from Pierre Deux, a French Provençal-themed boutique that was all the rage in the late seventies and early eighties. Then she would wrap her little hands around my little hands and we'd sit together talking. There was an intimacy between us, perhaps because she was so close to my mother, but maybe also because she had a gift for connection. My mother once wrote, "I think that I've never known anyone with a greater capacity for living than Ruth," and it was true. Ruth offered my mother a very different kind of role model than Baba.

Then there were those guests who visited infrequently but who were considered very important. One day when I was about six, my mother said to me, "Now, Natasha, tonight a dear friend of ours is coming over for dinner. His name is Sir Laurence Olivier, and he's the world's most talented living actor, so you must be very polite to him." The most talented actor I knew was my Daddy Wagner, so I told my mom: "He can't be the world's greatest actor. Daddy is." My mom laughed her wonderful laugh and later, when "Larry" arrived, I was introduced to him. Larry reminded me of a cozy grandfather and sounded just like my Daddy Gregson with his English accent. I immediately felt at ease around him.

Since I'd recently discovered knock-knock jokes, I decided to entertain Sir Laurence with a few of my favorites. He was kind enough to humor me by listening attentively, dutifully replying, "Who's there?" to my every "Knock-knock!" When I started laughing before all the punch lines, he even joined me in my hysterics. After dinner, I left the room and my mother told him the story about what I'd said about my father before he arrived. Before she got to the punch line, Larry interrupted. "Don't tell me," he said. "I'll bet I know what Natasha said: that her daddy is the greatest actor in the world." I walked back in at the precise moment he spoke the words ". . . her daddy is the greatest actor in the world." I smiled triumphantly and said, "See? He agrees with me!"

Most days around five o'clock, my mother picked up the phone to buzz the pool house and the guest house for my godfathers Mart or Howard. "Martino, Aitchey, when are you coming down here? Let's sit at the bar and have a drink." Like the nuts and cigarettes in the little silver cups on the bar, alcohol was always present at home. It was part of what made our household so lively and festive.

Various bottles were stacked deep in the liquor cabinet, and the liquids inside flowed freely. My parents always drank. All their friends drank too. Drinking was an everyday pastime in Hollywood in those days, often continuing late into the night.

Sometimes the fun took on an edge that bothered me.

My mom did not drink hard liquor, only wine, her favorite being white-wine spritzers. Around the time I turned eight years old, I'd start to notice if she'd had too many drinks. She seemed less attentive to me, and when this happened, I worried about her. I was used to having a somewhat vigilant, slightly bossy mother. When she had been drinking, if I tugged on her skirt because I needed her, she would no longer react right away. Instead, she'd brush me off with a far-away-sounding voice, as if she was too distracted by whatever conversation she was having with a guest to give me her full attention. Mommie was here, but at the same time, she wasn't really here. *Where's my regular mother?* I used to think.

Both my parents seemed to drink more when we traveled. In 1978, we rented a house on the beach in Hawaii for three months while my dad shot the miniseries *Pearl* with Angie Dickinson. Late one night, I was awakened by voices and walked out of the house to find my parents' good friend Tom Mankiewicz wearing nothing but his bikini briefs. He held a drink in his hand, and my fully clothed parents were drinking too. Mank was there to discuss writing and directing the pilot of a new series my dad was starring in called *Hart to Hart*. But this didn't look like a business meeting to me.

"Why are you in your underwear?" I blurted out.

"Well, Beano," he said, "I'm thinking of taking a dip in the ocean."

It was two in the morning. Why wasn't anyone talking him out of it? At eight years old, I knew that a grown man going swimming in his underwear in the middle of the night wasn't the best plan.

"But it's dark outside."

I looked to my mom and my dad, but they gave me no indication that anything abnormal was happening. My dad simply said, "You should be in bed."

I went back to my room, thinking, *What kinds of craziness do my parents get into when I'm not around?* I had the strong feeling that I needed to keep an eye on them.

The following summer, we went to the Las Brisas resort in Acapulco. My dad had made some commercials for a Mexican clothing company in exchange for a free trip there. The whole gang came along: Mart, Howard, Kilky, Courtney, and Katie. Early every morning, the hotel would put bright red hibiscus flowers in the pool outside our suite, and I remember waking up to see these beautiful flowers floating on the water, almost as if they had fallen from the sky. Guests at Las Brisas had access to pink-and-white-striped Jeeps with low bucket seats, and we rode through the winding hills of Acapulco Bay on old dirt roads, carefully turning corners to avoid getting the Jeep stuck in the deep ditches on the side of the road. It became a running joke; every time we turned a corner, Mart, Howard, and the rest of us would yell in unison, "Watch out for the ditch!"

One evening, my dad was driving, my mom was in the passenger seat, and Courtney and I were in the back. When we returned to the hotel, my mother was slumped over in her seat. My dad said, "Natalie, get up." She tried to move and ended up falling down onto the floorboard. "Natalie, you're scaring the kids," my dad said. "Get up." She mumbled, "I can't get up," from the floor. She looked like my mom, but she wasn't acting like my mom. It was scary to me. That was the only time I remember seeing my mom *really* drunk.

Was my mother dependent on alcohol? Or just someone who enjoyed a few drinks? Mostly I felt too shy and confused to talk to my parents about their drinking. On the few occasions that I did protest, they would assure me that there was nothing to be concerned about and that I was worrying too much. They were in control; everyone was safe. All was well in my world. Maybe at some point, had she lived, my mom would have realized the drinking was getting out of hand, and she would have turned to my dad and said, "R.J., it's time to take a break." She was a professional actress: when she needed to diet for a role, she was extremely disciplined, counting calories and working out to get into shape. Maybe she would have done the same with alcohol. I'll simply never know.

# Chapter 5

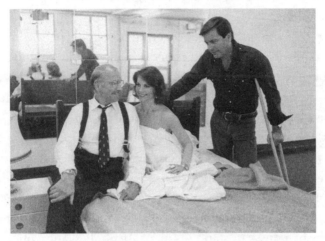

Sir Laurence Olivier, Natalie, and R.J.
in rehearsal for the 1976 British TV production
of *Cat on a Hot Tin Roof*.

Although her family was important to her, my mom was growing restless, less content with being a full-time mother and occasional actress. Nothing could entirely replace performing for the cameras, at least not for someone who had been starring in movies since kindergarten. She had planned and carefully constructed our domestic world, and now that it was up and running, she was ready to return to her career. It was more than a force of habit or an ego trip for her; acting was her lifelong passion.

In 1978, she began preparing for a role in the big-budget disaster movie *Meteor* (about which she later joked "the *movie* was the disaster!"). In it she played a Russian scientist, which meant she had to brush up on her Russian for the role. She found herself a Russian teacher and spent hours listening to the language on a tape recorder, perfecting her accent. I remember sitting next to her and reading my book or drawing as she listened and recited. This was the first time I can recall witnessing my mother's diligence when it came to preparing for a role.

After that she played a recovering alcoholic in the made-for-television movie *The Cracker Factory*, which was filming in LA. Kilky would bring Courtney and me to visit my mother on set. As always, she was thrilled to see us, beaming with pride as she introduced us to the cast and crew. I was just as proud to be her daughter. *This person that everyone wants is my person*, I thought. Because *The Cracker Factory* was a serious drama concerning alcoholism, suicide attempts, and mental hospitals, she allowed us to watch her shooting only lightweight, PG scenes. Her favorite moment in *The Cracker Factory* was when her character gives a defensive, angry monologue to her doctor, in which she refuses to stand up in an Alcoholics Anonymous meeting and "confess my ninety-proof sins to a bunch of old rummies who just crawled in off of skid row!" I can remember overhearing my mom memorizing that speech at home, and sensing that she loved saying the words as much as I loved listening to them. The speech was punchy, funny—strong.

The night the movie aired on TV, my mom was out to dinner, but she'd instructed Kilky, "When it comes to the scene where I take the pills, change the channel!" She didn't want me and Courtney to be traumatized by seeing our mom swallowing a bottle of sleeping pills and falling over. Meanwhile, I had overheard the phone conversation and was prepared. When Kilky switched the channel, I reached over and switched it right back. I wanted to watch that overdose scene! Later, when we got a copy of the movie on videocassette, Courtney and I watched our mother's monologue over and over again and memorized all the words, which we would repeat for each other at any time of the day or night.

Once *The Cracker Factory* was over, she took a part in a TV series based on the 1956 movie about Pearl Harbor, *From Here to Eternity*, alongside the actor Bill Devane. She played the Deborah Kerr role from the movie, an emotional and sexy role—which meant that we weren't allowed to watch her filming or to see the finished product once it was on TV. In the lead-up to filming, I remember she was excited, extremely focused, and watching her weight. Whenever she got a big part, my mom went on a diet. She was always petite, but she loved comfort food and usually put on a couple of extra pounds when she wasn't in front of the cameras, eating whatever she liked: her beloved lamb chops, beef bourguignon, borscht, and cold cuts from the Nate'n Al deli. She and my dad liked to have deli feasts of matzo ball soup and turkey or roast beef sandwiches on rye bread, topping it all off with her favorite Häagen-Dazs coffee ice cream. Then, right before a project, she'd do a grapefruit fast, a watermelon fast, or a cantaloupe fast. She ordered plain salads "with the dressing on the side." And of course her favorite chopped salad at La Scala, as always, "*without the garbanzo beans!*"

In 1979, Daddy Wagner shot a pilot for a TV series called *Hart to Hart*, and it really took off. He coproduced and starred as Jonathan Hart, one half of a chic, jet-setting couple who solved mysteries and were passionately in love. Stefanie Powers played his wife, Jennifer. They traveled, they sparkled, they called each other "darling." My mother had originally been offered the Jennifer role, but my parents decided it wouldn't be possible for them to raise children and both be working the grueling schedule of an hour-long weekly TV series at the same time.

I remember going to the Warner Bros. lot in Burbank to watch a screening of the ninety-minute pilot. My parents told us there was a surprise in the episode. Halfway through the program my mom appeared in one of the scenes dressed like Scarlett O'Hara. All in pink and carrying a parasol, playing an over-the-top movie star called Natasha Gurdin (her birth name). Yes, I was surprised and excited to see her on-screen, but it was also confounding to me. *When* did she shoot without me knowing? I considered myself the keeper of my mom's whereabouts, so the fact that she had fooled me actually bothered me.

*Hart to Hart* became a hit pretty quickly. Courtney and I weren't allowed to stay up late and watch it, but my parents taped every episode so we could watch the next day. Our favorite part was the opening credits. We memorized all Lionel Stander's lines: *"This is my boss, Jonathan Hart, a self-made millionaire. He's quite a guy. This is Mrs. H. She's gorgeous . . ."* Every few episodes, my dad would bring home a chunky VCR tape labeled "GAG REEL," containing all the blunders and mistakes the actors made on set. Courtney and I watched the gag reels over and over again.

Suddenly, millions of people were seeing my dad on TV in their living rooms every Thursday night. Strangers had always spotted my parents in public, but now fans were even more eager to ask for autographs, photographers more anxious to aim their cameras in our direction. Almost every time we left the house a trail of admirers would cluster around us. Because my mom and dad were both reared in the old studio system, they treated fans with respect, signing scraps of paper and smiling for pictures. I remember once a friend giving my parents matching T-shirts that said, "I'm not signing autographs, I'm on vacation." They got a kick out of that. But they rarely complained unless a fan behaved rudely or interrupted our dinner. Only sometimes after a particularly enthusiastic devotee left, my mom would roll her eyes and make a funny sound like "OYYYYYY" and they would both smile and that would be that.

By now my parents had also revived the production company they had first started together in 1958. The original company was called Rona (an amalgam of Robert and Natalie) and the new company was Rona II. Through Rona II, they contributed to the development of the hit series *Charlie's Angels*, so they received a profit from that show as well as from *Hart to Hart*. Ever since she'd become an adult, my mother made sure to stay in control of her finances. She was every bit the businesswoman, once saying, "You get tough in this business until you get big enough where you can hire someone to get tough for you. Then you can sit back and be a lady." (There's a famous picture of my mom wearing a black hat and seated at the head of a boardroom table, the only woman surrounded by ten men who worked for her: her lawyers, agents, business managers, publicists.) Both my parents were savvy about business and money. My dad's point of view was that "The only positive is the negative," meaning that owning "the negative"—or a piece of the film—is where you make the real money (not from your fee as an actor). After the success of *Hart to Hart* and *Charlie's Angels*, our family was definitely in the positive.

On the nights my parents socialized outside of the house, they left us in the care of Kilky, or with my mom's assistant, Liz Applegate. Liz was petite and delicate-looking, just like my mom, with wavy brown hair. "Hello, lovey, how are you?" she asked in her cheerful English accent whenever she arrived at our house. At four in the afternoon she drank black tea with condensed milk, so that became my favorite drink too. Liz referred to my parents as "mummy" and "daddy," as in, "Mummy's still out, she'll be home later," or "Daddy's on the set, you'll see him at dinnertime." Liz was my favorite grown-up outside of my parents. She was also in charge of the other people who worked for my parents: Coralia the housekeeper, Stanley the driver, Jamie the handyman, Helen and Gene, who cooked for us. These people were so much a part of my landscape growing up, they were like members of the family.

When my parents left me in the evenings in Liz's care, she told me stories she invented about two creatures named Billy Mouse and Morris Gerbil. Though I delighted in Liz's stories and company, not even she could allay my concerns about my mother after she went out. By the time I was nine, I had memorized the phone numbers of every restaurant my parents frequented so I could call them before I went to bed to make sure Mommie was safe. I knew the numbers by heart: La Scala, Orlando-Orsini, Dominick's, the Bistro, Morton's, L'Orangerie, the Ginger Man, Bistro Garden. I knew most of the maître d's by their first names. They recognized my voice and put my mom on the phone right away. If my parents were on the boat, I knew how to place a shore-to-ship call. "Whiskey-Yankee-Zulu 3886," I'd say to the operator, who would connect me to the *Splendour* via radio.

Some nights I would get so consumed with worry I could hardly breathe until I heard my mother's voice on the line. I was in fourth grade now and had made a new friend at school, Jessica, who had perfectly straight blond hair and loved to read as much as I did. Jessica would often stay over, and together with Kilky, she would do her best to keep me calm until I could get my mom on the line.

Our phone conversations never lasted long.

"Hi, Mommie."

"Hi, Natooshie."

"What are you doing?"

"We're just sitting here finishing up dinner. We've been having a great time, lots of laughs."

"Are you going out after or coming straight home?"

My mom would either respond, "We may go have a nightcap. . . ." or "We're coming back now."

If they were returning home right away, the knots in my stomach would loosen; I could take a deep breath and nod off to sleep. If they were continuing on for a nightcap, I'd hang up the phone and begin to panic. I could tell instantly if my parents had been drinking too much. Their voices got a bit louder and looser, their words sounding a little slurred like they had a cotton ball or two inside their cheeks. Kilky or Liz would try to soothe me and put me to bed. Sometimes I called a restaurant only to be told by the headwaiter, "They've already left." *Where are they?* I would think. *Are they on the way home, or have they had a terrible accident?* My mind would race in circles of speculation. Inevitably, the oak front door would creak open and they'd be home. Once I heard my parents' footsteps and laughter downstairs, I could fall right to sleep.

• • •

When Courtney and I were younger and my parents traveled for work, they often took us with them. For the filming of a British TV adaptation of the Tennessee Williams play *Cat on a Hot Tin Roof* with Laurence Olivier, our whole family traveled to England, renting an apartment in London. My mom was Maggie the Cat and my dad was Brick, the troubled wife and husband played by Elizabeth Taylor and Paul Newman in the classic movie. My mother had known Tennessee Williams, studied his heroines intimately, and hoped to perform in all his plays. Olivier took the role of Big Daddy, Brick's wealthy plantation-owning father. One day while we were in London for the rehearsals, Courtney and Kilky and I were downstairs and we could hear my parents shouting at each other upstairs. Kilky went up the stairs. "Hey, you two, everybody calm down now. What's going on?"

"Willie Mae," my mom replied, "we are just acting, rehearsing for the show. Don't worry!"

As we got older, it was harder for us to go with them on their shoots as our school wouldn't permit us to take so much time off. In 1979, when the BBC asked my mother to go to the Soviet Union to film a TV documentary about the Hermitage Museum in Leningrad with the actor Peter Ustinov, she told us she would be going without us. It would be the first time my mom had traveled to Russia, the country where both of her parents had been born. This trip was a big deal for everyone. Courtney was okay with Kilky as her substitute mother, but I felt like the separation was going to be unbearable. Before my mom left, she tried to ease my mind by coordinating strict phone-call schedules while she was away. This was actually part of her contract with the TV people. Of course, when she got to Leningrad, the Russians did not keep up their end of the bargain. She threw a fit and threatened to be on the first plane out of there if a telephone was not put in her room right away.

While she was in Russia, I remember standing sentinel by the phone five minutes before her calls, my heart racing. Inevitably my mind would start to run away with itself. *What if she doesn't call? What if something happened to her? How will I find her?* When the long, unfriendly overseas beep tone ended and the operator came on the line to say, "Person-to-person call from Miss Natalie Wood to Natasha and Courtney," I would shriek with excitement and pent-up longing.

I could barely contain myself. "Hi, Mommie, hi, Mama, I miss you so much, you got me a present, how many more days until you are coming home?" Each call would inevitably end in tears, with Kilky swiftly removing the phone from my hand and reassuring my mom that we were fine, busy, having fun. While I was talking to my mother, the warmth and love in her voice made my sadness and longing vanish—and I felt transformed. After the receiver clicked in its cradle, it was as if all the magic had gone.

Despite my concern for her when she was away from me, my mother's renewed attention to her career was paying off. Toward the end of 1979, she learned she had been nominated for a Golden Globe for her role in the TV series *From Here to Eternity*. She had won the award twice before, once in 1957 for *Rebel Without a Cause* and again in 1966, when she was given a special achievement award. This new nomination must have been so validating for her—she had only recently made her comeback and now she was being acknowledged for her hard work. I remember the afternoon of the awards, Courtney and I were swimming in the pool when our parents came outside to kiss us goodbye. They were all dressed up, my dad in a black tuxedo, my mom in a dark, elegant dress with layers of tulle at the shoulders, the golden ribbon cuff that my dad had given her that previous Christmas wrapped around her wrist. She carefully stepped over puddles of pool water in her heels to reach us.

Our parents bent down to receive our wet pool kisses, and then they left.

Later, we were allowed to stay up and watch the awards show. I felt a rush of excitement seeing my beautiful parents on TV looking the exact same way they had a couple of hours earlier when they'd walked out to the pool to say goodbye. I could see the expectation on my mom's face when they read her name and then the absolute astonishment when she won. The childlike glee in her eyes made us whoop and holler at home. "Mom won, look at that, Mom won!" Kilky chanted. Courtney and I hugged each other. We were so excited. We could see the look of love in my dad's eyes when the camera cut to him. He was always so proud of her.

After winning her award, she starred in the comedy *The Last Married Couple in America*, opposite George Segal, in which they played a couple struggling to stay happily married as their friends divorce all around them. In early 1980, my mom promoted her projects on the talk-show circuit, appeared in a commercial for Raintree products, and began work on the TV movie *The Memory of Eva Ryker*, about a woman whose mother is drowned after a German torpedo destroys a cruise ship during World War II. In the film, she played both mother and daughter at different points in their lives. The shoot took place partly in Long Beach aboard the *Queen Mary*. My mother organized a field trip for my entire fifth-grade class to visit her on set. We showed up on a yellow school bus, buzzing with curiosity to see my mom at work. In turn, she was so happy to have us there that she had prepped everyone on set for our arrival. She introduced us to the director, the director of photography, craft service people (my favorite), and a little girl named Tonya Crowe, who was playing my mother's character as a child. I was shocked. Why was there another little girl playing my mom? Tonya was about my age, and I instantly wondered, *Why didn't my mom ask me to play the part of her as a little girl?*

This was my first inkling I might want to be an actor when I grew up.

"Mommie," I asked her later, "why couldn't I have played that role?"

"When you grow up, you can make that decision," my mom replied, perfectly composed. "Right now you're a child and I want you to have a normal childhood."

If my mother was spending more time working and away from her kids, at least her kids were getting along better. As Courtney grew a little older, we started to make peace with each other. She was funny and creative and pushed the boundaries further than I would, so that added a colorful layer to our make-believe play.

Katie moved in with us when she was fifteen, in 1979, and was now a popular sophomore who wore a T-shirt that said "Blondie Is a Band" and wished she could wear her hair just like Debbie Harry. After she got her license, she drove around town in a white Honda Civic and seemed to be friends with all the coolest kids at Beverly Hills High. To me, Katie was where it was at. To her, I was practically invisible. For my ninth birthday, she gave me a necklace that expressed her opinion of me: a gold chain with two charms—one was engraved with the word "spoiled," the other "brat." Did Katie know something that I didn't?

Sometime around 1980, my parents' work schedules and social lives got pushed a little further to the extreme. There were too many parties, too many vacations. *Why can't everyone just slow down? Why can't we be a normal family where Mommie cooks dinner and has it waiting for Daddy when he gets home from work?* Most fathers I knew came home from work much earlier than my father, and most dads weren't wearing pancake makeup on their face when they walked through the front door.

Why was the phone always ringing, the intercom for the front door always buzzing?

I knew what that incessant sound meant. It was somebody coming over to distract my parents or to take them away from us.

Out to dinner, an event, the airport.

I felt my mother belonged to me, just like I belonged to her. If she was busy all the time, where did that leave me?

With a marker and a sheet of paper, I made a special calendar for myself—a chart of the nights they went out and the nights they stayed in.

I made another calendar for her.

"You're only allowed to go out two nights a week!" I told her. "The other five nights are reserved for Courtney and me."

My parents were sympathetic, they made all the right sounds as they tried to comfort and placate me, but even so, they didn't change their plans. The doorbell kept ringing, and off they went again.

I cried. I raged. I told my mom I wanted to go live with Tracey. Her mom didn't go out all the time; she was home in the evening. Tracey didn't have to worry about when her mom was coming back. Her mom was already right there.

It wasn't that my mother didn't listen to me. Her therapist, whom I'll call Dr. Fisher, told her that it was important for us to have special time together (my mom had been in therapy for many years, ever since her divorce from my Daddy Wagner). So my mother would make sure we had that. Many afternoons she would be the one to pick me up at school, taking me to my piano lessons. Even though her driving style was gas-break-gas-break, and I didn't much like playing the piano, I loved our car rides because I had her to myself. In her car she was my captive audience. I could ask her anything my heart desired.

"Who do you think is the most beautiful woman ever?"

"Well, I guess I would have to say Vivien Leigh."

I remember one day, my mom picked me up from school and said, "I have a surprise for you." She drove to the MGM lot, where she had arranged a private screening of *Penelope*, a silly comedy she made in 1966 that practically ruined her career. Though the movie was a colossal failure, she seemed to sense that her nine-year-old daughter would enjoy it. She was absolutely right. In one scene, she dresses up like an old lady and robs a bank at gunpoint. We both laughed and laughed. I think she was also proud of the song she sings in the film, a sweet ballad called "The Sun Is Gray." I felt so known and loved that afternoon. It wasn't about the movie; it was that she planned a special date for just the two of us.

When it came to her social life, however, my mother remained firm. She simply wasn't going to stay home five nights a week. Her therapist supported her independence from me, telling her that it was healthy.

Like my grandmother, I began orchestrating elaborate good-luck rituals to keep my mother safe. The carpet in the hallway leading to my bedroom was the same as the wallpaper pattern—bloodred roses and peonies entwined with green leaves, forming a garland of squares against a cream background. I made a rule for myself: when walking to my room, I had to step on the garland squares an even number of times or something terrible might happen to me or Mommie. I was gripped by the fear that my mother was going to die.

My best friend Jessica was the only one who noticed the little two-step shuffle I performed on the hallway carpet. When she came over to spend the night, she watched me quizzically. "What are you doing?"

"Oh, nothing," I'd say, trying to be as nonchalant as possible.

Once I made it safely into my room, I couldn't go to sleep until all twenty or thirty of my stuffed animals were lined up in a row on my brass bed, my Barbies perfectly positioned in their Barbie Dream-House. As soon as I finished brushing my teeth and turned the bathroom lights off, I had to switch on my swan night-light. I prayed every night, "Now I lay me down to sleep . . ." including a special prayer to God to please keep my mom safe. Then I had to walk one complete circle around the bed before turning off the swan light. If I was particularly worried, I had the locket around my neck with the holy flowers from my grandmother inside that I would palm feverishly. I was embarrassed by these rituals but felt compelled to do them every night.

When I flip through my mother's datebooks from 1980, they are packed with events: charity galas (she was the national chairperson for UNICEF), guest appearances (she and my dad were co–grand marshals of the Hollywood Christmas Parade), social functions, business meetings, parties, and dinners, and she still made time to entertain her inner circle at home. She kept up with Daddy Wagner's *Hart to Hart* schedule better than he did, jotting a running log of his call times and making sure he was there for every shoot. As for herself, she coordinated meetings with writers and producers about projects she was interested in with costume fittings and photoshoots for current projects.

At some point that crazy year, my parents were scheduled to fly to New York City for a week. I begged them not to go. My mother tried to talk it through with me. At first she comforted me patiently and listened to my concerns, but when that didn't work, she became increasingly exasperated. *What* exactly was I afraid of? She reminded me that she was just a phone call away, that I could have her number at the hotel (joking that I would have it memorized within ten minutes). She would let the front desk know I would be calling. On and on and on. Nothing could appease me.

Every time I even thought about my parents leaving for the New York trip, my heart would race and my stomach would flip over with fear. The idea of both my parents being on the other side of the country terrified me. I continued to beg them to stay. They actually considered canceling the trip, but my mother's therapist, Dr. Fisher, told her, "You have to go, or else Natasha will think there's something to worry about. Staying home will only confirm her irrational fears." So Mommie gave me Dr. Fisher's phone number in case I couldn't reach her in New York and I needed someone to talk to.

The evening after they left, Kilky told me to take a shower, brush my teeth, and put on my pajamas, and then we could call my mom. On the scratch paper pad next to the phone in our playroom was my mother's number at the Sherry-Netherland hotel in New York. There I stood in my footed flannel pajamas, long wet hair down the length of my back, ready to call. I dialed the number. The receptionist put me through to her room, but it rang and rang. I dialed again. And again. When I couldn't reach her, I started to cry. My friend Jessica was there, as well as Courtney. They tried to reassure me that she was probably just out for dinner, there was nothing to worry about, that I could talk to her in the morning. Jessica went back into my room to get ready for bed, but I could not fall asleep.

Next to the Sherry-Netherland number was Dr. Fisher's phone number. I didn't want to call him and humiliate myself but I was desperate. I called the number, but no one picked up, so I left a sobbing, near-hysterical message on his answering machine. Dr. Fisher never called back. The next morning when I finally reached my mom she said Dr. Fisher's wife, who was a teacher at Westlake prep school, assumed it was a prank call from one of her students. I felt the hot burn of shame knowing these important professionals in my mom's life had dismissed my cry for help as a hoax.

After that incident, Dr. Fisher referred us to a child psychologist for my separation anxiety. Thus began my twice-weekly visits to Dr. Murray's Beverly Hills office. Here I was, at age nine, with my very own "talking doctor."

I did not "connect" with Dr. Murray. His office was dim, gloomy, and stocked with brown and olive-green 1970s furniture that looked utilitarian and vaguely Soviet. He was over sixty and wore ugly brown polyester suits and thick glasses with big black frames, his few remaining strands of hair stuck to his sweaty, shiny head. He never smiled. Somewhere in the back of my mind, I remember thinking, *How can you help me with my anxiety if you look so uncomfortable in your own clothing?* My mom was such an intimate, cozy person who wore soft, pretty clothes and smelled good. *Why does Mommie think this guy can help me?* I wondered.

My mom sat outside in the waiting room while I sat inside with Dr. Murray. Sometimes he would ask her to come in for a little while so we could all talk together. But for the most part, it was just the two of us. Dr. Murray sat behind his desk. He stared at me, asked questions, and scrawled observations on his notepad. I thought we were there to figure out why I was so worried about my mom all the time, why I felt so unsafe whenever she was away from me. But I don't recall having one productive or meaningful conversation with him about my mother, her drinking, or anything else. Once, he had me play some sort of game with wooden blocks. I got so annoyed that I threw a block. It struck his forehead and knocked his glasses askew. I was horrified at myself, though he remained silent, his expression blank. He simply adjusted his glasses and continued staring at me.

I probably saw Dr. Murray for a year tops even though it didn't seem to help. I think my mother simply didn't know what else to do.

# Chapter 6

From left, Courtney, Natalie, Natasha,
and Tracey in Chinatown, 1981.

By the time I turned ten, the injustice and hypocrisy of it all really started to bother me. Suddenly the whole setup became crystal clear: my mother could go out in the evenings, work and travel whenever she wanted, but I had to follow her unwavering rules, whether or not she was home.

We started to clash.

As a little girl, I had long, straight, light-brown hair that was fine and tangled easily. I didn't want to deal with the tangles and I didn't want anyone else brushing them out either. In fact, I thought the knots were kind of cool, in a West Coast bohemian way. My mom, however, had zero patience for messy hair. She had grown up in the Hollywood studio system of the 1940s and '50s and was taught to look camera ready at all times, with not a single hair out of place. Her shining tresses always looked perfect and she wanted mine to look perfect too. "Natasha, if you don't start brushing your hair every day, I'm going to cut it all off," she threatened.

Did she want my hair straight and shiny and perfect because that was what her hair looked like when she was my age? In her childhood movies and photos, my mother always wore flawlessly braided pigtails that framed her face like two silken ropes. Did she really want me to be exactly like her?

Instead of doing as I was told, I started to try to trick my mom, to see if I could get one over on her. I began taking my bath and wetting my hair, but not using any shampoo. Then I would take a hairbrush and press down on the tangled hair without actually combing out the knots. I would walk into her room and tell her I was ready for bed, waiting to see if she noticed.

"Natasha, did you wash your hair?"

"Yes," I lied adamantly.

"Well, the knots are still there. Where's the No More Tangles? I will have to brush it myself."

At this point, I confessed that I actually hadn't washed my hair and my mother made her threat to cut it off all over again. Then I pointed out that my friend Tracey didn't have to wash her hair every day and her tangles looked more like curls—Farrah Fawcett curls. My mom didn't care about Farrah Fawcett's curls or Tracey's tangles.

"You are my daughter and my daughter will not walk around with knots in her hair!"

End of conversation.

My mom did not want anything to mar her precious daughter. Once, at Tom Mank's house in Malibu, I accidentally sat down on an empty wineglass. It cut the back of my leg and, when the cut healed, a little raised scar remained. The scar didn't bother me in the slightest. I felt like it gave me an edge. But my mom insisted on taking me to a well-known dermatologist in Beverly Hills, who injected some kind of miracle serum into the scar that made it completely flat and nearly invisible. Looking back, I wonder, was her concern over my appearance for me or for herself? I was Natalie Wood's daughter. I was a reflection of her. Did she worry that I couldn't be seen to be anything less than perfect?

I was spending more and more time with my friend Tracey at her mid-century house in the Hollywood Hills, becoming increasingly aware of the contrast between her family's lifestyle and ours. Tracey's parents were not fussy perfectionists like my mom; quite the contrary, in fact. At their house, you didn't need a code to enter the house. Tracey and I were allowed to eat cereal on their comfortable green-and-brown plaid sofas. This was life well lived, in my mind. If they were out of milk—or vodka, for that matter—Janis would think nothing of popping down to Rexall at ten at night, with Tracey and me in the back seat, no seat belts, along for the ride. *Why are there so many rules at home?*

While Tracey loved the structure and organization at my house— our regular mealtimes and bedtimes, and the neat braids my mom would weave in her hair—I loved the lack of a regime and regulations in *her* house.

Now that we were getting older, Tracey and my other friends were allowed to play outside unsupervised. But my mother wouldn't even let me walk once around our block in broad daylight. Just as my grandmother had always been terrified of someone harming her precious Natasha, now *my* mother was terrified of someone harming *her* precious Natasha. She was convinced that if she gave me even the slightest bit of freedom, something terrible would happen to me. Didn't I know that the Lindbergh baby had been snatched right out of his crib? That Patty Hearst had been held for ransom only a few years earlier?

Around this time my mom decided to install a cream-of-the-crop security system. She hired a well-known security expert who had installed similar systems in many Hollywood homes. The plan was to create a safe space upstairs so that if an intruder ever entered from downstairs we would all be protected in our second-floor fortress. The upstairs railings on the landing were torn down, and in their place, a floor-to-ceiling bulletproof wall with a bulletproof window and a code-locked metal door were erected. My mother's bedroom door was also replaced with a thick metal door that clicked in place with a four-number punch on the keypad. This was our safe room where we could hide if needed. We were also taught a safe word and the protocol for hightailing it upstairs and locking ourselves in. The security expert told us that as safe as we were, the best deterrent were dogs, so we added a new large dog to our brood.

Meanwhile, I didn't care about security; I just wanted to be able to walk a couple of blocks around our neighborhood with my best friends. Tracey and I had started a Save the Whales campaign, which consisted of knocking on people's doors and asking for money. Why did Kilky have to trail behind? At Tracey's house, we were able to roam free.

Billy Joel's "My Life" was popular at that time, and I adopted it as my theme song. When my mom called me at Tracey's house from France or someplace she was visiting with my dad, grilling me with questions like, "Did you finish your homework?" and "What did you eat for breakfast?" I sang the chorus right into the phone at her, which ended with the lines:

> *I don't care what you say anymore, this is my life*
> *Go ahead with your own life, leave me alone!*

Then I hung up the phone defiantly. And immediately I would miss her, longing for her comforting hugs and feeling guilty for pushing her away.

Tracey and I decided to run away. We built a go-cart using wheels from old roller skates and a flat piece of plywood we found in her backyard. Her mother's friend Doug drilled holes in the board and attached the wheels, and once we could roll down the hill we were off. I left an ultimatum for my parents in the form of a ransom note that read, "I'm not coming back unless you give Courtney up for adoption." Tracey wrote a similar note to her parents about her brother Steven. We left the notes at Tracey's house and go-carted to our friend April's house, where we planned to hide out. The minute we arrived, April's phone rang. It was Tracey's mom, Janis. "Are Tracey and Natasha there?" April instantly caved in and said, "Yes." So much for our big getaway. Mommie was so angry when she came to pick me up. This was not a joke to her; she took it very seriously and quite personally. In the car, I gingerly ventured to ask, "Is Daddy at the house?" I'll never forget the fire in her voice when she snapped, "*Both* daddies are there!"

Daddy Gregson and Daddy Wagner were waiting in the living room when we got back home. Both of them seemed rather calm and slightly entertained. My mother turned to Daddy Gregson. "Richard, what are we going to do about this? Natasha needs to be grounded!" He looked at me and started laughing. So I started laughing. Then Daddy Wagner joined in. The only person who was not laughing was my mom. "This is not funny!" my mom said. "This is very, very serious." My dads tried to diffuse my mom's rage by explaining that this was *not* a major transgression. Together they reached a sort of compromise punishment: I was forbidden to see Tracey for a week.

The following Monday, Liz came to work and found me sitting at the top of the stairs with a wild grin on my face.

"Why do you look so pleased?" she asked.

"I ran away from home with Tracey," I whispered proudly. "I'm grounded from Tracey's for a week!"

I was over the moon with my mini-rebellion and the impact it had had on my mom. My mother had power over me *but I had power over her too*!

Clearly my mother and I were transitioning into a new phase in our relationship. My mother wanted me to become less anxious and obsessive when she was out in the evenings or away on trips. But she didn't necessarily want me to spread my wings and start doing things independently of her. I wanted my freedom, while at the same time, I struggled with being apart from her.

A few months later, I asked to go to a sleep-away camp in Malibu where I would take care of horses and live with other kids for five days. Daddy Gregson championed the cause, but in my mother's eyes, the very idea was scandalous. Her little Natasha sleeping away from home for almost a week? But I begged and pleaded. Somehow, my dad talked her into it.

"Are you okay?" she asked on the phone every evening, having gotten special permission to call. "Do you need me to come and get you?"

"No, I'm fine, I'm fine," I assured her. Then when I got into the shower each night, I let the tears stream down my face. I missed her so much. I tried hard to be like all the other kids, who seemed just fine—happy, in fact—to be away from their parents, but then the hard truth would hit me: I couldn't manage without my mother for longer than a day.

This may have been a natural, healthy phase of our relationship, but it bothered us both because we had always been so close. "Natasha wears her heart on her sleeve," I used to overhear my mom telling her friends. "I always know how she's feeling."

But I wanted a degree of distance from her. I didn't want her to know all my thoughts and feelings.

When my mother was annoyed with me, she tried hard not to show it, but I could always tell because she assumed a pleasant yet professional tone, a veneer of calm and control. "Well, Natasha," she would enunciate in her best on-camera voice, proceeding to explain to me why things must be done her way. On the rare occasions when she got *really* angry, I could practically sense the electricity in the air. Her whole body vibrated with feeling.

One Saturday afternoon, Courtney and I desperately wanted to go see the movie *The Blue Lagoon*, but she wouldn't take us. Though it was a story about two kids, it was not a movie for children, as indicated by its R rating. We wouldn't take no for an answer. We poked and pestered and drove her crazy until she finally snapped and said, "Fine! We will go see *The Blue Lagoon*! Get ready *now*!" We followed sheepishly behind her as she stalked out the front door shouting, "R.J., we're going to see *The Blue Lagoon*!" Courtney and I knew by her voice that she was seriously unhappy with us. The car ride to Westwood Village was a silent affair. We weren't sure if getting to see the movie was a victory or a defeat.

I knew my mom didn't enjoy having to get angry or discipline us. She would much rather laugh and have fun with her girls. She preferred to keep the mood upbeat, to call me "Natooshie" or her "little petunia." Or Courtney "little Court." She didn't like having to say, "Well, Natasha," in that affected tone any more than I liked hearing it. Despite our increasing clashes and my new desire to kick down the boundaries she set, the deep emotional bond we shared was unshakable. I complained to my friends, my dads—anyone who would listen—that she kept me on a tight leash, and yet I continued to sink into sadness whenever we were separated.

I was trying to figure out how I was different from her. It was already clear to me how much we were alike.


Another wedge between my mother and me soon appeared in the form of a new figure in my life: my stepmother, Julia. Although Daddy Gregson had a home in England, he was spending more time at his apartment on the beach in Malibu. He had fallen in love with his new girlfriend Julia, who I thought was the most glorious lady in the world, second only to my mom. I fell for her instantly.

I remember the first time I saw Julia. I was lying in bed at night at my father's place in Malibu. I heard soft footsteps on the wooden pathway leading to my dad's front door, so I crept out of bed and peered through the window. There she was—tall with long, curly red hair, full lips, and clear blue eyes. She wore flowing skirts and silver and brass bangles stacked up and down her arms, her bracelets ringing like bells as she walked. She looked like a model, so different from my tiny, dark-haired, dark-eyed mom with her tight jeans and high heels. I knew right then I was going to love Julia. I crawled back into bed and fell asleep, dreaming of when we would meet face-to-face.

When I did meet Julia the following weekend she was everything I had imagined that night and more. Along with her beauty, she had one of the loveliest English accents I had ever heard. I discovered that she was a journalist and a former model. Later she became a successful novelist.

Julia loved dogs, horses, cooking delicious food, and telling stories. I loved dogs, horses, eating delicious food, and listening to her stories. She told me about growing up in the wilds of Australia, breaking horses, foraging for berries with her sister, Caroline. Julia had the kind of childhood I dreamed about, with endless freedom to roam, discover, create. I could tell that my mom was slightly annoyed by my love affair with Julia and so I used this awareness to needle her. I told her how beautiful and *young* Julia was. That she was a true bohemian and that she had bouncy curls, "just like Farrah Fawcett." I said I may want to live with Daddy Gregson and Julia in England when I got a bit older but that I definitely wanted to spend "all my weekends" at their apartment in Malibu until then. Mommie was not happy about my new infatuation with my dad's girlfriend. Maybe she felt hurt and left out. There was something about my life at the beach with my British dad and Julia that threatened her.

At my dad's place, Julia and I hung out in the kitchen while she prepared shepherd's pie, rhubarb crumble, leg of lamb, and rich English trifles for dessert. On hot summer evenings, the three of us went for long walks on the beach in Malibu. Along the way we collected stones and driftwood, sometimes building fires or stone sculptures. On Sundays we went horseback riding in the hills of Calabasas, setting off down the 101 freeway in my dad's Mercedes convertible, my long brown hair and Julia's red curls blowing like streamers in the wind. My friend Tracey often joined us. Although the horses were pretty tame and mostly just trudged up the hills good-naturedly, once Tracey's horse actually took off on a canter over the mountain, with Tracey screaming into the wind, "JULIA, DOOO SOMETHING!!" Julia immediately set off galloping behind Tracey, speaking some kind of horse language that not only stopped the horse in his tracks but silenced Tracey's hysterics too. Nothing worried Julia. She never lost her cool. This was new for me. She was the first female figure in my life who taught me that scary things can happen and you don't need to panic.

When we stopped at Denny's for lunch on the way back, my dad and Julia let Tracey and me sit at our own separate table. We pretended we were on our own—maybe we were runaways or orphans, or we worked at the stables and were taking our lunch break. Daddy and Julia gave us just the right amount of distance between tables. They could watch to make sure we were safe while allowing us to feel separate and grown-up. I wasn't used to having this kind of space, this much room to breathe. At my dad's place, I could roam up and down the beach with a friend for hours, talking, dipping my toes in the sand and surf, playing with dogs, whatever. It was no big deal. Daddy and Julia called me in when it was time for dinner. This was a radically different environment than our gated, bulletproof house on Canon Drive.

One of my British dad's biggest fears was that I would somehow be spoiled growing up in a "lotus-eating la-la land," as he called it. He wanted me to be self-reliant. He wanted *me* to be the one mucking out the horse stables, putting the saddles and bridles away, using the farrier rasp to clean the horses' hooves. This directly clashed with my mother's desire to insulate me from the harsher aspects of life. My mom would have preferred me to just ride the horse and let the stable staff do the rest. It wasn't so much that she thought I was above doing those kinds of things; it was that those types of things posed a risk to my safety. What if the horse accidentally kicked or stepped on me?

My British dad wanted me to enjoy the kind of freedom and responsibility afforded most kids my age. When he came to visit, he'd ask me questions like, "Did you walk around the block today?" and I'd say, "I'm not allowed to walk around the block." Then he'd confront my mom. "Natalie, Natasha is ten years old. She should be able to leave her house and walk around her own block." She would say, "Are you crazy? Absolutely not! She can walk around the block if somebody's with her, but not by herself."

Our problems were not insurmountable, but they were real. My mother had made me into a princess locked in a comfortable Beverly Hills tower and herself into an obstinate palace guard. I wanted to unfurl my long, tangled locks of hair to the street below, like Rapunzel in my favorite fairy tale. But at the same time, I was afraid of what might happen if I did.

# Chapter 7

Natasha and Natalie in Newport,
California, 1981.

As my grandparents approached their seventies, their health took a
turn for the worse. Deda had always suffered from heart problems;
now he had to have bypass surgery. I remember him in his hospital
bed, a scar across his heart and little white stickers on his chest. He
never fully recovered. He still had his gentle and kind smile, his warm
eyes, and his soft, accented voice, but each time we saw my grandfather he was increasingly frail.

Not only was my mother dealing with her father's failing health, she was also all too aware that when the time came—and Deda passed away—Baba was going to fall apart and would need a lot of caretaking. My grandmother suffered from fainting spells and now she had arthritis in her hands, her fingers curling at the joints. Her blood pressure had begun to rise and she needed to take pills to lower it. I remember hearing my parents' clipped conversations about how best to deal with Baba when Deda died. My mother told the nurses to call her first so she could let Baba know. It was clear to me that my mom was parenting her parents and not the other way around.

Deda passed away in November 1980. He was the first person in my family who had died, but because he had been sick for some time, I don't remember feeling sad. Instead I felt curious about my mother's reaction to his death. I took my cues from her, calibrating my emotions to hers. My mom threw herself into organizing the funeral. She was the one to let her mother and sisters know Deda had died, she planned the services and arranged for the priest; she did it all.

At Deda's funeral, I watched my mom closely. She was going to be the one to read his eulogy. I remember her standing at a podium at the front of the church, delivering her tribute to her father, surrounded by flowers and candles. Courtney and I were seated next to our dad and Baba. As my mom said the words that she had carefully written to honor her father, her voice caught. The emotion of the moment was too much for her, and she paused to swallow and reset herself. That moment is imprinted on me, so rarely did I see her lose control: my beautiful, self-composed mother, taking a beat and then righting herself so she could carry on with her tribute.

Many years later I found in her datebook a pencil sketch my mother made of the profile of my grandfather's face on the day he died. It was as if she were trying to hold on to him, to stamp his features in her memory before he left her forever. Their relationship had been complicated by my grandmother's ways, by my mother's need and desire to break free from her parents' control, by my grandfather's bouts with alcohol dependency and melancholy, yet there was always love between them.

No one could have ever guessed or predicted that almost exactly a year later, we would be attending another funeral, this time for my mother.

In the months after Deda's death, my parents' lives continued in high gear. My mom's datebooks list the directors she wanted to collaborate with—"Alan Parker, John Schlesinger, Scorsese, Fosse, Milos Forman, Sidney Lumet, Sydney Pollack"—right alongside her reminders to take me and Courtney to ballet, piano lessons, gym class, math tutoring, and social events ("Natasha to Tracey's overnight"), Katie's class trip to Europe, doctor appointments, black tie affairs ("Dinner at 20th Century-Fox for king and queen of Spain"), and on and on.

My mother felt a pull to try live theater, which she had never done, and was planning to star in a stage version of *Anastasia* at the Ahmanson Theatre. The play was based on the true story of Anna Anderson, a young woman who insisted she was the only surviving member of the Romanov family, having escaped execution by the Bolsheviks in 1918. My mother felt connected to the story for obvious reasons, and she was hoping her old friend Laurence Olivier might direct her in the play (in the end, the timing wasn't right for him). Live theater was going to be the ultimate challenge for her, the biggest moment of her career since *Splendor in the Grass* in terms of stretching herself as an actor. She always said that her voice was her Achilles' heel—she worried it wasn't loud or deep enough to project to the back of a theater. As much as she was scared to try acting in a play, she was also electrified by the possibility.

She had lots of plans. In August, she signed a contract to executive produce and star in a suspense thriller called *Mother Love*. She hoped to play Zelda Fitzgerald, the wife of F. Scott Fitzgerald, in a biopic. When that fell through, she accepted a role in a sci-fi feature called

*Brainstorm*, costarring Christopher Walken, who had recently won an Academy Award for his role in *The Deer Hunter*.

I could tell my mother was readying herself for the camera in the late summer and early fall of 1981, because she was eating light and trying out different weight-loss tactics like the Scarsdale Diet. Sometimes she let me observe her Pilates sessions, or even sit on her lap, "if you sit quiet as a mouse," she said. I would follow her to the pool house and watch with fascination as her instructor taught her to use the machine. She also got regular massages, which, in those days, were thought to help people lose weight. (It was another time. . . .)

In early September my mother told me she would need to go to North Carolina for a few weeks in September and November to shoot some scenes for her new film project *Brainstorm*. My dad was also going to be shooting *Hart to Hart* in Hawaii in November. This was the first time both of my parents would be away from us for work simultaneously.

I knew my dad wasn't too happy about the situation. Although he always supported my mom's career, he also understood the realities of having three children. Someone needed to be our anchor at home, keeping things grounded and in place. My dad was working long hours on a TV show. He couldn't be that person. But now my mom seemed to be just as busy as he was. I think even my mom knew it was getting to be too much. She had started talking to him about relocating us to New York, away from the Hollywood circus.

One of the hardest parts of her being in North Carolina was that she was going to miss my birthday at the end of September. In our home, birthdays were celebrated to the max. All our friends came over to our house. We opened a towering pile of presents. Each year the cake was a slightly different theme, but it was always something extravagantly girlie: a princess, pink roses, butterflies, rainbows. Last birthday I had turned ten—double digits!—and my parents had taken six of my girlfriends and me for a weekend on our boat in Catalina.

My mom sat down with me to break the news that she was going to be away for my big day. "Now, Natasha, you know I have to go to North Carolina in November to work," she explained, "but I will also have to be gone for a week or so in late September." Pause. "I am going to miss your birthday, my darling, but I will be able to fly home for the weekend so we can have your party, and then you and Daddy are going to go on a special date on your actual birthday to the Bistro. How does that sound?"

I was sad and scared to be without her, but I remember trying to be brave because I was turning eleven, which I knew was a grown-up age. I tried to make her feel better by reassuring her. I told her that not only was I going to be okay without her on my true birthday but also I was excited to have my dad all to myself.

After she left for North Carolina, she and I mailed letters back and forth to each other. They were just simple notes. "Dear Mommie, I hope you're having fun, I miss you," I wrote in one. I illustrated the bottom of the page with a little drawing of a tear. In case she missed the symbolism, I wrote "tear" next to it. In late October, Courtney and I joined our dad in Hawaii, where he was shooting, and when we got back in early November, the house was empty without her.

I called her at her hotel. "When are you coming back home?"

"Soon," she said. "I miss you and Courtney so much, Natooshie."

Earlier, in September, when my birthday had come around, she'd flown in the weekend before, just as she had promised she would, for my party. We had a piñata and lots of candy. All my girlfriends came and Courtney was there too. I was having so much fun I didn't even mind that my mom would be heading back to North Carolina that night. On my actual birthday, I went out to dinner with Daddy Wagner, me in my fancy new Pierre Deux dress that my godmother Ruth had given me, Daddy looking dapper in one of his *Hart to Hart* suits. The waiter brought a cream-colored rotary phone over to the table. It had a long cord. My mom was on the other end wishing me a happy birthday. I was happy; I felt loved.

• • •

When my mother finally came home right before the Thanksgiving holiday, I showered her with kisses and gave her one of my strangulation hugs. How could I ever think of this beautiful, warm, radiant soul as an overprotective nuisance? She was my mom. I wanted to hug her forever, to never let go. My Mommie, my love, my everything.

Thanksgiving was right around the corner. Just like birthdays, any holiday at Canon Drive was a big deal. My parents threw New Year's Eve parties, Easter lunches, Christmas dinners with friends and relatives over, presents, and plenty of food. Thanksgiving was no exception. Helen and Gene, the married couple who cooked for us, arrived the day before with bags filled with groceries, then came back early the next morning to start the cooking. Smells of turkey roasting in the oven, candied pecans frying in a pan, oranges being hulled out to make room for the mashed sweet potatoes filled the house. My friend Tracey came home with me after school on Wednesday and would be staying over Wednesday and Thursday and then I was going to spend the weekend at her house. On Thursday morning Courtney, Tracey, and I woke up early, excited for the day ahead. My mom was also early to rise, returning calls, picking daisies and chrysanthemums in the garden and arranging them in vases, calling out to my dad with questions and requests.

We kids knew we needed to bathe early. My hair was diligently washed and combed, prepped, and ready for curlers. I could never dream of arguing about my tangles on Thanksgiving morning. After we finished washing, Kilky helped Courtney and I put on our pretty, newly purchased just-for-the-occasion dresses, brown and forest-green velvet with little white lace collars. Then we went to find my mom in her bathroom. She was in her robe, curlers in her hair, eye makeup already applied. Brushing her teeth with the Macleans toothpaste she always used, spritzing herself with her Jungle Gardenia. A second set of hot rollers was waiting for us on the side, so that she could fix the rollers in our hair with a pin before we went off to play.

Soon enough our guests arrived: Baba; my dad's mother Chattie; my godfather Mart; Katie and her brother Josh Donen, who was living in our guesthouse at the time; and Delphine Mann. We all went downstairs to greet them. My dad behind the bar in the den, my mom welcoming everyone. Nuts in shiny dishes, cocktail napkins perched on coffee tables, fresh wooden matches with their forest-green tips in silver match strikers throughout the house, just as they always were for a party. In the dining room, the food was served buffet-style. We gathered our plates and sat in the living room or den. On sofas, in chairs, on the carpet. Everyone dressed up yet nobody minding if they wound up on the floor. Over the course of the evening the piano was played, toasts were made, jokes and stories told. Then a confection of desserts appeared: pumpkin, pecan, and apple pies; ice cream; and pumpkin pie cheesecake (my favorite).

If there was any pall or sadness—even a frisson—between my parents that night, either I didn't notice or I don't recall. In my memory, our last Thanksgiving together was just as it had always been: full of food, warmth, good friends, and happiness.

But we were about to be separated again. That weekend, my mom and dad were planning a boat trip to Catalina with Christopher Walken, the lead actor in my mom's new film project. Mommie asked Courtney, Katie, and me to go on the boat too, just like we often did, all of us together. I didn't want to go on the boat—I wanted to spend the weekend with Tracey. As usual Courtney wanted to do whatever I did, so decided not to go either. Katie was a teenager and had her own plans. My mom invited Delphine Mann and a couple of other friends, but no one could make it. And so she was going to go alone with my dad and Christopher.

My internal conflict never raged harder than on that Friday in November. I wanted to be independent—I knew I had to stop clinging to Mommie and be my own person, to make my own plans like Katie—but at the same time, I wanted to be with my mom. I had to fight hard against my desire to prevent her from going or to go along with her so she would be within my sights and I would know she was safe.

I ended up asking her to stay home.

"Don't worry, Natooshie," she said. "Everything will be okay."

I knew she must be right. Everything would be okay. We would spend the weekend apart—she was going on the boat; I was going to Tracey's house—and we would see each other on Sunday night when she returned.

It had stormed Thursday night, and that Friday dawned dark, cold, and drizzly. My mom, my dad, and Christopher were sitting and talking at the bar in the den before the trip. The weather and the mood felt dangerous to me, and after she went upstairs to finish getting ready, my old anxious feelings started up again. Suddenly I was crying; my heart was pounding; I could barely breathe.

Maybe it was because we had already been separated for several weeks, and my mom had only just come back home. Maybe it was because of the rainstorm the night before. Maybe because I didn't know Christopher Walken. Maybe because it was a holiday weekend. . . . I don't know, I just knew I wanted her to cancel the trip and stay home.

I went to find her upstairs in her bathroom.

"Mommie, I don't want you to go," I told her.

"Natooshie, we'll be fine," she said. I could tell by her sweet smile and the way she brushed my long hair out of my face that she wasn't taking me seriously. I often told her I didn't want her going away. For my mom, this was just a reenactment of so many familiar scenes from our past.

She probably just assumed I would have a great time with Tracey that weekend, that I would enjoy the haircut she had booked for me that Saturday morning at the proper grown-up salon she had just started going to. In hindsight, I imagine she thought that as soon as she was back from the weekend and *Brainstorm* wrapped we would reconnect, take a long look at our separation issues, maybe hire a new therapist, and start planning for Christmas.

To my mom, this was all business as usual. To me, it was something more.

My dad came to find us. "Daddy, I'm scared," I told him. "I don't want you guys to go."

He reassured me. "Oh, Natooshie, what do you think is going to happen?"

"I don't know," I said. I knew I sounded whiney, like a little child. I was eleven now—not a clinging baby anymore. But I couldn't shake this feeling. *Why won't they listen to me?*

Once more, in a small voice, I asked my mother to stay. With a sweet, understanding but firm tone of voice, she made it clear that she would be going. That was final.

My mother was wearing a soft, fuzzy, light-colored angora sweater with pastel appliqués on it that day. I twisted the soft strands in my fingers. Finally she knelt down to give me a long hug goodbye. Her eyes locked with mine.

"I know you don't want me to go," she said. "But I promise you I am going to be okay."

"You promise?"

"I promise."

Usually when we had a heart-to-heart conversation and I looked deep into her eyes, I would be comforted for the rest of the day. But not this time. About an hour after they left, Mommie called to check on me when they stopped off in Marina del Rey to get a bite to eat before boarding the boat. Once again I broke into tears and pleaded with her not to go. Once again she reassured me. That Friday night, while I was staying at Tracey's house, my mom called from a hotel on Catalina Island, explaining to me that she had come ashore for the night because the sea was too rough and she was getting queasy. She asked me how I was feeling and if I was still worried about her. I told her that I had calmed down a little and was enjoying myself. That was the last time I ever spoke to her.

PART 2

# Without

# Chapter 8

Natasha, circa 1981–82.

After Kilky came to get me from Tracey's house that terrible Sunday morning, after my dad came home and confirmed it was true—that my mother was gone and not coming home ever again—the sensation I most vividly remember is pure terror. *Did the one thing I've been most scared of my whole life actually just happen?* Was I cursed with a sixth sense? Did I foresee it? I was always so afraid of losing my mom—unnaturally afraid. And now I had lost her. Forever. *Why did this happen? Why did it happen to me?* In my traumatized eleven-year-old mind the answer was obvious: it happened because my mom was so famous and beautiful and everybody knew that we were so close. I had been blessed with this gift of an extra-special mother. So this must be some kind of punishment. The Lord had given, and the Lord was now taking away. Perhaps I was being punished for striving for independence when she died, for not appreciating her as much as I used to. Is that what had caused her death?

I remember the next several days in patchwork flashes; some moments come back with clarity, while others are missing.

My dad went to bed and stayed there. He was incapable of functioning.

Liz told me that Baba fainted when she heard the news. She had only recently lost her husband, and now fate had taken away her dearest Natasha too. It must have been the darkest day of Maria Gurdin's life. I don't remember seeing Baba in the days after my mother's death. I think they tried to keep her away from Courtney and me because she was too hysterical.

I stayed close to my dad. I didn't want to let him out of my sight. Kilky and Liz were doing their best to mother Courtney and me. My little sister—who was, at age seven, too young to understand what had happened to her mom—reacted by attaching herself even more strongly to Kilky. I chose to latch onto my dad, even though he was practically insensate with grief. He was the next best thing to Mommie. He was the person I most closely associated with her.

I remember spending a lot of time in their bedroom right after she died. I napped in her bed. It was a way to feel close to her, to smell her perfume, to inhabit her space. The room was still filled with her energy. On the little notepad by her vanity, she had scribbled a dinner date:

"Herbert and Nora Ross December 6th 7pm Orlando-Orsini."

I stared at that note a lot. I couldn't make sense of it. December 6 was coming up, just a few days after her funeral. She had planned to meet her friends at Orlando-Orsini, but now she wasn't going to be there. What would happen? Would Herbert and Nora Ross scratch that date from their calendar? Would they show up at the restaurant? She must have made all kinds of plans for the future that were never going to happen. How could life just continue without her?

That first week was the strangest of my life. Nobody went to school. Nobody went to work. There was no structure—no bedtimes, no mealtimes, no rules. Calendars, schedules, and clocks became meaningless. It was like being on a long plane flight; it gets dark and you don't know what land you're over or what time zone you're in. Nothing happening down on earth seems to matter.

The house was full of people. The first person who showed up was Daddy Gregson. He arrived from England, picked me up as if I were a baby, and carried me into my room. There he held me in his arms for what might have been an hour or longer—it just felt like forever. He told me that he loved me very much, that he had loved my mother, and that I would be okay. My dignified British father seemed so over-come with emotion, unable to find words. This was completely out of character for him and therefore a little awkward for me. The person I usually went to for intimacy and comfort was my mom, not my dad. Yet on that awful black Sunday, he knew that I needed to feel a tight connection to my birth father, my only living biological parent. And I did. After he comforted me, he went in to talk to Daddy Wag-ner. I later found out that he offered to take me back to England, but R.J. wanted Courtney, Katie, and me to stay together. In my mom's will she asked that if anything ever happened that Courtney and I be raised together. Daddy Gregson agreed. Any further loss or separation would have been detrimental.

My godfather Mart was at the house, as well as Howard, Del-phine, and, eventually, every single person my parents ever knew, or so it seemed. Friends, family, acquaintances, church officials, neigh-bors, celebrities, well-wishers, mourners, deliverymen appeared on Canon Drive at all hours of the day and night. I remember thinking, *Don't these people ever sleep?* They filed into the living rooms, the den, and the kitchen, hugging me and Courtney and Katie, crying, and saying how sorry they were. Adults I barely knew were so nice to me. I remember Kate Jackson from *Charlie's Angels* handing me a scrap of paper, saying, "This is my phone number. This phone is right by my bed. You call me if you need me." Paul Simon, who was one of my mom's favorite musicians, came by with his wife at the time, Carrie Fisher. There were the drinks, the nuts in silver bowls on the bar. It was like the biggest party we ever had, but this was not a celebration.

My girlfriends came with their parents. There was an Atari system in Kilky's room, and I played Pong and Hangman there with my friends. I remember one time when my friend Caprice was starting to win at Hangman, I quickly pushed a button to prematurely end the game. *I can do this*, I thought, *because my mom just died*. Caprice looked at me like she was about to tell me off, and then stopped herself. It was like I was testing everyone around me to see how real this was. *If Caprice gets mad at me, maybe my mom didn't really die.* But my friend didn't get mad. She let me win the game. It was real.

The parade of people at home continued. My dad remained upstairs in his bed. In the coming days, I witnessed all of these adults, many of whom I'd grown up around and trusted completely, falling apart at the seams like the Velveteen Rabbit. I could see their buttons and threads fraying and unraveling. People consumed glass after glass of alcohol and broke down wailing or laughing hysterically, sometimes both at the same time. I was used to my parents and their friends getting tipsy, but I had never seen grown-ups lose total control like this before. I often felt like the sanest, soberest person in the room, able to observe everything. Once, I went downstairs and saw Mart standing with a small crowd in the dining room. He was clutching a silver ice bucket that had belonged to my mom, holding it close to his chest and sobbing, "I'm taking this! I'm taking it!"

On the lawn just outside our front gates, hordes of press perched day and night with their Kodaks, their microphones, and their video cameras on tripods, swarming on anyone who entered or exited the house. I had never seen so many photographers before. They made us prisoners in our own home. The police were there too, trying to suppress the crowds and traffic outside. Cars were parked all up and down our street. News coverage of my mom's death was on the radio and television constantly. I didn't want to see it on TV. I didn't want to hear about it on the radio. If the news—or any mention of my mother—appeared on a television set, I changed the channel.

After my mom died, Kilky wheeled a TV set into my bedroom on a portable table. When my mother was alive, she never allowed me

to have a TV in my room. But now I was breaking that rule. *I like watching TV in my room*, I thought, *but Mommie would not be happy about this.* I suddenly had the freedom to do all the things she had prohibited. R.J. was in bed and so no one stopped me from eating junk food, staying up late, or playing video games . . . but the victory left me feeling guilty and confused. Not only was my mother gone; all the rules and routines she had so carefully established were gone too. Were the rules she made not valid anymore? Or was I allowed to break them because everyone felt sorry for me?

I silently bolstered myself: *I have to get through this. I can't go down.* And then I realized: *I need to see her, that's what I have to do. I have to see her.* Something deep within me knew that it was not acceptable for me to live my entire life without ever seeing my mother's face again. I had been told there was going to be a closed casket at the funeral service, so that meant I had to get to her before the funeral happened. I told Daddy Gregson, "I need to see Mommie." He told Daddy Wagner, and they had a therapist come to the house and discuss the pros and cons. Daddy Wagner was afraid I would be traumatized by seeing my mother in a coffin, but it was eventually decided that, though it might be a little scary, it might help me to accept her death and give me the chance to say a belated goodbye. Daddy Wagner knew he wouldn't be able to take me to the mortuary, that he couldn't bear it and wouldn't be able to cope.

"I can't take Natasha," I remember him saying. "I can't go."

So Daddy Gregson said, "I'll take her."

I decided to write a letter to my mom, so I could give it to her the next day at the mortuary. In my bedroom, I sat down at my white wicker desk and opened the drawer that held my stationery. So many times I had written thank-you notes or birthday cards to my parents or other adults from this spot. Only a few weeks ago, I sat here writing love notes to my mom while she was filming in North Carolina. Now she had gone away and she wasn't coming back. I knew that

she would never read this new note, but even so, I needed to write it and she needed to have it. I pulled out a piece of my stationery and sat there at my desk, writing. When tears fell on the paper, I wiped them away with my hands and kept on writing. I think the note went something like this:

*Mommie,*

*You took up a lot of space in our lives. It's going to be really hard to live without you. I don't know if Courtney understands, but I do. Daddy Wagner and I are taking it the hardest. But I'm going to be okay, I'm going to help him be okay, and Courtney will be okay too. But I really miss you. I love you.*

*Natooshie*

Then I neatly folded the letter.

My dad's driver, Stanley Stork, drove Daddy Gregson, Liz, Kilky, Courtney, and me to the mortuary in a limousine. I remember arriving at the cemetery, driving through wide-open gates, past a park laid out with green grass and rows of white headstones. A small brown house came into view at the end of the lot. It looked cozy and comfortable, completely out of place in a graveyard. My dad explained that this was the mortuary. We got out of the car to go inside. I kept my head down, holding on to his hand, letting him lead the way. He was in charge this morning.

Inside, the mortuary smelled like sadness. A mixture of old furniture and the same wood polishing spray we used at our house. We were led into a room. There were chairs against one wall and a casket at the far end. Liz, Kilky, Courtney, Stanley, and Daddy Gregson sat down in the chairs. I slowly walked toward the casket. Behind me I could hear muffled chokes and sobs and so I turned around. Stanley was crying. I had never really seen adults cry until a couple of days ago—now it seemed as if they couldn't stop. My little sister, Courtney, was dancing around, not really focused on the situation.

"Can I please be alone with her for a few minutes?" I asked.

This was my last chance to talk to my mom. Just the two of us. Everybody left the room.

I walked up to the casket.

I don't know what I expected my mom's dead body to look like, but the woman in the coffin did not look like my mother. Her face was harder, her nose pointier, her skin rubbery. It was as if all the warmth and light and coziness had been sucked out of her. Her makeup hadn't sunk into her face; instead it sat on top of the skin like it didn't belong there, a translucent mask that didn't quite cover up a small bruise on her forehead and another one near her cheekbone. Then there was her hair. I thought, *That's not her hair. The color is wrong and it's falling the wrong way.* Her feet looked weird too. Instead of lying straight, they were flopping out to the sides. She was wearing white low-heeled pumps and panty hose. The feet looked like the feet of an old lady, not my mom's.

I knew I needed to find a way to feel connected to her. That's all I wanted. A moment to feel close to her again. So I stood there, waiting to get used to her pointy features, the strange hair that didn't look like hers, the feet splaying out awkwardly to the left and right. At least her hands still looked like her hands—the perfect French-tipped manicure and the gold Cartier wedding ring were in place. Diamond studs in her ears. She had her Elsa Peretti gold cuff on her left wrist, covering up the bump. There was a thin cream-colored blanket folded underneath her shoes. I had never seen this blanket before.

I reached out to touch her hand and jumped back when I felt it. Her skin was not soft and warm. I told myself, *Okay, that's just because she's dead. She isn't in her body.* I waited a minute and touched her hand again. *This is what a dead body feels like. It's not so scary. She is right here. I am right here. I can do this.* I lifted my mom's heavy, cold hand and placed the folded letter underneath it. I wanted to say something to her. I started to talk to her in a soothing voice, mimicking the soothing way she used to speak to me. A blend of a whisper and a song. I told her that I loved her so much and I missed her. "I don't really know where you are now," I said, "but I'm going to stay in touch with you. I'm going to figure out a way to stay connected to you." And that was it. I was done.

I told the grown-ups I had finished. Now Courtney wanted to see our mom and give her something too and so Stanley took off the scarf he had around his neck and handed it to her. When Courtney stepped up to the coffin, I think she got scared. She sort of haphazardly threw the scarf in and ran off. I was not happy when I saw the scarf had landed right over my mom's face. I asked Liz to fix it. "It can't be on her face," I said adamantly. "You need to move the scarf."

"I will, lovey," Liz said in her kind way.

Then I asked Liz about the blanket. She told me the plan was to pull it up to my mom's shoulders before they closed the top of the casket. I asked to speak to the man in charge. I told him calmly and clearly that I needed to be the one to pull the blanket up over my mother. Together the three of us went back into the room. He and Liz helped me pull the soft, cream-colored blanket from under her feet. Then they left me alone. I gently pulled the blanket up to her shoulders. I smoothed it over her chest. I patted it down gently on the side of her body that I could reach. I tucked her in the way she had tucked me in. "Good night, Mommie. I love you," I said. Then I walked out of the room.

Later, I learned that my mother's friends had gone to great lengths to make her look as much like herself as possible. They asked her hairdresser, Sydney Guilaroff, to fix her hair—which had become hopelessly matted after being in the water. Somehow, Sidney managed to shampoo her hair, blow-drying it and combing it over a dark brown hairpiece or fall that had been worn by Ava Gardner. Eddie Butterworth, her longtime makeup artist, had done her makeup. Liz told me that he kept having to stop because his tears would drop onto her face and smudge his handiwork. Of course, the first thing I said to Mart after viewing the body was, "That wasn't her hair." He looked crestfallen. "Are you kidding me right now, that wasn't her hair?" he said. "We worked so hard, and the first thing you say is, 'That wasn't her hair'!" But I was right, it wasn't her hair, and it wasn't even her hairpiece. Poor Mart. Everyone wanted to contribute their services, but they were in a state of shock.

After the viewing, we went back home to get dressed for the funeral.

First I had to take a bath. I remember easing myself into the bathtub, the heat of the water spreading through my body, hotter than I can ever remember it being before. This was the same bathroom I had taken baths in for eight years, my own bathroom with the pink carpet and the Vitabath bubbles. But nothing was the same.

I could hear Kilky calling to me from the other side of the door.

"Tasha, you wanna wear the dress that Ruth gave you? The one from Pierre Deux?"

"Okay," I said, looking at my limbs under the water. They appeared blurry.

The Pierre Deux dress was my special dress for special occasions. *This is a special occasion*, I remember thinking. *Mommie has been dead only a few days and now we are burying her. Why is everything happening so quickly? Why do people have funerals so soon?*

Looking around the bathroom, everything was familiar; everything was different. *What's going to happen to me?* There had been a dull ache and pale ringing in my head constantly since Mommie died. *Who am I? Do I even exist? Is this a dream?* Now that I couldn't define myself by her moves, her love, her attention, I felt raw and alone, so small.

I washed my hair, remembering to add No More Tangles because the smell reminded me of her. *Mommie never wants me to have tangles in my hair. If I do, she will cut it off. But now she is in a coffin. I have just seen her this morning.*

After my bath, I got dressed and put on my shoes. I looked in the mirror. I was wearing the brown-and-yellow-flowered dress that my godmother had given me for my eleventh birthday only two months ago, the same special dress I wore to the Bistro for my birthday dinner with Daddy Wagner. The next time I had planned to wear the dress was on Christmas Eve. Instead, I wore it for my mom's funeral and never wore it again.

Daddy Wagner somehow managed to get out of bed, take a shower, shave, and put on a suit. I don't know who helped him get ready but somebody must have because he could barely move or walk or talk. We drove back to the cemetery together.

The service was on a lawn underneath a big tree. All the most important adults in my mom's life were there. These people who were usually smiling and happy seemed far away, their faces flat with sadness. Crisp white gardenias lay on top of my mother's closed wooden casket. Gardenias in November, her favorite flower. They were everywhere that day, stitched into the men's lapels, held dearly in the grasp of all the women's hands. Someone gave me one to hold.

The speakers were her close friends Tommy Thompson, Hope Lange, and Roddy McDowall. The sky overhead was gray and overcast, but as Hope spoke eloquently about my mom's heart and her warmth, the sun emerged from behind a cloud.

After the speeches stopped, Daddy Wagner walked to my mother's coffin and placed a gardenia on it. He kissed the casket. I remember feeling so worried that he would just fall down dead right in front of her, he was so distraught. As she was lowered into the ground, I understood that this was final. I didn't want to cry in front of all these people, but I could not stop myself. My limit had been reached and I couldn't hold my tears in any longer.

Many years later, I found a picture of me in my flowered dress that day. I am holding a gardenia and crying. Daddy Gregson is behind me, looking down in my direction, his face filled with concern. Daddy Wagner is kissing me, his hand on my hair; he is touching my head and my hair exactly the way my mom used to.

When the service was over, we left in a limousine. I remember looking out of the car window as paparazzi snapped picture after picture. Even then I knew people were taking my photo so it could be printed on slick paper and neatly wedged between a gossip column and an advertisement, to make money.

After the funeral, everyone descended on our house. Frank Sinatra, Gene Kelly, Fred Astaire, and who knows how many other movie stars were there. Elizabeth Taylor, heavily made up and fresh from her performance of *The Little Foxes* at the Ahmanson Theatre. She brought Anthony Geary from *General Hospital*; I was starstruck. I remember Shirley MacLaine going to see my dad in his room. She was wearing a gauzy, flowing dress and beaded necklaces, reminding me of Agnes Moorehead as the character Endora in *Bewitched*. I was most impressed with the appearance of Joyce DeWitt, the actress who played Janet on the sitcom *Three's Company*. Liz Taylor I didn't care about, but meeting Joyce DeWitt I thought, *Wow, your mom dies and Janet from* Three's Company *shows up in your home.*

I don't remember interacting with Baba at the funeral or the wake, but my godfather Mart recalls Baba coming up to him that day. "If you had been on that boat, my daughter would still be alive," she told him, as if it were all Mart's fault. Baba may have been lashing out at Mart, but I wonder if she actually intended the remark as a compliment. But who knows what was going through her mind? She and Mart and everyone close to my mom were beside themselves.

Hundreds of cards, letters, and Western Union telegrams were delivered in bundles all day, every day, for weeks. I remember Liz Applegate sitting at my mom's desk going through all the condolence letters—sorting them, wrapping them with rubber bands, putting certain ones aside for my dad. Heartfelt words of sympathy arrived at our doorstep from people my parents knew—David Niven, Blake Edwards and Julie Andrews, Cary Grant, Jimmy Stewart—and people I didn't know that my parents had ever met: Luciano Pavarotti, Maria Shriver, John Travolta, Brooke Shields, Anthony Hopkins, Lana Turner, Mickey Rooney, and so many others. Queen Elizabeth and members of the British royal family sent wires from England. Condolences arrived from the US Coast Guard, the Los Angeles District Attorney, the governor of North Carolina, the owners of all my parents' favorite hotels and restaurants, and the clowns from Ringling Bros. and Barnum & Bailey Circus, which my parents had taken us to every year. The staff at the Beverly Hills Western Union office even sent their own telegram—my mother's death had certainly kept them busy. So much sincere appreciation of my mom and dad; so much love and empathy and heartbreak—no judgments or criticisms or accusations. That would only start much later.

No one in my world questioned my dad's love for my mom or his utter despair at her loss. Everyone in our lives wrapped their arms around him. R.J. had loved Natalie "more than love." When it came time to choose the inscription on her gravestone, my dad made sure to add those three words, the same phrase my parents had always used to describe their love for each other. He asked if Courtney and I wanted it to say anything else. We told him we liked it just the way it was.

Mart later told me that in the days and weeks after my mom died, R.J. tried over and over again to make sense of what happened that terrible night, to figure out exactly how she got into the water. He kept asking if there was anything he could have done differently. They had all been drinking. At a certain point, my mom had simply gone off to bed. After that, what had happened? He had been right there on the boat that night, but he'd had no idea my mom had left to go down to the dinghy. Did she go down to the deck to move the dinghy? Did she somehow fall into the water at that point? Or had she gone out to the deck because the sound of the dinghy knocking against the boat was bothering her and she wanted to tie it up more securely? Did she slip and fall as she bent down to tie up the boat? Finally, the only thing he could come up with was that my mother *must* have tried to secure the dinghy to starboard.

In the week after the funeral, he barely left his room. One evening, I remember he came downstairs to take a phone call. I was in the next room, and I heard him talking in the den, then hanging up the receiver. He came out and announced, "I just got off the phone with the president of the United States, Ronald Reagan. He called to give his condolences for your mom." I couldn't tell by my dad's voice if he was impressed or bewildered. I remember thinking, *Is a call from President Reagan supposed to make me feel better?* Could that make my pain go away? No. A friend of my mother's would show up with presents.

Could that make my pain go away? No. Liz wanted to take me to get ice cream. Could that make my pain go away? No, that didn't do it either. I couldn't even use my happy memories of my mother to make me feel better because the good times were too painful to relive. So I shut out the past and began eking out a life that hinged on merely surviving from day to day.

Some of our favorite moments as a family had been spent on the boat at Catalina. My dad donated the *Splendour* to the Sea Scouts and none of us has ever been back to Catalina Island.

# Chapter 9

Courtney and Natasha, early 1980s.

After the funeral, Daddy Gregson and Julia went back to England. The troops of mourners, flowers, and telegrams that had been filling our house dwindled. Soon the paparazzi outside the front gates were the only ones left. The press clearly had no intention of leaving us alone.

Before long, most of my mom's rules were put back in place—except for some reason the TV was allowed to remain in my room. I felt a sharp pang of guilt every time I turned it on. Things were supposed to return to normal. But how could we go back to normal when normal no longer existed? It was like living in a house that had been struck by a meteor, and we were expected to walk past the gaping hole in the ceiling and step around the smoking boulder on the floor as if they were part of the decor.

At least my dad was finally out of bed. Nine days after my mom died, he went back to work. He was needed on the set of *Hart to Hart*. Two weeks prior to my mom's death, Stefanie Powers's significant other, the actor William Holden, had died in his home after drinking too much and falling, injuring his head. I remember the seriousness in my dad's tone when he told us that Stefanie's boyfriend, Bill, had died. Stefanie was still in the throes of her early mourning when my dad lost my mom. They were already close, but their shared grief deepened their friendship.

The same Monday morning my dad returned to work, I went back to school. My best friends Jessica, Tracey, and Caprice formed a protective force field around me, taking it upon themselves to make sure I was okay. My teachers were very kind to me—the expressions on their faces a mixture of pity and sympathy—but I was embarrassed that so much of the focus was on me.

Before my return to fifth grade, the Curtis School held some kind of assembly to break the news to my fellow students and to encourage them to be respectful. Even so, there were stares and whispers as I moved through the halls and classrooms. Some kids made bad jokes. "What kind of wood doesn't float?" was a popular one, the punch line, of course, being my mother's name. I had avoided hearing about her drowning from the TV news as much as possible, but I couldn't avoid the murmuring behind my back. I assumed it was happening because my parents were famous and my mom had drowned at night. I wasn't old enough to understand why people gossiped. I just knew that everyone was interested in my life and I hated that feeling. I pretended I was fine, smiled a lot, and pushed the intense feeling of longing for my mother aside until nightfall, when I would cry for her in my bed, my stuffed animals absorbing my tears.

Nothing was right. Mommie had been our wizard and fairy godmother. She was our everything. Without her, all the color and sunshine seemed to have gone out of our home. The curtains stayed open, and yet it was as if they were pulled closed, leaving the house in shadow. The house was quiet in a way it had never been in the past. It had become a place where people cried and spoke in whispers.

On December 12, once the autopsy was complete, the coroner, Thomas Noguchi, and the lead Los Angeles County Sheriff's Department detective, Duane Rasure, concluded that my mother's death had been an accident, without any evidence of foul play. They surmised that she had gone down to the dinghy and then likely missed a step, slipping and falling into the water, and that the bruises on her face and body were consistent with this sequence of events. The case was officially closed.

We all knew my mother often got annoyed if the dinghy wasn't tied down tightly. If the wind picked up and the sea became rough, it would bang right up against where her head rested in her bed. She was a light sleeper and she hated noises. She was also a feisty woman—our trusty first mate—who didn't need a man to do things for her. It was so like her to get up in her nightgown and socks to go tie down the dinghy herself. At home she often ran downstairs in her nightie to investigate if she heard anything that disturbed her, not wanting to wake up my dad if he was asleep.

The swim step that led to the dinghy was wet and slippery, and she had had too much to drink. If she lost her footing and fell into the water, how could anyone have heard her struggling? They were all inside the boat. She was wearing a heavy down coat that absorbed the seawater and would have quickly dragged her under before she could hoist herself out. She was not a strong swimmer. It was November, and the water that night would have been cold.

But we could only guess at these details. No one knew for certain. My mother had been alone that night. For my part, I didn't want to think about the details of her death at all. It was too painful. I didn't care *how* she died. I just cared *that* she died. I put up a wall against analyzing or discussing it with anyone. It was too devastating, too horrific for me to picture her drowning alone at night in the dark, cold water. I didn't see the point in dwelling on those thoughts. After all, she was gone, and that was all that mattered.

• • •

My mom dying confirmed all my worst fears. I had been in therapy for more than a year to overcome my terror that she was going to die. Now I should have been able to put all my ridiculous good-luck rituals to rest. Instead, what happened only confirmed that I had been right to be terrified. I should have performed *even more* rituals, not fewer. Obviously, I hadn't done enough and this was why she had died. What if, like my grandmother, I really did have some sort of sixth sense about things? Was this why I had obsessed over the thought that my mom was going to die? If I foresaw it, did that mean it was partly my fault for not preventing it? In my grief-stricken, eleven-year-old mind, I managed to convince myself that my mother's death had somehow been my fault.

I became more frightened, anxious to the point of hypervigilance, on high alert for the slightest bad omen. I doubled down on my nightly rituals, lining up my stuffed toys with newfound meticulousness. I had gotten my hair cut on Saturday morning, November 28. I was never getting my hair cut on a Saturday again. Anything I did that weekend, I never wanted to do again, including waking up to the sound of the radio. To this day, I do not fall asleep with a TV or radio on. I can't trust them.

I wanted to find a way to stay in touch with my mother. My grandmother, firmly believing herself to be psychic, was happy to help me. We began holding séances in my parents' linen closet, with Courtney also in attendance. The closet was warm and dark, with just enough room for the three of us to sit comfortably on the floor, the neatly folded linens and towels lined up on shelves all around us. Baba lit a candle, then we closed our eyes and held hands as she tried to reach our mom and Deda. The bottom shelves in the closet were covered in a soft white plastic, and I remember picking nervously at the material in the dark, as Baba commanded the spirits in hushed, dramatic tones. My dad and Kilky obviously didn't know these séances were happening or they would have been furious. This couldn't have been a healthy way for children to handle a parent's death. But Baba was always a mystic.

I began to wonder if I was a mystic too. Each night, I lay in bed and asked my mother to show a sign that she could hear me. One school night, a week or two after she died, Jessica was sleeping over and Liz was telling us one of her made-up stories about Billy Mouse and Morris Gerbil. She was just about to turn out the lights when I asked my mom out loud if she could send me a sign. Suddenly all the lights outside flashed on and off. Jessica, Liz, and I held our breath and then I started to cry.

"It's okay, lovey," Liz told me, trying to comfort me. "That means Mummy heard you. She is with you all the time."

I was stunned and a little scared that my request had so much power, but at the same time, it devastated me because it made her death feel all the more final. Another time, I held a séance on my own in the closet with my bird Smokey. I turned the lights out and asked my mom to make Smokey chirp if she heard me. He did. Again, I wasn't comforted. Instead, I was terrified of this new world without my mom in it.

We had been a famous family that everybody admired and now the worst thing imaginable had befallen us and everyone knew it. I'd be carrying my books across the school grounds or shopping at the mall, and people would point their fingers in my direction and mutter, "That's Natasha Gregson Wagner," adding, "Natalie Wood's daughter." I had never been pitied before. I had always been so proud to be my mother's daughter, but now the association filled me with embarrassment and regret. In public, I wished to be anyone but Natalie Wood's daughter. If only I could just be some anonymous girl—normal, safe, and unremarkable. In private, I felt small and lonely.

Sometimes after school Courtney and I would go with Kilky to our neighborhood market, Food King. Kilky was friendly with all the baggers and checkout people but I felt embarrassed when they looked at Courtney and me—seeing the pity in their eyes. Then just as I would look down or away in shame and dismay, there next to the checkout counter would be the *National Enquirer*. Inevitably, my mom and my dad would be on the cover, with a headline about her death, some new "revelation": that my mom was drunk that night, that she was allegedly having an affair with Chris Walken, that my parents had been fighting. I'd grown up with celebrity parents—I understood not to believe a single word printed on the cover of a tabloid. But it still hurt. In the checkout line, I tried to turn away, to block out the words and the images, but I was getting the message that there was no safe place for me these days. Home was filled with memories of my mom, and the outside world was filled with people pitying us or judging us with accusing headlines.

I spoke more and more quietly, hoping to disappear. In school I never raised my hand or volunteered to answer questions. I participated as little as possible. I think I was afraid that if I opened my mouth to talk, the tears would overwhelm me. I tried to learn, but I couldn't really concentrate on my studies because my heart hurt too much. I failed algebra and geometry and had to take them again in summer school.

Without my mother as my mirror, I started to see myself in a new light. I had been so assured of my mother's approval that I could be a bit of a bossy girl. Katie had called me a spoiled brat, and maybe she was right. I was a pampered little princess who grew up believing I was fragile. But now the worst possible catastrophe had happened. Did that mean I was cursed? Not a princess anymore? I felt more like a paper princess torn apart and pasted back together—a sham.

I played our last moments together over and over in my head. I could hear my mother's voice telling me there was nothing to worry about. I remember how she said my nickname in her special way, "Natooshie." My mom promised she would come back and I had believed her. She didn't lie to me, and yet and yet . . .

That one last gardenia-scented hug with her, in her soft angora sweater. I'd had no way of knowing it would be our last moment.

• • •

I was so worried Daddy Wagner would be next. I begged him not to go out for dinner. I called him on the set of *Hart to Hart* to make sure he was safe. I burst into tears whenever he left me. When I said my nightly prayers I pleaded with God to let me keep my dad. Maybe if I prayed hard enough, He wouldn't punish me as He had done when He had taken away my mom.

Like many men of his generation, my dad had been raised to stifle his feelings and so he handled his grief by throwing himself into his work. He couldn't sit still. Maybe one day a week, he came home early from work. He hugged me and I smelled his familiar smell. I sat next to him or on his lap. His blue eyes were always ringed with pale red those days and his face looked just as sad as mine. For those moments, we were partners in grief. But it was short-lived. The phone rang, a friend arrived, a dinner date was waiting, and despite my protests, off he went. While our dad could leave our house of pain, Courtney and I were stuck there. He could hug us and tell us he loved us, buy us presents, but he was not capable of filling our mom's shoes.

This is where Katie stepped in. As our dad's first child, she had the most experience dealing with him. After we lost our mother, Katie served as the bridge for me and Courtney with our dad. If I had a problem I felt he wasn't listening to or couldn't deal with, I went to Katie and she would work it out with him. With her steadfastness, her maturity, and her dependability, Katie morphed from a stepsister to something of a substitute mother for me.

My relationship with Courtney also began to shift. Suddenly Courtney and I were no longer vying for our mother's attention. My sister was just as devastated and, because she was younger, even more confused than I was. One day shortly after the accident, Courtney was looking at some jewelry my dad had bought my mom recently that was still in its box. Liz said, "Oh, lovey, don't touch that. That's going back," and Courtney said, "Is Mommie coming back to get it?" She couldn't really comprehend that our mother was gone forever.

Though we bore only a faint resemblance to each other, we both looked like our mother in different ways. Just looking at my sister's face could be healing for me; she was a living, breathing reminder of Mommie. One Sunday morning, I remember Courtney came into my room. She pushed the door open and saw me playing with my Barbies. She sat next to me. I flinched slightly. Was she about to wreck my things? But she didn't. She watched and listened. "Toosh, can I play too?" she asked sweetly. For the first time, I said "yes."

This was the beginning of a new closeness between us. A mutual understanding that we had both lost our favorite person, our dearest protector. No longer the squabbling sisters we were before November 29, we had become motherless overnight. The cells in our bodies had shifted. Courtney at seven became more tender with me. At eleven I became more protective of her. I don't know if I would have been okay if it wasn't for Courtney.

Everyone in the family coped in their own way. Baba responded to the death of her beloved daughter by clinging to her memory with fierce tenacity. Maria Gurdin gave the world Natalie Wood, managed her career, kept her in the spotlight. By sheer force of will, she had parlayed her little girl's natural gifts into wealth for her family. Even before my mother died, the fact that Natalie Wood had been her daughter was completely fused with Baba's identity, her self-worth, her reason for living. Afterward, Baba's focus was mostly on herself and her famous daughter. Now, whenever I saw her, she would tell me about how some group was honoring her for being Natalie Wood's mother. This validated my grandmother's existence, but it made me cringe.

Ever since her daughter first got into the movie business, Baba had taken care of her fan mail, and after my mother married my dad, Baba started looking after his mail too. Though my mother was gone, Baba didn't stop—she kept on sending out photos. She had stacks of eight-by-ten photographs of my mom and dad that she would auto-graph and mail to fans. I often wondered if anybody knew that it was Baba signing my mother's ones. She even took the eight-by-tens to my mother's grave site and sat there, so that when fans came to pay their respects, she could give them a signed photo.

My aunt Olga—my mom's older half sister—lived in San Francisco and had three sons, and so she stayed in close contact with us via phone, calling regularly, sending us presents for birthdays and Christmas, and visiting when she could. My dad truly appreciated her support. When we saw her, she would share stories about my mom and show us pictures of them when they were young.

Then there was my aunt Lana, my mother's younger sister. My mom's relationship with her younger sister was much more complex than the one she shared with Olga. Theirs had been a troubled relationship for many years—with periods of closeness followed by periods of estrangement. Clearly, there was once a lot of love between my mother and Lana, but by the time I was born, their relationship had become strained. Though my aunt was at our house for the holidays, she was never part of my parents' inner circle.

My parents liked to surround themselves with people they trusted, and as far as they were concerned, Lana was not that person. At their second wedding, Lana's then husband, Richard, had been allowed to photograph the ceremony on the condition that the photos were private. Later, my parents found out that the photos had been sold to a fan magazine. A lot of the arguments between Lana and my mom revolved around money—I remember walking into my mom's bedroom and hearing my mother tell Liz that Lana had asked her for money yet again. Liz remembers that Lana would go to boutiques where my mom had house accounts and charge clothing. "Put it on Natalie's account!" she would say. At the end of the month, Liz would receive the bills for clothes my mother had never purchased. When my mom would ask Lana about the charges Lana would become defensive and another cold front would move in between the two of them. Another story I've heard from those times is that Lana asked my parents for seven thousand dollars so her daughter, Evan, could go to private school, but instead used the money for her own plastic surgery, having her nose narrowed to look more like my mother's.

It can't have been easy for Lana to grow up with a sister who was a star. Even though she was able to carve out a brief career for herself in

Hollywood, she was always overshadowed by her sister's fame, not to mention her own mother's obsession with Natalie. Years later, I read an article about Lana where she told the interviewer: "Natalie was the embodiment of what my [mom] longed for in life. She worshipped Nat, I was the forgotten daughter. . . . After Nat died, it turned out that she was stuck with the daughter she didn't really care about that much."

In my mother's will, it stated that Lana was to have her wardrobe, perhaps because the sisters had always worn similar clothes and traded outfits when they were girls and teenagers. My mother probably never imagined she would die so young and suddenly and that Lana would take the bequest so literally. She had been dead for less than a month when Lana came to take away her clothes. Courtney and I had stayed home from school that day because some kids were teasing us about our mom's death. Liz looked out the window from my mother's office, which was in her bedroom, and saw Lana and two friends pull up with a U-Haul. Lana rang the doorbell and told Liz that she had come to get our mom's clothes. Liz told her that the will had not even gone to probate. Lana replied that she had come to take what was rightfully hers. She told Liz she was worried pieces of the clothing would get lost or misplaced if she didn't come sooner rather than later. Liz called my dad at the studio and told him what was going on. He said, "Just let her come in and take the clothes." Courtney and I were both upset and afraid. We were worried about what the closets would look like without any of our mother's things.

I remember sitting on my mom's bed and watching as Lana and her two friends pushed rolling racks into the room. They commandeered her closet with the efficiency of a military operation. I watched them go in and out with armfuls of clothes. In and out. Back and forth.

I do not recall any comfort or tenderness from Lana that day. She coolly went about her business. At some point, I went into my mom's smaller closet, where her nighties and bras were kept. The room was dark and still smelled like her. I wanted some of the pale, puffy bras she always wore. I took a couple and some nighties and then got back into her bed.

I asked Lana why she was taking my mom's bras, underwear, and nighties. She told me, "Your mom wants me to have them."

Three hours later, Lana and her friends had emptied my mom's closets. Every thread of my mom's beautiful and elaborate wardrobe—her original Edith Head gowns, her striped T-shirts, her soft lavender dresses, her rainbow of silk shirts, the fancy outfits she wore when she went out, her shoes, coats, handbags, even the rest of her nightgowns and undergarments—was gone. Only blank space was left behind.

My dad offered to pay Lana for some important pieces, sending her a check for eleven thousand dollars for a few fur coats that he wanted to keep for Courtney and me. She returned the furs, but she wouldn't allow him to pay her for anything else. A few weeks later we found out that Lana had sold all my mom's clothes to a resale store, even though she had promised my dad she wouldn't. Apparently she didn't have room in her apartment to keep them all. The resale store hung a sign in the window advertising that the clothes "Belonged to Natalie Wood." My dad was furious. My mother would have hated that her clothes—right down to her undergarments—were on public display, ending up in the closets of strangers and collectors. None of us were able to forgive Lana for that. After that, my aunt was no longer welcome in our home.

# Chapter 10

R.J., Katie, and Natasha, Gstaad,
Christmas, 1981.

"I think it would be too painful for us to stay here for Christmas," my dad said as December wore on.

For my mother, Christmas was the supreme festival of the year. When the holiday approached, she lit Rigaud Cypres candles that smelled of pine needles and cedar. This rich, wintery fragrance meant December was here, and even more merrymaking than usual would consume the house; more friends, more relatives, more presents, more food and singing. My mom loved to sing and knew every word to every Christmas carol. She would sing them all in her sweet high voice, and I would sing right along with her.

Now that she was gone, how could we do anything—caroling, tree decorating, present unwrapping—without accentuating her gaping absence? It was decided that the whole family, along with Kilky; Mart; Delphine and her two kids; Liz and her husband, Adrian; and Katie's half brother Josh Donen, would spend Christmas at a chalet near David Niven's house in Gstaad, Switzerland. David, known to us as "Niv," helped my dad immensely during this time. He had lost his first wife, Primmie, in a sudden and tragic accident in 1946, which had left his sons motherless. He knew firsthand what Daddy was going through. We didn't want any reporters following us, so the trip was kept top secret. Niv waited on the side of the road in the snow for four hours while our flight was delayed by a blizzard. When we finally left Geneva Airport, we all piled into a van and found David's car by flashing our headlights in a prearranged signal. It was like being in a James Bond movie. Niv led us through the snowbanked roads to our rented chalet.

The Switzerland trip was meant to be an escape, a time to get away from home and all its changes and enjoy ourselves despite everything. Niv was so sensitive to our needs, meeting our sad eyes with such compassion in his own. He was the perfect British gentleman, but with his ribald, freewheeling sense of humor, he was also able to make my dad smile and laugh again. I remember one time during the trip we were driving in the car, and both Niv and my dad had to go to the bathroom so we pulled to the side of the road. Niv told my dad to pee to the right, pee to the left, pee to the front, and pee to the back. "Now you've peed in all the great rivers in Europe." They both laughed like schoolboys.

My primary memory of that trip, however, is the feeling of being petrified if Daddy Wagner moved more than five feet away from me. I didn't want to let him out of my sight. After Switzerland, we went to see my British dad in Wales for New Year's. He and Julia had bought an old farmhouse with an enormous stone fireplace. "The fireplace is as big as you," he told me. I was happy to visit him. But when New Year's Eve came, the celebration seemed out of step with my feelings. When everyone gathered at midnight to ring in 1982 with a chorus of "Auld Lang Syne"—"should old acquaintance be forgot and never brought to mind?"—I may have been forcing a smile on the outside, but inside I was thinking, *How can I ever be happy again?* After New Year's, Daddy Wagner had to take Katie, now age seventeen, to Paris to see about enrolling her in the Sorbonne, leaving me in the care of Kilky and Daddy Gregson. I remember the early morning, standing at the window of our bed-and-breakfast, watching my dad and Katie leave, my dad in a dark blue peacoat, his head covered by a wool hat, a waiting van making puffs of smoke in the icy air. He kept coming back in to give me one more hug . . . one more hug . . . and one last hug. After they drove away down the winding forest road, I climbed back into his bed, which was still warm and smelled like him. Under the covers, I held myself and cried until I fell asleep again.

When we returned to Canon Drive, the paparazzi pack lingered, and reminders of my mom were everywhere. Her night table was still there next to her bed, with her Limoges boxes on it and the books she had been reading, a funny novel called *High Anxiety*, by Mel Brooks, and another one, *Gorky Park*, by Martin Cruz Smith. The silver tray outside her bedroom that held the multitude of her sunglasses. Her vanity and all her makeup, brushes in silver cups, trays with pots of black powder, pink powder, the cut-glass carafes in her bathroom that held mouthwash, bubble bath, fragrance. All of those things sitting safely on their shelves like they were waiting for her to return from a trip. If those things were still here, why couldn't she be here too? It was as if she had just stepped out for a day or two.

By now my dad had found me a new therapist, Mrs. Malin, the wife of his own therapist. Like my mom, my dad had been in therapy for many years, dating back to the time of their divorce. I didn't like seeing Mrs. Malin at first. I was aware that my dad was paying for me to have intimate conversations about my feelings with this woman once a week, and when my hour was up I had to leave. Before, I had intimate conversations with my mom for free, whenever I wanted and needed to. Now I had to squeeze my feelings into a therapist's forty-five-minute schedule.

Mrs. Malin did not work with children, only adults, but she made an exception for me. I remember I hated that I was the only kid going in and out of her office. Why couldn't my dad have found a shrink who saw children and teenagers? Mrs. Malin had black hair parted in the middle that fell to her shoulders. She wore no makeup, silk shirts, and pleated gray pants. She said I could call her Naomi, but I decided to call her Mrs. Malin because she felt like a teacher to me.

In our early sessions, I was shy and uncomfortable.

"I have nothing to say. I don't know why I'm here," I told her.

"If you have nothing to say, just sit quietly then," was her reply.

I quickly realized that I wasn't going to be excused to leave just because I didn't want to talk, so I might as well start communicating. Slowly I began to open up. I told her about a disagreement with Courtney or a funny thing that happened at school, what Jessica and Tracey and I had planned for the weekend.

Mrs. Malin was the perfect combination of intelligent, insightful, and nurturing. "What's the trigger?" she would ask when I felt sad or anxious or depressed or ashamed. She taught me to observe and analyze my own thoughts and emotions. If my heart started to beat or my armpits pricked with sweat, she taught me to slow down and observe the feeling. Maybe my dad was going out of town in the next couple of days and I had just remembered? The mother-daughter luncheon was coming up at school. Was I worried about that? Could I go with Jessica or Tracey? Or was it best to stay home?

Soon, her home office became my weekly sanctuary. Slowly I learned that the bad feelings came and went. That I could rage, yell, and cry and that Mrs. Malin calmly allowed me to sit with those feelings, waiting for them to pass.

I think I knew my dad would not be single for long. How could he be? There were women all over the world chasing after him. After my mom died, wild-eyed women penciled their eyes with dark liner in an attempt to look like her. They would hand me their phone numbers to give to him, hopeful tears glistening in their eyes. It was Valentine's Day 1982 when my dad told me that Tom Mankiewicz was "bringing over a friend." Courtney and I were in the pool house playing on a new Pac-Man machine when Jill St. John walked in, a svelte, stylish woman in a burgundy cashmere turtleneck sweater. She introduced herself and brought us each a handcrafted folding fan made with purple feathers. Courtney and I exchanged glances. *Why is this woman bringing us presents?* Later, Daddy, Jill, Tom, and Katie went out to dinner. I was left behind wondering, *Why can't I come?* I felt betrayed by Tom. He had been my mom's close friend, and now he was bringing home a date for my dad. Where was his loyalty?

My dad told me that when they were little girls, my mom and Jill had been in ballet class together with Stefanie Powers. He showed me the black-and-white photo of the three of them clad in leotards, their smooth hair knotted at the backs of their heads. Baba had been friends with Jill's mom and Stefanie's mom. Even though there was this connection to my mother, I found it very hard to bond with Jill. She didn't have children of her own and was not a naturally maternal woman. Jill had bright red hair held in place with hairspray. She wore tight cashmere sweaters and figure-hugging leather pants to show off her incredible body. My mom was an intimate person who would lounge around the house in her nightie or robe, her hair tied in a pony or hanging loose around her face. I loved to touch my mom's soft hair or snuggle up in her lap. Jill was not that kind of a woman. My mom was a furry kitten, whereas Jill was a smooth-haired cheetah. I was intimidated by her.

My dad was in an impossible position, because he really liked Jill and he needed her to help him through losing our mom. He tried so hard to be sensitive to his kids, always struggling to bridge the gap between Jill and us. "Jill was thinking of you today," he'd tell me and Courtney, "and bought you a present." Or, over the phone, he'd say, "Jill's right here, let me put her on so you can say hello." We would roll our eyes. *Please, let us end the call without you bringing Jill up again*, we would think to ourselves.

Soon, Jill was around constantly. She traveled with us every time we took a trip and started spending all the holidays with us. It became clear that she was here to stay, so we better get comfortable with this new arrangement. At the time, I resented my dad's focus shifting to this other person. Later, as Daddy and Jill grew closer and I grew more mature, I became aware of what a difficult and precarious position Jill was in, stepping right into a family that had been leveled by loss.

We managed to stay in the Canon Drive house for a year after my mom died. After that, we moved to Brentwood. The new house on Old Oak Road was designed by the architect Cliff May and it couldn't have been more different from our white Cape Cod in Beverly Hills. This property was Western, with carved wood, adobe, Spanish tile, and a wide-open feel, with lots of glass and walls so thick no air-conditioning was needed. There was a pool, horse stables, and a trail that led right up into the Santa Monica Mountains. We didn't abandon the old house, but made a slow, gentle transition into the new one. A long goodbye and a fresh start.

Delphine, one of my mom's best friends and our real estate broker, sat with Courtney and me and talked with us about the things we wanted to bring. All my stuffed animals, of course, and my swan night-light. The large brass bed my mom had bought me the year before when she redid my room. My wicker desk. The photo albums.

After we moved to the new house, I turned thirteen. I had begun to develop a connection to horses and riding, taking weekly lessons at a house near Sullivan Canyon. For my birthday my dad gave me a beautiful Arabian horse named Fa-Da-Li, a chestnut gelding. My dad and I shared a love of horseback riding. Neither Katie nor Courtney was into horses, so this was something just for the two of us. When my dad and I rode up into the Santa Monica Mountains together, I followed behind him, falling into the rhythm of my horse and instantly feeling lighter. Once we made it to the top, we could see the ocean. This is where we would stop, the horses grabbing mouthfuls of wild green grass. My dad would inhale the air deeply, pointing out how beautiful this place was and how lucky we were to live here. The sunshine casting its yellow light on the oak and sycamore trees. The lizards on the rocky earth darting to and fro. The clippety-clop of the horses' hooves on the black asphalt as we made our way down our street and back home. Out riding together, my dad and I didn't need to talk to communicate how we felt about each other.

At other times, our relationship wasn't so easy. Mrs. Malin suggested that my dad occasionally join me in our therapy sessions. She encouraged me to be honest with my dad and express my true feelings. So I did. I shared with him that I felt he was going out to dinner too many nights. I was confused about his relationship with Jill. Now that he was dating her, did that mean he didn't miss Mommie anymore? Where did all his love for my mom go? Did it evaporate into thin air? Why couldn't he be more like other dads who came home after work and stayed home? Why did he travel so much? My dad sat there in Mrs. Malin's office, shifting uncomfortably in his chair. He couldn't deal with my questions, my poking and prodding about his private life with Jill. After about ten minutes or so he would simply get up and walk out of the session, down the creaky wooden steps, and out to his car, where he would drive away. Mrs. Malin and I would sit there trying to make sense of what had gone wrong. She would explain to me that my dad was not able to "hear" me because his grief was overwhelming him. I felt guilty and ashamed. Terrified my feelings would somehow cause his death. Frightened that he would send me back to Wales to live with Daddy Gregson. Ashamed that my questions were more than he could bear. On those afternoons Mrs. Malin had to drive me home.

The message from Liz and Kilky was clear: "Don't upset your dad with your sadness and suffering. He has his own and they are bigger than yours." The last thing I wanted to do was cause my dad more trouble.

Daddy Wagner continued to work and travel. Instead of resting when he was on hiatus from *Hart to Hart*, he took on other movie roles. Daddy Gregson used to call long-distance from England to check on me. "I don't understand why he's working all the time," he'd say to me. "He's got enough money. He should be spending time with you."

In the spring of 1982, not long after my dad started seeing Jill, my best friend Tracey and I flew to visit him in the South of France, where he was filming *Curse of the Pink Panther* with his buddy Niv. This time we visited Niv at his house on the Cap Ferrat, overflowing with food, drink, and laughter, a lot like our own home in the old days. Niv was tanned, with a gold ID bracelet around his wrist. He was so kind to us children, giving us handmade Easter baskets filled with chocolates. I was mostly quiet to the point of silence, but he was garrulous and as hilarious as ever. The elegant French model and actress Capucine was their costar and another good friend of my dad's. Beautiful and kind, she seemed to truly enjoy spending time with Tracey and me. One day, she and my dad took us to a bustling outdoor market, the kind you find all over the South of France. Capucine bought a bag of reddish oranges. She peeled the burnt-orange skin and handed Tracey and me the reddest sliver of orange I had ever seen. "These are blood oranges, the sweetest you will taste," she said. To this day, every time I eat a blood orange I think of Capucine.

During our visit, my dad made a huge effort to be present, to take Tracey and me out and show us the town. He taught us to play endless rounds of gin. He drove us to the Loews Hotel Monte-Carlo in Monaco to celebrate Tracey's thirteenth birthday. We saw showgirls dance in a chorus line, and the waiters brought out a chocolate birthday cake and a glass of champagne for each of us. I felt so close to my dad that week, his attention firmly centered on me. When it was time to say goodbye and fly home without him, I fell apart. I was crying so hard in the back seat of the car as Tracey and I rode to the airport that the driver actually turned around and asked if I was okay. *"Est-ce que ça va?"* Did I want him to stop the car? *Stop and do what?* I thought.

"There's nothing anyone can do," I replied.

I just couldn't stand to be separated from my dad.

A few months after the trip, David Niven died of Lou Gehrig's disease. An understanding, supportive friend was gone. Seven years later, Capucine would jump to her death from her eighth-floor apartment in Switzerland.

Soon after Niv died, I learned that Howard Jeffrey—Aitchey—my parents' close friend and a crucial part of our family, was sick with a strange illness known then as GRID, later identified as AIDS. Howard was sick for a number of years and died in 1988. My mom's death seemed to have set off a chain reaction of loss.

As a child, I was always told how much I looked like my mother. But puberty was changing my looks. At thirteen, my body began sprouting painful, hard lumps where my breasts would be. My light-colored eyebrows grew dark and bushy, like two furry caterpillars perched contentedly on my forehead. My nose was too big for my small face, and my skin, which had always been clear, now felt greasy and two-toned. Tiny little pimples popped up everywhere. As a teenager, my mother had flawless skin and iconic looks. In 1956, *Life* magazine had even named her the Most Beautiful Teenager in the World. My adolescence was so very different. It was as if when my mom died she took with her any beauty that I may have had. I felt embarrassed for people to know I was her daughter. She was beautiful Natalie and I was the little ugly duckling Natasha.

In addition to weekly visits to my therapist, I now paid weekly visits to the Beverly Hills office of Dr. Sutnick, dermatologist. He'd inject my blemishes with a small needle, and then close up the wound with what appeared to be magical mystery smoke. "Lorraine, get me the dry ice," he'd bellow to his nurse after popping my pimples. "Now you gotta look great," he would say when examining my face, "because Ted Sutnick's here, and he's not lookin' at you through rose-colored glasses!"

One day after school, Daddy Wagner and I were in the backyard. "Why do you think your skin's so broken out?" he asked. "How should I know?" I wanted to respond. Does any teen know *why* their skin breaks out? But I didn't have the confidence or self-awareness to answer him truthfully. I quietly replied, "I don't know," and tried to play it off like I wasn't bothered by his criticism.

Right around that time Katie, Courtney, and I decided to get our hair chopped off. There was a trend in the early eighties for girls to have close-cropped, feathered hairdos, and so on a trip to London, we went to the Vidal Sassoon Salon and proceeded to get the worst haircuts of our lives. Mine was layered, helmetlike, and profoundly unflattering to a face stricken by puberty. Immediately after we walked out of the salon I knew the haircuts were bad. Not just bad, but truly awful. When my dad saw Courtney and me in the lobby of our hotel he paused to take a breath. I knew right away he did not approve. The new haircut only cemented my feeling that all my childhood beauty died with my mom.

Now that I was no longer in the bubble of her unconditional acceptance, I felt constantly lost and ashamed. If I could no longer see myself reflected in my mother's eyes, who was I? I clung tightly to my best friend Jessica. If she was okay, then I was okay. Though she was my age, she became my strength and my protector. Jessica was beautiful. She too was sprouting little breasts, but her face remained smooth and clear. The thought of being separated from Jessica terrified me so much that I followed her to a small private school in Studio City for a year, even though Kilky had to haul me more than twenty miles to and fro every day.

I built a composite mother from parts of Liz, Kiky, Katie, Mrs. Malin, and Tracey's mom, Janis. I looked to each of them for different things. Liz reassured me that nothing bad was going to happen to my dad. Kilky gave me the familiar consistency of the life I had before my mom died. Katie was magnetic and beautiful and took me under her wing. Mrs. Malin made me feel safe. And Janis was the

My grandmother Maria Gurdin.

My grandparents Maria and Nicholas Gurdin with baby Natasha, as my mother was originally known, San Francisco, December 15, 1940.

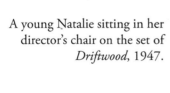

A young Natalie sitting in her director's chair on the set of *Driftwood*, 1947.

MISS
NATALIE WOOD

Maria, Nick, and baby Lana watching
Natalie practice ballet at home, 1948.

Orson Welles with Natalie during the
filming of *Tomorrow Is Forever*, 1946.

Natalie and
James Dean
in a scene from
*Rebel Without
a Cause*, 1955.

Maria and Natalie at home, circa 1955.

Natalie and R.J. on their wedding day at
the Scottsdale United Methodist Church,
Arizona, December 28, 1957.

Natalie as Maria in *West Side Story* (1961),
about to perform her rooftop ballet.

Robert Redford
and Natalie on the
set of *Inside Daisy
Clover*, 1965.

Natalie and my father, Richard Gregson, on their wedding day at the Holy Virgin Mary Russian Orthodox Cathedral in Los Angeles, May 30, 1969.

Daddy Gregson holding me at our house on North Bentley Avenue, Los Angeles.

Richard and Natalie, heavily pregnant with me, in Los Angeles, late summer 1970.

Natalie and R.J. on board the *Ramblin' Rose* on their second wedding day, July 16, 1972.

Daddy Wagner and me
at the house on Canon Drive.

Family portrait,
clockwise from
top left: Natalie,
R.J., me, and my
sister Courtney,
1977.

My mother with her signature Elsa
Peretti cuff, Hawaii, 1978.

Sean Connery about to take flight
with Courtney at the house on
Canon Drive, New Year's Eve,
1977.

Me and my mother
in the backyard.

From left, me, Katie, and Courtney in an
unfortunate phase of eighties hair and makeup.

Courtney and me playing
dress-up, 1981.

Daddy Wagner and Daddy Gregson with me and my niece Emma Webster at my first wedding at the house on Old Oak Road, 2003.

Me with my stepmother Julia (above) and with my sisters Sarah Gregson and Poppy Gregson Wall on a family vacation in the South of France, 2008.

Willie Mae Worthen, aka Kilky, and me at Daddy Wagner's in Westwood, California.

Happy as can be and very pregnant with Clover at 3 Square in Venice, California, 2012.

My mother aboard the *Splendour*, looking radiant, circa 1971.

Clover and me in Malibu, 2012.

freewheeling, fun mom that I wished my mom had resembled a little more before she died.

And of course there was Julia. The year I turned thirteen, Daddy Gregson called to say that Julia was pregnant and I was going to have a new sibling in November. I was thrilled. I adored Julia. The more the merrier as far as I was concerned. Their dog Daisy was pregnant during Julia's pregnancy. They told me they were going to keep one of Daisy's puppies. There were two names on the table. Apple and Poppy. The puppy would have one of the names and the baby would have the other. Daisy gave birth to nine fluffy, golden-haired puppies. The puppy they kept was named Apple. My sister they called Poppy.

Despite my discomfort with my body and my looks, I was a teenager now. I knew I was supposed to start thinking about clothes and parties and boys—and maybe looking outside myself for answers that would help distract me from my grief. One evening, Jessica and Tracey invited me to a taping of the TV series *Silver Spoons*, a sitcom starring a young blond actor who most girls my age—including Jessica and Tracey—had a crush on, Ricky Schroder. I did not have a crush on Ricky, nor was I a fan of the show, but I went along for the ride.

As it turned out, Ricky's agent, Flo Allen, was a friend of my dad's and she recognized me. "Would you and your friends like to come backstage and meet Ricky?" Of course we would! Jessica and Tracey were over the moon with excitement but trying to play it cool. Before we left, Ricky asked in a quiet voice, "Can I have your number?" Naturally, I assumed he was talking to Jessica, the beautiful one, so I said nothing. Ricky looked right at me and reiterated, "Natasha, can I have your number?" *Wow*, I thought, *somebody special noticed me for the first time since my mom died.* Clearly, my terrible haircut had grown out.

The next day Ricky sent me a hundred red roses. I was shocked and thrilled. Was I dreaming? Soon I was going to Universal Studios every Friday night and watching as he taped his weekly *Silver Spoons* episode. Ricky had been a child star—like my mother—and was coming into his own in Hollywood at that time. Until now I had experienced the industry only via my parents. Now I was experiencing it with Ricky.

Ours was a very innocent romance. Ricky and I would sit in the back seat of his town car and hold hands. I especially liked spending time with his sister, Dawn, who was dating Miguel from the boy band Menudo. I also loved Ricky's mom, Diane, a no-nonsense woman who managed his career, and spending time with Ricky and his family at their house in Calabasas. Soon I was joining them on their family vacations, being immersed in that comfort and stability. More than a boyfriend, what I longed for was a mother.

We dated for about a year. At some point, a photo of Ricky and me appeared on the cover of a tabloid magazine under a headline that said something like, "Puppy Love for Natalie Wood's Daughter." Diane sat Ricky and me down for a serious talk.

"Natasha, we've had a decline in Ricky's fan mail since the magazine story," she said. "From now on, you both need to tell the press that you're just friends."

Ricky was appalled. I was compliant. I felt like such an imposter. When my mom was my age, she was on the covers of many magazines, practically on a weekly basis. She always looked stunning and proud. She was an actress; she had a reason to be on display. It was the opposite for me. I hadn't known I would be on the cover, I didn't like the picture, and the only reason they had bothered to put me there was because I was the daughter of Natalie Wood and the "girlfriend" of Ricky Schroder. I was thirteen.

Ricky and I were still dating around my fourteenth birthday, but we were so young I think we both realized it wasn't going to last. The year was 1984, and my big sister Katie had started hanging out with the Brat Pack actors that were currently taking Hollywood by storm. When I walked into my birthday party that year, Katie had arranged to surprise me by inviting Rob Lowe and Judd Nelson, one of the stars of *The Breakfast Club* movie, which I loved. "Happy birthday, Natasha," Rob said, and gave me a kiss on the cheek. Rob's girlfriend Melissa Gilbert was there too. They seemed to enjoy the excitement on my face and on all of my friends' faces as we realized they were there to celebrate with us.

My close friends like Jessica and Tracey appreciated Ricky, but my wider circle of school friends were more impressed by Rob, Judd, and Melissa. They let me know that it was time to send Ricky on his merry way. I was so insecure that I succumbed to peer pressure and broke up with him. I let him down gently by parroting things I had heard adults say on television: "I feel like this relationship isn't working out. We need to take some space, some time off from each other." Ricky was a good and sweet boy, with no dark or rebellious side that I was aware of. I was starting to be drawn to guys with more of an edge. Broken boys that I could mend.

I knew I had made the right choice, even if it was for the wrong reasons. Would it have been different if my mom had been there to help me find my way? There were so many moments where I missed her, longed for her guidance, her complete and unconditional love.

Later that same year, I got my period. I noticed the brownish-red streaks in my underwear and immediately told Jessica. I was the last one in my group to get it, and so I understood what was happening.

My mother had always been open with me about her body and what would happen to mine when I grew up. I remember one time, standing in her bathroom as she prepped for a night out and glancing in the toilet to see a ruby-stained piece of puffed white cotton floating there, a tiny string trailing behind.

"What is that?" I asked, perplexed.

She looked at me and smiled.

"Oh, that is my tampon, Natasha. I have my period. You remember what I told you about when ladies have their periods, right?"

I sort of did and I sort of didn't.

The next day a large box arrived with a plastic body inside it complete with all the organs and body parts. My mom sat me down at the round wicker table in our playroom and gave me a lesson on all the various body parts and what their functions were.

Later that evening, after Courtney went to bed, my mom told me the story of the first time she got her period. Baba had not told her anything about it. One day she was on a movie set and she started bleeding. My mother thought she was dying. She ended up confiding in another adult on the set and they explained to her that she had just gotten her first period. She truly had no idea. When she became a mother herself, she wanted to make sure that I understood my body and that I was prepared for puberty. She wanted me to feel safe and empowered.

Even though she was gone, her lessons had stuck with me, and getting my period didn't worry me at all. The next morning at breakfast I told my dad. He looked at me long and hard. His eyes got a little teary. "Well, Natasha, you are on your way to becoming a woman," he said. That afternoon when I came home from school there was a present on my bed. He had bought me a navy leather purse. A sign of becoming a woman, I guessed.

# Chapter 11

Natasha and Courtney at the house
on Old Oak Road, mid-1980s.

During these years, crying felt as natural and automatic as breathing to me. Many mornings, I would arrive at school with the puffiest of eyes. One day my friend Shingo asked me why I looked like a salamander. He wasn't being mean; he just didn't understand why my eyes were always so swollen.

Time was passing but my feelings about my mother had only grown stronger, threatening to overwhelm me. Whenever I left the house, I put on a brave face, desperate to blend into the background, to convince everyone I was okay. I could cry alone in the shower or on my pillow, but to the outside world I played the game that I was fine. It was exhausting. *I have my act together. I am not sad or upset or lonely or missing my mother. It's all in the past and I never even think about it.* I had too much pride to let people see my ugly feelings, and yet they must have been fairly obvious: they were written all over my face. It was as if the pieces of a jigsaw puzzle had spilled from the box and scattered across the floor, but because I wasn't yet mature enough to figure out where each piece fit, I just jammed them together and hastily bound them with Scotch tape. "It's all fine" was the message I tried to convey. "Just don't look too closely." I kept my crying jags private even from Courtney, who was becoming my closest friend.

To leave the house was to constantly risk exposure to other people, their pointing fingers, the looks of pity on their faces and whispers behind our backs. Before my mother died, our parents' fans never seemed scary to me. Now they felt different—looming, overly emotional, locking me in with their eyes and their body language. One time I remember Courtney and I went with our dad to a charity benefit. Courtney and I dreaded these events, as it meant we would be surrounded by a lot of strangers. At this particular benefit, I remember my dad was shepherded away from us and we were left alone in a banquet room, where guests were filling their plates with food from a buffet. As soon as people realized who we were, they swooped. Suddenly we were surrounded by older women with made-up faces telling us how much they *loved* our mom. How *sorry* they were that she died. How much we *looked just like her*.

"Oh my God, we're so sorry for your loss, we loved your mom," they lamented.

It was like being trapped in a scene from a Fellini or Buñuel film.

"Oh my God, look at you, Natalie's daughters!" one woman said between bites from the buffet. She was wearing a sequined blouse and had food stuck in her teeth. Then she shouted to her husband across the room, "Natalie Wood's daughters!" before turning back to us. "Oh my God, what a terrible tragedy! Your mother was so beautiful. Your father is gorgeous. Look, I can see the sadness in their faces!"

I think because my mom had grown up in front of the cameras, people felt they somehow knew us and were entitled to speak to us, ask us questions, invade our personal spaces as if we were objects on display in some Natalie Wood museum. I didn't want to talk to these people, I didn't want to be showcased for them to see, I just wanted to get through the day.

After her death, the press maintained a strong interest in my mother, especially around the anniversary of her death. Each November when the tribute articles appeared, I did my best to block them out. They always seemed to say the exact same thing, speculating again about her "tragic death," how my parents had fought that night, that my dad had somehow been "jealous" of my mom's closeness with Chris Walken. At a certain point, the tabloids even started implying that my dad had somehow been involved in my mom's death, that he could have saved her but he didn't. I knew this couldn't be true, so I simply shut out the chatter. My mom and dad had loved each other more than love. There was nothing in the world that would have stopped my dad from rescuing my mom if he could have. When the media started talking about foul play, our family was always told by our publicist and lawyer to remain silent. *Do not respond. That is what the rumor mill wants. These reporters are baiting you. Do not dignify falsehoods with a response.* So we remained silent. As did our close circle of family and friends.

My aunt Lana felt differently. In 1984, less than three years after my mom's death, she wrote a gossipy book about my mother's life. My dad was upset but not surprised. I remember my aunt Olga was horrified that Lana had done this so soon after my mom's passing. My mom was close to many people; she had a large circle of loyal and intimate friends and family members. No one else had sold their story in the way Lana had been prepared to do.

As I entered my mid-teens, I started to have a social life of my own. Going out at night became my escape from the big, empty house on Old Oak Road. Jill and my dad traveled frequently and we were often left home with Kilky and Liz. At fifteen, I began to discover the Los Angeles nightlife with my friends. My big sister Katie knew the door-man at *the* nightclub at the time, Vertigo, and so he would let my friends and me in too. Before our nights out, I always made sure to raid Katie's closet, filled as it was with one-of-a-kind designer pieces from her mother Marion's clothing boutique. I was certain Katie's beautiful clothes made me look older, although they probably only accentuated my underdeveloped frame. My goal was to look exactly like Rosanna Arquette in *Desperately Seeking Susan*. Even if I merely carried one of Katie's Judith Leiber purses or wore her black silk bomber jacket with a sequined Felix the Cat on the back, I felt anointed. My coolest-of-the-cool older sister's clothes were my armor against the world.

Some of my friends were starting to drink and experiment with cocaine. It was the 1980s and coke was the drug of the moment. When my friends did lines, I did them too, not because I particu-larly enjoyed being high, but because I wanted to fit in. I didn't like the way the powder burned my nose or the weird metallic taste in the back of my throat, but I wanted to be like everyone else. So I did the tiniest of lines, or I'd rub some on my gums so I wouldn't have to snort it. I watched the movies *St. Elmo's Fire* and *The Breakfast Club* religiously. That's what I wanted. A group of friends who were as close as family.

Once dressed and equipped with fake IDs, my friends and I had to figure out how to get a ride downtown. Of course, I would lie to Kilky and my dad and say that Jessica's mom was picking us up. In fact, we would call a taxi and tell the driver to wait a few doors down from my house. The drivers never seemed to mind or notice that we were underage; they were just happy to have a fare. Eventually we met a driver who liked coke. Soon we were bribing him with folds of cocaine we had bought downtown to take us to and from Ver-tigo. Out on the dance floor, we spun around to Madonna, Prince, and George Michael, the strobe lights blinking in our eyes. I moved through the experience robotically. I didn't love it. I didn't hate it. I just went through the motions as if I were in a dream.

I began dating a seventeen-year-old guy named Jack. He was tall and thin with sandy-brown hair cut short and spiky. Handsome, but with an edge. I had met him through neighborhood friends. One night he drove me in his vintage Mercedes convertible to Bonnie Brae, a sketchy street just west of downtown. "I'm taking you out to dinner," he told me, "and then we're going to score some coke." I remember thinking: *Wow, I must really have him fooled. He thinks I'm cool enough to score coke with him on the street.*

We were cruising along when suddenly his old Mercedes put-put-puttered and stopped dead. "What's going on?" I asked.

"I don't know." He got out and lifted the hood. "Oh, the gas tank is busted," he said. "I think we ran out of gas. We're going to have to walk to a gas station."

"Okay." I felt a little nervous because we were in a somewhat deserted area, but I wasn't frightened. Somehow, my feelings of isolation and sadness gave me a strange kind of courage. I remember secretly hoping that I would get jumped by someone and fatally stabbed or shot, and at the same time, I knew with perfect clarity that this wasn't going to happen, because I had no such luck.

We hiked to the gas station, got the gasoline, and filled the tank, and Jack drove me home. The streets were quiet that night, no trouble to be found. I don't even remember if we bought the coke. What I really wanted was to go home and drink warm milk and Ovaltine. I wanted socks on my feet and pajamas on my body. I wanted to watch Mister Rogers and be a little girl again.

A couple of days later, Jack confessed that he had arranged for the car to run out of gas on purpose. "I wanted to see what Natalie Wood's daughter would do if she had to walk through the streets of downtown LA looking for gas." He smirked.

That was the end of my relationship with Jack.

After *Hart to Hart* was canceled in 1984, my dad went straight into another series, *Lime Street*, about a widower raising his two daugh-

ters, a role to which he could clearly relate. My dad had just finished shooting the pilot episode in England and we were at London's
Heathrow Airport together, en route to Switzerland for a vacation,
when suddenly my dad was paged on a loudspeaker to take an urgent
phone call. This was unusual, and I started feeling panicky. When
he came back from the call, the look on his face told me something
horrible had happened. His *Lime Street* costar, a young actress named
Samantha Smith, was flying back to the States from finishing her
work with my dad. Her plane had crashed and she and her father had
been killed instantly. She was thirteen years old. My dad was devastated, stunned, barely able to get the words out. As soon as we arrived
in Switzerland, he turned around immediately and flew to Maine to
be with Samantha's mother and attend the memorial service. I stayed
on with Jill, Kilky, and Courtney. I was rocked and blindsided. I
couldn't stop thinking about Samantha's mother. She had just lost her
daughter and her husband. What must she be going through? How
could one person cope with so much loss?

Three days after that, the phone rang. Jill answered, listened, and
then hung up. "Natasha, I'm so sorry, Ruth Gordon died today." She
spoke the words plainly. There was no hand-holding, no hugs. Just the
cold hard facts. My darling godmother had passed away from a stroke.
Whomp, another punch in the gut. I took it in and pretended I was
fine. I don't remember if I cried. I just knew that I needed to hold on
tightly to the people in my life because death was all around us.

I became terrified to travel. Every time I landed in the UK to see
my Daddy Gregson, I panicked, becoming convinced that something
catastrophic had happened during the long flight. As I walked off the
plane, my pulse would race and my lungs would tighten up. I anx-
iously searched the faces and body language of whoever had come to
pick me up for any hints of impending bad news. "Is everyone okay?"
I would ask before saying as much as a hello.

For our family, the 1980s was an entire decade of loss. Was death
going to be a constant presence in our lives now? With each passing, the grief I felt over my mom was compounded. I became con-

vinced that we were a cursed family and that Daddy Wagner would be next.

I lost my virginity in the summer before my sixteenth birthday. Jessica did it first, so naturally I wanted to do it too. Paul was a year younger than me and went to another school. He was smart and funny and sophisticated, one of those people who made you feel like the most important person in the room when they focused their attention on you.

Before Paul and I had sex for the first time he put on the song "Tonight's the Night," even though it was the middle of the afternoon. Losing my virginity hurt, but I did it anyway. It had nothing to do with Paul and everything to do with being like my best friend Jessica.

One night right around my sixteenth birthday, my dad took me out for dinner at Valentino, an elegant Italian restaurant on Pico Boulevard. He told me he thought it would be a good idea if I started taking birth control pills.

"I know you and Paul have been spending a lot of time together lately," he said.

"Don't worry, Daddy, Jessica and I already went to Planned Parenthood and got the pill."

I could see the relief in my dad's eyes. What my dad was not able to see was how much pain I was still in over losing my mom.

When Paul and I began dating, he called regularly, and we'd chat or make plans to see each other. After we started sleeping together, he'd say he was going to call, but then he wouldn't—and he wasn't home when I called. My friends told me they saw him out with other girls. I would wait by the phone, my heart pounding, my palms sweaty, my anxiety mounting with every minute. I knew this feeling. It was the same feeling I had as I waited for my mom to call when I was a little girl.

Unlike me, Jessica had a good and kind boyfriend and they were spending all their time together. I began to feel as if I was losing her. She was my safe person and without her I was not safe. I was also about to start a new school where I knew no one. My relationship with Paul was clearly going nowhere.

My dad was in England working when things reached a breaking point. It was a warm June night. I could smell the sweet jasmine outside my bedroom window. I could see my beloved horse in his stall. I had so much to be thankful for, and yet I still felt so alone and insecure.

Courtney and I loved my mom's movie *The Cracker Factory* about a woman going through a nervous breakdown. We watched it a lot on the VCR at home. Whenever we got to the scene where my mom's character attempts suicide I would think to myself, *If it all gets too much, I can do that. I can take the pills and check out.* For some reason, the image of her downing the pills comforted me. It helped me to know I had a way out of my suffering if I really needed one.

That night, I found a bottle of Tylenol in my bathroom medicine cabinet. On impulse I reached for it, popped it open, and swallowed a handful of pills. I didn't want to kill myself. I was somehow emulating my mom's character in the movie. Jessica was in my bedroom watching TV. Courtney was in her room, and I could hear Kilky through the wall talking on the phone to her best friend Velma. I washed the pills down with a glass of chocolate milk.

Almost immediately after I swallowed them, I panicked. I didn't want to die but I had done something very serious and I knew it. Now I might be in real danger. Could I rewind the tape, make it all go away? This wasn't a scene in a movie. This was my life.

I walked into my bedroom and told Jessica. She immediately called Tracey, who put her mom on the phone.

"Natooshie, it's Janis. Are you okay? What's going on?" Her voice was like warm milk and honey.

"Did you take some pills?"

"Yes," I admitted, and started to cry.

"How many did you take?"

"I don't know. Maybe a handful."

"Natasha, I'm going to hang up the phone and call the paramedics."

"Please don't!" I begged.

I knew I needed Janis to save me, but I also knew I was about to be in very big trouble.

During this conversation, Jessica had raced down the hall and told Kilky what was going on.

Kilky came running into my room.

"Tasha, what did you do?" she screamed.

Kilky grabbed me, steered me to the toilet, and put her finger down my throat. I could feel her long nails scratching the back of my throat. I gagged and threw up but only a little.

"Tasha, what is wrong with you, why would you do something like this?"

By this time Courtney was standing in the bathroom too.

"Courtney, go get Jamie," Kilky shouted. "We have to get to the hospital right now!"

Jamie worked for our dad helping around the house, and happened to be there that evening. He scooped me up and put me into the car, Kilky by my side.

We went to St. John's Hospital in Santa Monica. The nurses brought me a thick, pasty black charcoal drink and a blue bucket to throw up in. The charcoal tasted bitter and chalky. It was not like *The Cracker Factory* in here. There was no kindly doctor who took an interest in me and made me feel safe. I did not get to let all my feelings out with an on-the-nose emotional monologue. Instead, the doctor on duty, bearded and stern, told me I was very lucky not to have done irreparable damage to my liver.

"Had you taken any more pills or waited much longer, you would be in a much more serious situation," he lectured.

Sitting there in my thin blue paper gown, I felt like a thrift-store Thumbelina.

Jamie, Kilky, and I drove home silently that night. By morning both my dads had been notified of what I had done. I braced myself for the fallout. Courtney, Kilky, and I were leaving for the UK in a couple of weeks to visit Daddy Wagner in London, before heading to see Daddy Gregson at Whitebrook Farm for the rest of the summer. When I arrived in London, my two fathers were waiting for me at the hotel. I remember a tense dinner at Langan's restaurant.

"Things have got to change," Daddy Gregson told us. He reprimanded my Daddy Wagner for working and traveling too much, and laid down the law: it was time to reprioritize and spend more time at home with Courtney and me. Daddy Gregson also felt he needed to be more present for me. I would spend the summer with him in Wales, and then *he* would decide if he thought I seemed stable enough to return to Los Angeles. Because he was my legal guardian, the final word about my welfare rested with him.

Of course neither of my dads was really to blame. I hid my suffering from Daddy Wagner, terrified that if he knew I was still so sad it would be too much for him to bear. I hid my pain from Daddy Gregson, worrying that if he knew I was still struggling with the loss of my mother he would make me come live with him and Julia in Wales. The truth is, I was afraid to share my pain with anyone because I felt like I should have bounced back by now. Everyone else seemed to have moved on.

Thank goodness for Daddy Gregson, an unwavering force who righted the ship when it veered off course, so full of certitude and direction, caring and concern. As August came to a close, he and I took one of our long walks in the forest behind his farm. I could feel his attention focused directly on me, searching my face for the slightest shadow, probing for clues about my well-being. He was always like that, laser-focused on making sure I was okay, ready to provide counsel, assistance, support. After a summer together, my dad trusted me enough—or perhaps believed in my fortitude enough—to let me go back to America and find my way.

• • •

Back home, I settled into a new school, Crossroads, a private progressive school in Santa Monica. It was a small, caring environment where students and teachers called each other by their first names. I took a newfound interest in my studies, reading Franz Kafka, Langston Hughes, and Philip Roth's *Goodbye, Columbus*. I particularly loved my Film Studies class, guided by Jim Hosney. Jim was famous at Crossroads. Tiny and bespectacled, with his beloved pit bull mix Rona always at his side, he had seen just about every movie there ever was. He delighted in his students' discoveries. No question was ever too stupid or uninformed for Jim. His classroom was a safe place to open your mind, especially to the great screen classics.

One day Jim took me aside. "Natasha, would it be okay with you if I show the class *Splendor in the Grass*?" I was touched that he requested my permission to screen one of my mother's movies. This was the film my mom considered her best work, directed by Elia Kazan, the man I'd grown up calling Gadge. I had never watched the film in its entirety and certainly not in a room full of my peers. I surprised myself by saying yes.

We were studying melodrama at the time and so we watched the film in the context of the class. This took the onus away from me and my mom. I felt I could discover her performance and the film along with my classmates. Jim screened the film over two or three class periods as he always did. I don't even know if the whole class knew that Deanie was my mom. I watched and I listened and I learned from Jim about that movie just like everyone else. I was just a student. I was not the child of a movie star.

*Splendor in the Grass* is set in the 1920s. In the movie, my twenty-one-year-old mother plays Deanie Loomis, a small-town girl from Kansas who falls in love with Bud, the son of a wealthy local family, played by Warren Beatty. Deanie's mother (played by Audrey Christie) warns her to wait until she is married to have sex. Meanwhile, Bud's father tells him to look elsewhere to satisfy his desires, which he reluctantly does, leaving Deanie heartbroken. After she is almost raped by another man, Deanie attempts suicide, and her parents put her in a mental institution.

One of the most famous scenes in the film is the bathtub scene. Deanie is soaking in a hot tub and her mother comes in to check on her. Her mother asks what's the matter and if she's upset about Bud. She tells Deanie she's going to call that boy and give him a piece of her mind! Deanie erupts into anguished screams—"Don't you dare, don't you dare!"—and she threatens to do something desperate if her mom does call. A worried look passes over her mother's face and she asks if Bud has "spoiled" Deanie—in other words, if they have had sex.

"Did he spoil me?" Deanie asks, laughing wildly, then submerging her entire head face-first into the water before coming up for air. "No, Mom, I'm not spoiled!" she spits sarcastically at her mother. "I'm just as fresh and as virginal as the day I was born!"

Then she gets out of the bath, fully naked, eyes wide and arms outstretched, crying, "I'm a good little girl! A good little, good little girl!"

The scene ends with Deanie running from the bathroom, wild, naked, lost. As I watched the film in Jim's class, the scene sent a flicker of recognition coursing through me. The character felt so familiar to me; the heightened emotion, the woman-child on the cusp of adulthood. I recognized Deanie in my mother and in myself.

I felt proud to share her with my class that day—her beauty, her artistry, the emotional vulnerability she showed as Deanie. Everyone could see how amazing my mother was. Instead of shrinking under the weight of the comparison, I felt as if I were a reflection of her radiance.

At Crossroads, we had a weekly class called Mysteries. The teacher turned off the lights and lit a candle, which was placed in the center of the room. The students sat cross-legged in a circle. A talking stone was passed around. We took turns sharing our feelings in the dark. I loved Mysteries. I felt safe in this candlelit room. Here, I took the first small steps toward revealing my true self.

When a boy in our school died of a congenital kidney disease, the impact was felt throughout Crossroads. That week in Mysteries, other kids discussed the difficulties of accepting his death. None of the kids, however, had lost anyone close to them, and I remember thinking,

*These people don't know anything about grief . . . but I can teach them something about it.* This was my moment. There, in the flickering candlelight, I finally opened up about losing my mom. "Grief rocks you to your core," I told my classmates. "You feel unsafe. You feel afraid. You feel alone. And it never goes away."

I surprised myself that afternoon by speaking so openly in class. I think I surprised my classmates too, as I had always given them the impression that everything was fine with me. I was discovering how cathartic, how healing it can be to speak about your pain. Tentatively, I was finding my voice.

# Chapter 12

From left, Richard Gregson, Natalie Wood,
Robert Evans, and Ali MacGraw
at the Moss Hart tribute, April 1970.

"Oh, Natasha, you are so dramatic, you are going to be an actress when you grow up!"

My mom said these words to me so often during my childhood that I think some part of me always assumed that when I did finally grow up, of course I would become an actor. Both of my parents were actors. All my parents' friends were actors, directors, filmmakers, or in the business. My mom and I were so alike in every way that if she was an actress it made perfect sense that I would explore that path as well.

My mom's only stipulation was that I had to wait until I was eighteen. She didn't want me to work in the business before then.

I was in my junior year at high school when I brought up the subject of acting with Daddy Wagner. On some level, I think I was hoping it might even bring me closer to my mother. After all, acting had been foundational to her life since early childhood.

My dad set up meetings with various friends within the industry so that I could get some perspective on the business. I understood how lucky I was. When my dad and I were on the East Coast looking at colleges, we went to see Elia Kazan at his brownstone in New York on the Upper East Side. Gadge was just as I remembered him. A friendly Elmer Fudd, sitting at his long wooden desk in a cozy flannel shirt. I felt an immediate familiarity; he had spent so much time at our house on Canon Drive when I was a child. I remember mostly listening as Gadge and my dad spoke about my mom, about making *Splendor* and Method acting. Gadge took an interest in me and felt that I might have some talent. I told him about my desire to study. He was someone who looked at you deeply as you spoke. That afternoon, he told me to listen to my most inner voice.

Back in Los Angeles, I met with the director, producer, and actor Sydney Pollack. Sydney had directed my mom in *This Property Is Condemned*, his 1966 movie based on the Tennessee Williams play and set in the South during the Great Depression. In the movie, my mother played Alva Starr, a young woman stuck and frustrated in her small-town life who meets a handsome stranger, Owen Legate, played by Robert Redford, whom she sees as her way out. My mom was superb in the film—her emotional range visible in all its glory. In one scene she barges into Owen's room wet from skinny-dipping in the lake, furious at him for misunderstanding her. She rages and then she seduces him. She was nominated for a Golden Globe for Best Actress for the role.

I went to meet Sydney at his office at one of the studios in the valley. He came to greet me, giving me a hug, before sitting down at his large wooden desk, his eyes kind behind thick glasses.

He was very matter-of-fact.

"Do you think you have any talent?" he asked.

"I don't know," I answered honestly.

"Can you think of anything else you could do besides acting?"

"No," I answered.

"Well, give it a shot."

Unlike me, my mom never had a chance to choose acting as her vocation. As a child, she simply played whichever part came next. No one had to teach her. She had a natural gift for make-believe. It was only as she got older that she decided to become a student of acting. After she won the part of Judy, the girlfriend character in *Rebel Without a Cause*, her costars Sal Mineo, Nick Adams, and James Dean and director, Nicholas Ray, introduced her to Method acting. This movie set my mom on a lifelong quest to become a great actress. To know herself deeply, to be able to use herself as a vessel to communicate her emotions to the world. She was much less interested in being a star than in her craft and the chance to learn from directors like Kazan and costars like Redford and McQueen.

Thanks to my mother's example, I knew that if I wanted to become an actor I had to become a serious student. During my senior year of high school, I took a scene study class, memorizing lines from playwrights like Tennessee Williams and Sam Shepard. Sitting with a script in my lap going over the words felt so familiar—familial, in fact. I remembered this about my mom: her focus when she memorized her lines, her discipline when she worked with her dialect coach learning Russian for her part in *Meteor*. I remember how strict she was with her diet and her exercise when she was preparing for a role.

Onstage, I loved the emotional and physical vibration I felt in my body as I connected to a character or the dramatic arc of a story. So much of my grief and suffering suddenly had a place to live. Yet I was creaky with my emotions. I had spent so many years denying my feelings around others, expressing them only in the darkest of nights or in the safety of the warm water streaming on my face in the shower, that I did not know how to bring them into the light of day. I didn't know how to be emotional without getting overwhelmed.

I decided to go to college, and when it came time to pick a school, I chose Emerson College in Boston, a college with a strong performing arts curriculum, where I would be located halfway-ish between Wales and California. My parents had been considering relocating us to upstate New York, away from the bright lights of Hollywood, right before my mom died. I knew my mother had adored the East Coast. To me it felt like where the smart people went.

As excited as I was about college, I was deeply conflicted about leaving Courtney. We had grown so close, and I knew she depended on me. Our age difference was less important now. We had long discussions about my impending departure. I made her promise me that she would stay in touch by phone. I think we even scheduled regular check-in calls, just like our mother used to do when she was away.

My dad came along to get me settled into my dorm in Boston. I was so anxious that, instead of moving into my dorm room right away with my new roommate, Tory, I stayed in my dad's hotel every night. My dad put a letter on my pillow the day he left. Whenever I tried to read it, tears would blur my eyes and drip-drop onto the paper. It took me over a month before I could actually read his supportive words. The mature part of me knew that coming to college was the right thing to do. The childlike, insecure part of me wanted to get back on the plane with him and return to my life at Old Oak Road.

I took my first real acting class at Emerson. I was intimidated by the new surroundings, lonely for my loved ones in Los Angeles, daunted by the task of acting. Many of the students in my class had taken musical theater and drama starting in elementary school. They were so far ahead of me. Mostly what I learned in those acting classes was how much I still needed to learn.

I started immersing myself in different characters. I discovered how powerful that can be. I also discovered so many of my limitations. My high voice, my small size, my insecurities, my fear of failure, my perfectionism, even my vulnerability worked against me. Sometimes I felt that losing my mother at eleven had wiped away my developing self so completely that all I had left was an outline, a rough sketch of who I could have been. The idea of acting professionally felt further away than ever.

I had a hard time in those early days justifying my right to even try to be an actress. Compared to my mother, a woman whose beauty seemed made for the camera, a natural-born star who was acting professionally from the age of five, how could I possibly measure up?

I ended up staying in Boston for only one year. While I was away, Courtney began having panic attacks, suffering from such acute anxiety that she literally refused to go to school. Most mornings, her sense of dread was so intense that she could not face first period at Crossroads. I decided to leave Boston and return to LA. I wanted to be closer to Courtney. I also realized I wanted to commit myself to acting full-time.

I called Daddy Gregson in Wales to let him know. I knew he was not going to be pleased. He had been so proud of me, so supportive of my East Coast excursion. He would come to Boston every couple of months and take me and Tory, with whom I'd become close, out for dinner. He and I would go to museums and walk and walk. Boston also held a special place in his heart, as he had produced the play *Cyrano* there in 1973 with Christopher Plummer in the title role, and he had fond memories of that time.

"Hi, Dad."

"Hi, darling."

"I want to talk to you about next year."

"Yes," he said tentatively. I could hear the worry in his voice.

"Well, you know how I have been studying acting here. Um . . . I think that is what I really want to pursue. So I'm going to go back to LA and study acting there and apply to USC and try to get an agent. . . ."

Click. The phone went dead. I knew what that click meant. Sure enough, a couple of days later, he called Daddy Wagner and told him in no uncertain terms that he was not on board with my plan. I'm not sure how Daddy Wagner responded, but Daddy Gregson didn't speak to me for six months.

For my sophomore year, I transferred to USC and moved back to Old Oak Road. By now Courtney was fifteen years old. She had matured from a young girl to a gorgeous teenager. She hadn't gone through an awkward phase like me, but transitioned smoothly from childhood to young womanhood, looking a bit older than her years, her complexion remaining flawless—just like my mom's. Bright blond hair, long tan legs. A real stunner. After I moved back, we would meet in her room, talking or reminiscing, or we would raid the fridge in the kitchen late at night, sitting on the kitchen counters and laughing our asses off. We nurtured each other and we liked and loved each other.

I knew she had an older boyfriend. I knew she was drinking and going out with an older crowd. Beautiful, funny, and game, my little sister was a rebel and a magnet for men. They loved her and she loved their love. Everyone was partying at this time. I was doing my share, but I did it in moderation, to have fun and to fit in with my friends. With Courtney, I could tell it was different. Alcohol emboldened her, and she could take three shots of vodka in a row without skipping a beat. In a flash she would cease to be my little sister and fly out of reach, becoming unknowable.

One night we were at a club. I was waiting in line for the bathroom, the smell of spilled, warm beer and cigarette smoke making me feel sick. A tall blond girl told me I had cut in line.

"No, I didn't," I said. We started to argue.

From behind me my supernova of a little sister pushed herself through the crowd and punched this girl right in the face. They both went down, kicking each other, pulling each other's hair. I started screaming, "Courtney, *stop it*!" Katie appeared and was able to extract Courtney from the floor. When she stood up she had a giant egg-shaped bump on her forehead. Soon the bouncers arrived and we were swiftly kicked out.

Though I was grateful for Courtney's protection, I was shocked at the feral intensity that had come over her. Eyes glazed and fiery, she was ready for more.

Not long after I returned from Boston, a friend who had moved into my bedroom while I was gone told me that one night, Courtney had drunk too much and had driven herself home. I instantly felt the all-too-familiar pang of panic. Courtney was the only other human being on this earth who lost exactly what I lost on that night in 1981. She was my sweet, hilarious sister. Our insecurities and shortcomings made sense to each other. Though we were very different in temperament, we had so much in common: we had the same voice patterns, we moved the same way, we were like two halves of our mother's whole. Being with Courtney was as close as I would ever get to spending time with my mother. I couldn't lose my sister, I just couldn't.

When I wasn't worrying about Courtney, I was determined to work on my acting skills, so my dad helped me to find a teacher, Chris. He did little to bolster my confidence. I had gained the obligatory "freshman fifteen" pounds during my year at Emerson, and I remember him telling me, "Listen, it's clear you aren't going to be a beauty like your mom. You are not a leading lady. Let's focus on character actress roles for you." I felt my chubby, acne-spotted self burn with shame. I knew I was not as beautiful as my mom, but why must I be compared to her at all? I had my own brand of beauty. Maybe it wasn't the head-turning, traffic-stopping kind my mom had, but it was enough that I shouldn't have to be shamed for not looking exactly like her. I swallowed Chris's words and pretended I agreed with him, nodding matter-of-factly. *Of course he's right*, I said to myself. *He's just stating*

*the facts. So now let's move on to some monologues that would be good for
a character actress.*

Later, I told my dad what Chris had said to me. "I'm so sorry, darling. You know that isn't true." It felt good to tell him, and good to be
reassured. We never talked about it again, and Chris soon moved to
New York, so our lessons came to an end. But no matter what my dad
said, part of me still believed what Chris had told me, and I carried it
around for many years.

Luckily, my confidence was bolstered in other ways. Not long
after I returned to LA, I started seeing a new boyfriend, Josh Evans.
My friend Robyn had gone on a date with him first. "Josh is not right
for me," Robyn told me, "but I think you and he would hit it off."
She was right. It turned out that Josh and I already knew each other
tangentially, and not only because he had been a junior at Crossroads
when I was a senior. As Robyn predicted, we did indeed hit it off.

Josh was an actor who had already played the younger brother of
Tom Cruise in Oliver Stone's *Born on the Fourth of July* and was working on his second Stone film, *The Doors.* He was gorgeous, with the
dark refined looks of his father, the legendary movie producer Robert Evans, and the sensual, soft features of his beautiful mother, the
actress Ali MacGraw. Ali explained to me that she had met my mother
through Bob and that she and my mom were both pregnant—with
Josh and me—around the same time. She had brought Josh to my
first birthday party and I had attended his first birthday in return. It
seemed like we were meant to be together.

Josh was different from anyone I had come across in my life so far.
He was confident and mature. I was older than him by six months,
but he was years older in terms of wisdom and experience. We shared a
passion for movies and for acting, and similar backgrounds as the children of famous parents. Josh felt familiar to me from the beginning.
I recognized his love, his ways, his breath when he was sleeping. He
adored me in that intimate, all-encompassing, larger-than-life way that
my mom had. This love strengthened me, enabling me to put one firm

foot in front of the other as if I were heading toward some kind of destination. We would see one another off and on for the next six years.

Once again I was interested in my boyfriend's mother as much as I was interested in my boyfriend. Ali lived by the ocean and had all kinds of animals, like my parents. She drove a little Mercedes just like my mother had. My mom had dated Steve McQueen for a short time after she divorced my Daddy Gregson, and Ali was later married to Steve. Although my mom and Ali were not close friends, they liked each other. After I started seeing Josh, Ali took me under her wing, taught me about clothes and furniture and design—areas my mom and I hadn't gotten to. She introduced me to yoga and spirituality. Separate from my relationship with Josh, Ali and I formed our own friendship, one that thrives to this day.

On our one-year anniversary, Josh gave me a three-sided silver frame with three photos in it: the first was of Bob, Ali, my mom, and Daddy Gregson when Ali and my mom were pregnant with Josh and me; the second was of Josh and me at my first birthday party; the third was a quick, casual snapshot that Helmut Newton took of Josh and me after a day at the beach when I was twenty-one. Josh inscribed the bottom of the frame with the word "Destiny." It felt like it.

He had helped me at a pivotal moment. Not long after Josh and I began dating, my dad and Jill announced they were getting married. I was nineteen and Courtney was sixteen. Daddy and Jill had been together for more than seven years, but still the thought of our dad making that serious commitment filled my sisters and me with sadness and fear. I knew I should have been okay with it. Jill made my dad happy and that was important. But even so, I was terrified. Josh had gone through his own experience of his dad marrying multiple times and he could relate.

"You want him to be happy," Josh pointed out. "You're living your own life now. You're studying. You've got me. Let him live his own life."

Even so, the morning of the wedding, May 1990, I woke up feeling terrible, my throat sore and my head pounding. Josh held me and talked me through it. I left his place feeling fortified by our growing relationship, and miraculously recovered from my flu symptoms.

A couple of hours later, as Courtney, Katie, and I stood in the backyard of our house on Old Oak Road to give Daddy and Jill our blessing, we could not control our tears. I loved my dad so much and wanted him to be happy. I knew that life was for the living, and I knew that my mom would want him to be with Jill, a woman who loved him honestly and completely and still does. My brain knew this, but my body was unable to stop the flow of tears. The grief and fear I felt that day were not rational. My tears were for my mother and all that we had lost when we lost her; they were for my dad, onto whom I had projected all my needs, and who was moving on with a new chapter in his life.

But my boyfriend was right. I was moving on with a new chapter of my life too. Encouraged by Josh and his mom, I worked on my career. Josh had an acting teacher that he loved named Harold Guskin, so I met with Harold and decided to study with him. Harold was warm and dynamic and would hold these renowned five-day intensive Shakespeare and Chekhov workshops. I signed up for as many as I could.

I remember Josh and I went to a workshop at the Loews Hotel in Santa Monica. The class sat in a semicircle with Harold at the front. I looked around and noticed a few familiar faces, some strangers, and one man who appeared to be around sixty, with shoulder-length, unkempt hair and a scraggly brown beard peppered with gray. His disheveled ensemble was that of a person obviously down on his luck: faded black jeans, an old worn T-shirt with holes in it, dirty black boots. Santa Monica has always been a haven for hippies and beach bums, and because Harold is so open and accepting, I assumed that our teacher had allowed one of the homeless men who hung around the hotel to sit in on his class. *How cool of him*, I thought. By lunchtime Josh was acting strangely—anxious and self-conscious—and I wondered why.

"This class is intense," I prompted.

"Yeah," he agreed. "I wish I had known that Kris was taking the class."

"Who?" I asked.

He pointed to the disheveled man.

"That homeless guy is upsetting you?" I said in total bewilderment.

"That's not a homeless guy, Natasha. That's Kris Kristofferson, and he broke my mom's heart a few years ago."

Josh taught me about a new world of actors and directors. My parents had known an older Hollywood generation, but thanks to his producer father, Josh seemed to know pretty much everyone else.

After I had been back in Los Angles for about a year, I decided to get a place of my own. My British dad came to town and helped me find a cozy two-bedroom on Doheny Drive. The building was painted my favorite color, pink, and there was a courtyard surrounded by eight apartments. Josh's mom, Ali, helped me to set up my new home. She was a minimalist, the complete opposite of my mom. With Ali's help, I covered my sofas in mattress ticking; we found vintage rugs and rattan baskets to put around my apartment. She bought me a beautiful carved Buddha. Ali taught me how to make a fruit bowl look pretty, how to arrange flowers in a vase, and how to make a still life from a stack of books, a little bowl of nuts, a candle. There were so many missing pieces in my mothering; Ali was helping me to replace them.

# Chapter 13

Natasha on the set of David Lynch's *Lost Highway*, 1997.

One morning in the spring of 1990, Courtney and I headed off together in my black Jeep Wrangler, making our way out of our protected cocoon on the west side and onto the tangled freeways of the 405 and 101. For the first time since our mother died, we were going to visit the storage unit in Glendale where all her belongings were kept. My dad had decided he was ready to revisit the items that had been put in storage and he thought that Courtney and I might also want to take a look and see if there was anything we wanted to keep now that we were older.

Liz had organized the day. Since my mom's death, Liz had kept working as my dad's assistant. I remember feeling a nervous thrill when she called to ask if I wanted to go with her and Courtney to the storage unit. I was excited that my dad thought we were old enough to take care of our mom's possessions. What treasures might we find?

On the drive over I was filled with anticipation, but as soon as we walked into the storage facility I felt the back of my neck stiffen. It was a sort of gripping tension, a burning. There was Liz waiting for Courtney and me. Everything about Liz felt safe to me, her English-accented "Hello, lovey," her complete confidence in organizing our lives. I trusted her. *Why does my body feel like this?*

I followed closely behind Liz as we walked toward the back of the building and entered the storage unit. Long tables had been set up along the walls, covered with what seemed like hundreds of objects. All my mom's possessions, waiting to be rediscovered by Courtney and me. To be held, touched, looked at, and listened to. The flotsam and jetsam of a well-lived life. These artifacts from the past had been loved by my parents and they were waiting to be loved by us. Maybe if we loved them hard enough, if we made space for them in our own lives, they could tell our mom's story.

There were the silver goblets that Spencer Tracy had given my mom and dad for their first wedding. "Bob and Nat, all my love, Spence." I remember they had sat in our wooden bookshelves in the living room. When Jessica and I played "ladies" in that room, often we would pretend the goblets were tall wineglasses. We would take ladylike sips and try to imitate our mothers' voices. "Now, Natooshie, tonight will not work for a sleepover with Jessie. . . ."

In the middle of one of the long tables was a cluster of Limoges boxes that had rested on my mom's night table. There was an oblong box with the words "You are witty and pretty," a reference to the lyrics from a *West Side Story* song, with pale blue forget-me-nots circling the top and bottom. A box in the shape of a heart had been given to my mother for her birthday by Howard Jeffrey the July before she died. Pink and green flowers wound tightly together in friendship.

Then there was the sloppy rabbit I made out of clay for her in fourth grade. Painted dark mauve and molded with immature hands. She loved that rabbit and kept it next to her on her bedside table.

Novels that had once been piled on the floor next to her bed were now piled on the tables in the storage unit. I remember one called *High Anxiety*. Was that what I was feeling now?

Liz was the lightness in the room that day.

"Natooshie, look at Mommie's little shoes! Your grandma had them bronzed. Do you remember these sat on the mantel in their bedroom? And here are your little ballet slippers and Courtney's sweet little shoes. Look, Mummy did the same thing to your shoes. Take them with you today, lovey. They are beautiful!"

Courtney and I, discovering and rediscovering, what? Our childhood, our mom, our younger selves when life was safe and sweet?

A silver box with my parents' wedding invitation engraved on top, "the second time around."

Another plain rectangular silver box. I opened it and it read, "For Lady Wood, with continuing affection, Redford."

"Look, Toosh," Courtney called to me. "Remember Mommie's music box? I wonder if it still works?"

The box was large and square, made of dark, inlaid wood. Courtney opened up the lid, turning the old crank handle. Suddenly the bells started ringing, playing their familiar tune. Inside, there was a little drum and butterflies and flowers that hit the brass bells, chiming and chirping. The sound of our mother filled the room. I ended up taking the box home with me, to the magical delight of any small child that happens upon it.

That morning I lost track of time. I don't know how many hours went by before I remembered I had an appointment with my therapist, Mrs. Malin. I was still seeing her once a week. It was time to go, but where were my keys?

The three of us looked on every table and around every object, to no avail. What had I done with them? I felt foolish and insecure. This was a grown-up thing, to be invited to the storage unit. Now I was back to being an irresponsible child. I had lost my keys and I would miss my therapy session, dammit.

I can't remember who found my keys or how but they were finally retrieved after we turned that room upside down. I had missed my appointment.

When I finally made it to my therapy session the following week, Mrs. Malin asked what I had been doing when I lost my keys. I casually mentioned that Courtney and I had gone to the storage unit. Then I kept talking about some inconsequential argument I'd had with Josh.

Mrs. Malin stopped me. "Natasha, was that the first time you had seen the contents of Canon Drive since you moved out?"

I remember her gaze so clearly. Steady and deeply focused on me.

"Yes," I answered.

"Well, no wonder you lost your keys. That must have been an incredibly emotional experience. Let's talk about it."

I shifted in her noisy leather chair.

"Why?" I asked. "It's all fine now. I picked out things I wanted and I found my keys."

I did not want to talk about it.

Mrs. Malin looked at me again, her eyes filled with kindness.

"Okay," she said. "Maybe another time."

Not long after the visit to the storage unit, my mom's datebooks arrived at my home in narrow black boxes. Looking back, I can't precisely remember how they ended up there. Maybe I had asked Liz to send them to me? What I do remember is staring at them in the entry hall of my apartment. Each box had a year printed on top: the first year was 1964 and the last was 1981, when the boxes ended. I found the box that said 1970 and took it into my bedroom. I sat down on my bed and I opened up the box. Inside were twelve tiny, black, spiral-bound notebooks. One for each month. I remembered these datebooks. My mother kept them within reach on her table, her desk, her bed, usually opened to the current day of the week, so she could easily jot something down: a reminder, an appointment, a number, an address, a moment she didn't want to forget.

I picked out the book for September 1970, the month of my birth. My mom's loopy, happy, Natalie Wood handwriting was on every page, slanting upward and to the right. Sometimes she used black ink, sometimes blue, sometimes pencil. Sometimes she wrote in block letters, sometimes script. In the front of the book were the names and numbers of all her doctors, emergency numbers, numbers of her friends and her family and all her favorite restaurants. Some of them were the numbers I had memorized by heart as a child. I flipped through the pages to find September 29, 1970, the day of my birth. At the top of the page, in pencil, she had written, "cleaning crew." Then "1:45 Bentley's chop house Lana—Wilshire." After that the words: "At 2:30 hospital." Then, at the bottom of the page in big purple letters, she wrote: "Natasha born 9:11 p.m. 6lb. 8 ounces." My mom drew the *N* of my name exactly the way she drew the *N* of her name. Tall and proud but ladylike. A brick dollhouse.

Sitting in my room that day, I read the words over and over: "Natasha born." *I am born. I am here. If I am born, then how could it be that she is gone now?* These were the confusing strands of thought tangling in my mind. I know my mom wanted me so, so, so much. I know she was over the moon to become a mother. I remember how much she loved and adored and cherished Courtney and me. How much fun she'd had planning our parties, buying us velvet holiday dresses, curling our hair with her big hot rollers.

I pulled out the book for 1971. August. On the first page of the beginning of the month, my mom had written in turquoise cursive, "Sat 7:45 Dinner Langes." Beneath that in large, black, cursive letters, "End of Marriage," with a black line down the page. *Okay, so this is the day my parents' marriage ended.* I knew a couple of weeks later my mom, my aunt Olga, Mart, and I boarded the SS *Raffaello* for Europe. A disastrous trip but a journey that my mom somehow needed to take.

On the back of the datebook she had made a list: "Richard did not want me to continue breastfeeding after three months." "Wanted me to go back to work when Natasha was just a baby." "Did not understand why I needed to call home and check on her when we were out to dinner." "When she became of age wanted to send her to an

English boarding school." So here are my mom's reasons for leaving my dad right in front of me? If she were still alive and I asked her, "Why did you and my Daddy Gregson break up?" these would be her answers? Or would they?

Discovering this vulnerable time during her breakup from my father was too much for me. Sitting there with the datebooks, I realized I had been without my mother for nearly nine years. Her love no longer felt sturdy or solid. It felt far away, like cotton candy clouds in a dream that I could reach for but that disappeared in my hands. I was supposed to be a grown-up or very near a grown-up, but I still felt so much like a little girl. I might live by myself, have a boyfriend, drive my own car, and work as an actor, but I felt as if a big gust of wind might blow me away. I was looking for guidance in the datebooks. I needed to lean on my mother's trusty strength. If she had periods when she felt scared and insecure, then that meant I would have periods when I felt scared and insecure—and what would the outcome be for me?

I closed up the datebooks and sent them back to storage. Around this same time, Mart told me about my mom's suicide attempt. The year was 1964. She was divorced from R.J., filming *The Great Race* with Tony Curtis, and feeling particularly lost and alone. One night, Mart heard a banging on his door, and when he opened it, Natalie fell into his arms. She told him she had taken too many pills. Mart immediately called her doctor, who came to the house and said she needed to go to the hospital. My mother stayed in the hospital for the weekend, getting her stomach pumped, and was back to work on Monday, always the professional.

I heard what Mart was telling me, but I barely processed his words. I was nowhere near strong enough to come into contact with my mother's fragility. I didn't want to read her datebooks. I wasn't ready to revisit her intimate possessions from Canon Drive. I could only feel the anxiety gripping the back of my neck, mislay my keys, and cry in the shower when nobody could hear me.

• • •

While I was studying acting as a sophomore at USC, Josh was working with the producer Nick Wechsler. Nick invited me to audition for *Fathers & Sons*, an indie drama starring Jeff Goldblum and one of my teenage idols, Rosanna Arquette. I got the part of Lisa, a lost waif of a girl searching for love.

By now Daddy Gregson had started speaking to me again. One day, out of the blue, he called me up, and we were back to our old relationship. I think he realized I was serious about my acting career and he had better go along with it. He warned me that I would never be able to focus on acting *and* finish college. "You need to pick one," he said. The choice was obvious. I wanted to be an actor. Instead of going back to college for my junior year, I headed to Belmar, New Jersey, to start shooting my first movie. I had never acted professionally before, and I had no idea what I was doing. But I felt lucky to be among such an exceptional ensemble cast: Jeff and Rosanna, as well as Joie Lee, Samuel L. Jackson, Ellen Greene, and Famke Janssen. And I wasn't the only newcomer. The director, Paul Mones, had hired Rory Cochrane, also a first-time actor on a film set.

I had been on many sets as a child and I quickly felt at ease. The camaraderie was familiar to me. After all, most of my mother's dearest friendships had been forged on movie sets. I bonded with many of my castmates, the director, makeup artists, hairstylists, the first assistant director. I was especially drawn to people who could teach me, guide me, mother me. I was still looking for that kind of connection. The freshly printed scripts, collated and clean, reminded me of my parents and their scripts. When the paper changed colors from blue to yellow to pink, I knew what that meant. Rewrites!

What was not familiar to me were the inevitable discomforts of filming: the 4:30 a.m. wake-up calls, being so cold *all the time*, the way they called the next meal "lunch" even though it was clearly dinnertime. Night shoots . . . My very first day I had a love scene on the beach in New Jersey with Rory. It was January but we had to pretend it was summer, which meant we were freezing and sandy and all-around uncomfortable. Even so, I found I could easily relate to Lisa's search for love and connection.

I remember calling Gadge to give him an update on my career. He, of course, wanted to know all about the director and if I liked the way he talked to me about the character. I did.

Next I landed a small part in the film of the moment, *Buffy the Vampire Slayer*. One day on the *Buffy* set, I was waiting inside my trailer, only a little bigger than a bathroom on an airplane. I had my vampire teeth poking out of my mouth when I noticed another brunette actress wandering the parking lot with her own vampire teeth poking out of her mouth, waiting to be called to set. Despite the fangs, I recognized her from Bar One, the nightclub we both frequented. She reminded me her name was Amanda and we had met on the dance floor a couple weeks earlier. I invited her to share my space. Amanda's dad was the singer Paul Anka. Her mother was English like my dad. She had four sisters to my five (including those from my dads' other marriages). We had both traveled a lot as kids and were both trying to be actors. That day in my tiny trailer we began a lifelong friendship.

After that I landed roles in TV series and some other smaller films, including the indie thriller *The Phony Perfector*, later known as *Dead Beat*. In the film, I played Kristen Biedermeir, and I treasured the part. Kristen was a spoiled, neglected rich kid who took up with Kit, an Elvis impersonator turned murderer in a desolate valley in New Mexico. I wore a polka-dot bikini for many scenes and bleached my hair blond. We hunkered down in Tucson, Arizona, for the shoot. The cast included Balthazar Getty, Meredith Salenger, and Sara Gilbert. The movie was loosely based on a true story. The dialogue was snappy, the director, Adam Dubov, was playful—like a grown-up kid—the costumes were fabulous. I found it easy to understand the ride-or-die love connection that Kristen and Kit shared.

I was immersing myself in the actor's lifestyle. My mother's lifestyle. I grew accustomed to the rigmarole of auditioning. Rejection was painful, and of course I questioned my talent, especially when I really wanted a role. But as rejection is more common than acceptance in the acting business, all the actors I knew, including my dad, supported me through the experience—they all knew what it felt like.

When I did win a part, I was jubilant. Each film or TV project, it was as if I had joined another patchwork. I was also getting to discover different aspects of myself by experiencing the varying emotions of a character. Playing Kristen in *Dead Beat* was a revelation in this respect. In real life I was too circumspect to live my life with the kind of wild abandon that Kristen did. She had a temper and I was only too ready to let Kit have it in the movie. Was this what my mom loved about acting? When she screamed at the actress playing her mother, Audrey Christie, in *Splendor*, was she feeling the same release? I found it hard to let go of a beloved character when a shoot was over. Did my mom have the same struggle? In her performances, she is so completely immersed in her characters. If I missed Kristen after *Dead Beat* wrapped, did that mean my mom missed Deanie Loomis or Gypsy Rose Lee? I couldn't ask her. The more energy I spent following a trail of gingerbread crumbs to my mother, the more acutely I felt her loss.

As much as I was looking for her, I did not watch my mother's films during this time. I knew that if I studied her performances too closely I wouldn't be able to find my own identity as an actor. When people brought her up, I shrank. I did my best to make sure most people did not know I had famous parents. I wanted to live or die by my own strengths and weaknesses. But it was inevitable that I would be held up to my mother's mirror. One of my teachers told me that my mom "held her emotion in her throat" and that I did the same thing. What he meant by that was she wasn't speaking from the deepest place in her body, that her voice got caught in her throat; therefore in a very emotional scene there was still a part of her that she was holding back. "My mom held her emotion in her throat?" I remember saying it back to myself over and over. I wouldn't have dared look at my mother's performances with anything but admiration and awe. She was famous for her vulnerability, the tremor in her voice, her

191

velvet brown eyes that told the audience everything we needed to know. She had been nominated for three Oscars and this teacher just picked apart her talent? I felt very confused. Were her flaws my flaws? Maybe I had only inherited her shortcomings as an actor and none of her talent? Her image loomed large, and I worked overtime trying to diminish our connection. I wanted this time to be about my teachers, my directors, about me.

My agent suggested I take weekly scene study classes with Larry Moss, the great actor, director, and acting coach. Amanda was going to be taking the class as well so we decided to work on a scene together. We chose *In the Boom Boom Room* by David Rabe, about two go-go dancers. I played Chrissy, a young, inexperienced dancer with a past history of abuse and dreams of making it big on the stage in Philadelphia. Amanda played Susan, the more mature of the two dancers.

I borrowed a Playboy Bunny costume from a friend and Amanda put together her interpretation of a stripper's outfit. Larry sat in his director's chair in a corner of the theater, watching us intently. He was tall and gangly, a real string bean, with glasses and a baseball hat. I was in awe of him and desperately wanted his approval.

The scene went from bad to worse—neither of us was up to the task.

Larry was kind but he made it clear there was a lot to learn. He gently told me the unvarnished truth about myself: that I was a little girl who needed to grow up.

"You need to work on strengthening your voice and breathing from your diaphragm," he advised.

Even at the age of twenty, my voice sounded like a child's voice. It had no power or resonance and it could sound nasal and whiny. After that assessment, I didn't go back to Larry's classes for a very long time.

While I focused on my acting, my sister was on a very different trajectory. Two years after I moved into the condo on Doheny Drive, Courtney bought a place in the same building. We fell easily back into the pattern of living close together. We each had our own space, but we knew the other was just a floor away. Courtney's love affair with drinking and partying was intensifying. Often, she couldn't remember what had happened the night before. Katie and I were constantly getting reports from Courtney's friends, telling us about her wild nights.

"You guys better do something about Courtney," they said. "We're worried about her. She needs to go to rehab or she will wind up dead."

Sometimes I would organize for Courtney to stay with me. We would talk about our mom, the pain we were both struggling with, our dreams for our future. I would remind Courtney of her strength, her courage, her talent as an artist, her beauty. Though Courtney had seen a therapist after our mother died, this relationship did not yield the same kind of emotional stability that I had gotten from Mrs. Malin. The family conferred. Doctors and specialists were contacted. What could we do to help her? Could we find Courtney another therapist, insist that she go to rehab, take her to Wales to live with Daddy Gregson and Julia for a time? Courtney would listen to us, aware that she had a problem, in agreement that she needed help. And then before we knew it, she'd be out on the town, drinking and partying with no plans to stop or slow down.

Worry and fear for Courtney's life soon dominated my days. My family and I took turns staying with her, watching out for her, praying for her. I knew that losing her would be more than my family could bear. My mother had died from an alcohol-related accident. I couldn't save my mom, but I was determined to save my sister. I clocked her moves, I called her and her friends incessantly, I stayed up at night wondering where she might be and what time she would be home.

Finally, Courtney hit rock bottom and, a couple of days later, checked herself into the Sierra Tucson treatment facility in Arizona.

My sister had been at the rehab center for a month when my dad, Jill, Kilky, Katie, and I arrived for family week.

The facility was a low adobe building in the middle of the stark Arizona desert, surrounded by cactus and tumbleweeds. We rose early, separating into different groups. For the rest of the day we worked with specialists alongside other families that had been through loss and addiction. At the hospital, they called Courtney the "identified patient," meaning she was the one our family was always focused on. We were told that we were enabling Courtney by trying to ameliorate her problems. They suggested that Courtney was using her addiction as a way to stay young, to continue to be a child because she felt that she had not gotten enough of a childhood.

My sister had once said to me, "You miss Mommie. I miss having a mom." Courtney had scarcely had a chance to get to know her own mother before losing her. Because I was three and a half years older, I had had more time with our mother before she died. I felt guilty about this: guilty that I knew our mom better than Courtney did; guilty that I had a stable second family in Wales that I spent summers with, and she did not. Courtney was often left with Kilky while I was in Wales, Katie traveled the world, and my dad lived his life with Jill. She did not have a therapist who was as wise and brilliant as Mrs. Malin. Thank goodness for Kilky, who mothered Courtney consistently, with every bit of her love and devotion.

We each had our time in a chair speaking our truth to Courtney. I told Courtney that she was the closest person to me next to my mother. I told her I loved her as my little sister but also as my best friend. I told her how much I needed her. I apologized for my judgment of her, the times when we fought and I was furious at her. I admitted I was afraid of losing her. Maybe if I pushed her away first, the pain of losing her wouldn't be so great.

On that trip to Arizona, Courtney and I talked openly about what happened after our mother died. Because our dad was traveling and working so much, we had felt left behind, longing for him and his attention. He always told us how much he loved us, how much we meant to him, and yet he was not able to *be* there for us physically. He would call us and buy us presents, but he was not able to tolerate our pain, to sit still, to just stay home. Courtney and I didn't want to travel to Europe and stay in the nicest hotels or go to fancy dinners; we didn't care what beautiful gifts he gave us. We just wanted *him*, his basic, unadorned self, at home, doing normal, unremarkable things, like making dinner, playing board games, watching a movie, taking a walk.

That week, I watched my brave dad sit in a chair across from one of the therapists and talk about his relationship with his own father. The heartbreak he carried with him of not having a father who supported him in his life. How much he wished they could have had the opportunity to talk like this. My dad apologized to Courtney and me for working so much, for not knowing how to support us in our grief.

Jill also became more open with us. We learned that she simply did not know how to be a stepmom to us. She explained that our dad had asked her not to try to take our mom's place and that was why she didn't engage with us as much as we wished she would. It was not rejection. Jill acknowledged she didn't know how to be our friend.

After Arizona, Courtney did well for a while. Her sobriety went on just long enough for it to be all the more heartbreaking when she relapsed. A small thing, and before we knew it, she was drinking too much again and we had to face the hard truth that this wasn't over yet. My mother's loss was like an earthquake, continuing to send ripples of shock through our lives, leaving cracks beneath our feet where there should have been solid ground.

# Chapter 14

Natasha on location with Jesse Peretz (far left)
and author Ian McEwan in Houma, Louisiana,
for *First Love, Last Rites*, 1997.

Courtney's breakdowns were dramatic. Obvious. On the outside I was the "good" daughter, capable, working, getting on with my life. But that was only the facade. My breakdowns were more secretive. Reserved for my boyfriends, my closest friends, or Mrs. Malin. I allowed Courtney to be the messy one so I could be the tidy one. I did not want people to worry about me, to pity me, to feel sorry for me—but I was living a total lie. My anxiety would sit itself in my stomach, knotting up my insides. "How do you stay so skinny?" my friends would ask me. "You eat like a horse." And I did. I ate anything I wanted. I think my adrenaline was running overtime ever since my mother died.

When I was alone with my journals I could describe my struggles, my fears, my insecurities about not having any talent, not being as beautiful as my mom. Then there was my fear of separation, which had been with me since the earliest days of my childhood. Sometimes I could barely catch my breath when Josh left for a weekend, so terrified was I to be apart from him. I learned to go home to my apartment on Doheny to cry into my pillow exactly the way I did as a child when my mom died, take a bath, and call a friend or one of my sisters, and then I would be okay. It was just the initial trauma of separating that was so painful. I hated to be alone, and airports left my palms sweaty, my heart beating like a hummingbird's. Even if I could talk myself through it, saying, *Josh is not my mom, he is not going to abandon me*, I could not stop the physical sensations that overtook me.

Josh was opinionated. Instead of arguing with him or standing my ground when he implored me to adopt his vegetarian lifestyle, I assured him that I had stopped eating meat—around him, that was. When he wasn't there, I devoured a cheeseburger with the best of them. We fell into the roles of teacher (Josh) and willing student (me), and I quickly grew dependent on his nurturing and his advice. The more intertwined Josh and I became, the more terrified and out of control I would feel. Sometimes I acted out with other guys, blatantly flirting with them in front of Josh or mutual friends who would tell him. It was as if I was testing him, pushing the boundaries to see how far his love for me would stretch. When he would confront me, I'd become enraged, petty, and jealous. I would scream and cry and fall apart. During these emotional outbursts, Josh would always tell me, "You need to call Miss Malin." It became an inside joke with Jessica and me, the fact that he called her "Miss." But Josh didn't seem to care if he got her name right. He was emotionally mature enough to know that I needed to process these unwieldy feelings with a professional, not a twentysomething.

One night I stayed out late. When I came home to Josh's apartment at 3 a.m. he had accidentally locked me out. I was outraged, humiliated. When he finally came sleepy-eyed to the door, I let him have it. A punch would have been cleaner. Instead I raged at him from the darkest places inside of me. He sat there, he listened, he jumped up and ducked when I threw things. It was too late for me to call "Miss Malin," so he didn't mention it. A couple of hours later I was beset with shame and sadness. How could I have treated the one I loved so deeply, so terribly? I cried, I apologized, I curled into a ball. Josh was that rare person who was able to withstand my craziness. He was a few months younger than me and yet he had an emotional fortitude that I lacked. He was patient and strong and kind. But I knew something had to change.

After that, Mrs. Malin and I doubled down on our therapy sessions. She'd sit there in her brown leather chair, a long necklace of pearls or a gold chain around her neck, her gaze focused on me. Together, we began to see a pattern. I had gone from dating Ricky to Paul to Josh, instantly fusing myself with these boys in the same way I fused with my mom. Courtney found drugs to ease her suffering; I found relationships. Neither ultimately could take our pain away. I wanted to be with my boyfriends all the time. When we were together, I could be my stable, fun-loving self. When it was time to separate for a day, a weekend, or longer, I disintegrated into a puddle of need. Sometimes my neediness was like a little girl's; other times I became angry, lashing out at the men in my life.

I could not make sense of my thunderbolt emotions. Where were they coming from? Especially my rage. I had had such a happy childhood. I had been adored by all three of my parents, coddled, nurtured, protected. But in therapy, Mrs. Malin helped me uncover the parts of my childhood before my mom died that were not as perfect as I remembered them to be. It was a slow and delicate process. In the beginning, I did not want to believe that my beautiful, loving parents were anything but perfect. Just like they looked in pictures. They radiated warmth and safety.

Mrs. Malin encouraged me to accept that sometimes my mother wanted to be away from me and that was okay. When I was very young, after my mom and Daddy Wagner reconnected, she would leave me for a handful of days with Baba to be just with him. Later, she was constantly out for dinners and events with my dad or traveling for work. Mrs. Malin explained that the comings and goings were on her terms, not mine, and this was why when a boyfriend left me for a trip or even for an evening, I collapsed into rage and grief.

I grew to realize that one of the reasons I had such a hard time being alone—why I would be so sad when a weekend at Daddy Gregson's or a long holiday ended—was because when I was a child my parents had surrounded themselves with so many friends. There were always people at our house visiting, staying with us, having drinks or dinner. The message to me was that being alone was wrong—it was lonely.

We also talked about my parents' drinking. As a child I would clock my parents' voices when they were drinking, often waking up in the middle of the night to make sure they were safely asleep in their beds. No cigarettes smoldering in their ashtrays, no candles still lit. Was the front door locked? I carried this vigilance into my relationships.

I needed to accept the fact that my parents were not perfect. That my mother had her own bouts of sadness and anxiety. That she drank too much sometimes. This was devastating for me. To me, she was flawless and all-powerful. I was scared to view her as weak in any way. Mrs. Malin helped me to see that it was going to be impossible for me to flourish in my life without accepting some of these darker, messier truths about my mother.

Slowly, I began to accept that my parents were fallible human beings, children whose own hearts had broken at various times in their lives. I forgave my dad for his physical and emotional absence after my mom died. I began to forgive my mom for abandoning me. She did not mean to die. She drank too much; she argued with her husband, whom she adored; she felt overwhelmed. I believe she was at an artistic crossroads in her life. I know with my whole heart that had she not slipped, hit her head, and fallen into the water, she would have retied that annoying dinghy to the other side of the boat and gone back to sleep. She would have woken up the next morning and had coffee with my dad and Christopher Walken. She would have pulled herself together and come home to her children and her life. If my parents were struggling in their marriage, they would have reached out for help. My mother was a self-preservationist. She was a fighter, stronger than them all, as my godfather Mart always tells me. She would have figured it out, and my parents would have figured it out. It was a terrible, terrible accident and the only thing to blame was too much alcohol that night. My parents were not perfect like I thought they were and that was okay.

At some point, Mrs. Malin suggested I meet with a psychopharmacologist. She felt that the trauma I had experienced with my mother's death and my subsequent emotional highs and lows could be ameliorated with medication. I was prescribed 20 milligrams of a relatively new drug called Prozac, also known as fluoxetine. About a week later, I felt so much more secure in myself. I did not wake up with anxiety every morning, my heart pounding, my stomach somersaulting. I felt like the layer of skin that had been removed when my mother died was growing back—not as strong and elastic as it had once been, but at least it was there.

While I continued with my therapy sessions, my work life took a positive turn. In 1996, I got a part in David Lynch's movie *Lost Highway*. I played Sheila, the sweet girlfriend of the lead character played by Balthazar Getty. The film set my career on a new trajectory. It was my first time working with a real auteur. I knew I wasn't a great actress yet, but when you have an artist like David Lynch in your corner, it instills you with the confidence that you can do anything, even if you don't really believe that.

Soon after *Lost Highway*, I got my first leading role in the film *First Love, Last Rites*, Jesse Peretz's adaptation of the short story by Ian McEwan. I loved my character, Sissel, a complex individual who would erupt in flashes of anger. I related to the aloof and frustrating way that she showed her feelings for her boyfriend, Joey. Sissel was young and experimenting with her looks, her sexuality, her power over people. I knew her. Under Jesse's direction, I let the hair under my arms and on my legs grow out, wore long vintage dresses and shoes made for boys. Jesse got me as Sissel, and he also got me as Natasha. We became close friends. Through Sissel, I began to understand a certain part of myself—the part that could shut down so easily on people, the selfish, impatient side of me that wanted complete control in my relationships.

*First Love, Last Rites* was a true independent film, a labor of love with a minuscule budget, filmed on location in Houma, Louisiana. I adored every moment of it. I loved my sad, tired motel room. I loved our pink-and-blue location house on the bayou. I loved that we all rode together in one van—cast, crew, producers, and director. On the weekends, we all gathered in somebody's room and cooked a simple and inexpensive dinner like pasta with tomato sauce. Everywhere we went it was hot and sticky and buzzing with mosquitoes. I couldn't have been happier.

The 1990s were the golden era of indie films. I found myself drawn to projects that were small, irreverent, and experimental. I was not my mother, nor did I aspire to do what she had done. I had no interest in big-budget studio movies. I wanted to work a little bit under the radar. I wanted to take risks creatively and steer clear of the center of attention. If I stayed away from mainstream Hollywood, I thought, I could avoid the scary parts of the business that had made me feel anxious in my childhood: the throngs of fans, the magazine covers, the gossip. I felt safer in the world of indie films. There was room for *me* in that world.

Around the time we were shooting *First Love, Last Rites*, I purchased my first home, a 1,200-square-foot post-and-beam beach house on Malibu Road with white beadboard walls, hardwood floors, and large picture windows looking out over the ocean. My mom had made good business choices in her life, which in turn afforded me the kind of financial security that I knew most young actors did not have—I was so grateful for that. The house had been built in the 1950s and was painted Pepto-Bismol pink. The heavy salt air hung like a cozy blanket around me. I woke up to the sound of the waves in the morning. The frogs sang their ribbit ribbit in the evening. Every day, as soon as I got home, I opened my front door, took off my shoes, and headed toward the beach with my Westie, Oscar. The soft sand between my toes, the dark blue ocean unfolding before me, the rhythm of the tide lapping forward and backward—all of this comforted me, reminding me of childhood weekends in Malibu with Daddy Gregson and Julia. I decorated the house simply with white sofas and a few antiques from my childhood—my mother's music box; a faded red wrought iron bench that my dad had bought when he was married to Katie's mother, Marion; the Marcel Vertès painting of a ballerina that had once hung in our home on Canon Drive.

I was feeling grounded and confident when I auditioned for the comedy *Two Girls and a Guy* in the living room of a Santa Monica hotel suite. Robert Downey Jr. was there with the writer-director, James Toback. I had known Robert slightly through my sister Katie. A couple of years earlier, Robert had spent a funny Thanksgiving with us at Katie's condo. The oven broke and Jill put the turkey in the dishwasher on the steam cycle to finish cooking it. Frank Sinatra had just released an album with Bono, and my dad, Robert, and I all sang along to "I've Got You Under My Skin."

Robert and I clicked at the audition. I remember his wide brown eyes growing even wider after we read our scene together. I overheard him on the phone with his wife at the time, Debbie, saying, "Katie's little sister Natasha just read for the movie and she is fucking awesome in the role!" I pretended I didn't hear what he said. I had originally read for Carla, eventually played by Heather Graham. My agent called me a couple of days later to offer the role of Lou instead. Heather and I would play Robert's two girlfriends, each believing she is in an exclusive relationship with him until we encounter each other outside his building. I was fine with playing Carla or Lou. I just wanted to be in a movie with Robert Downey Jr., who had recently gotten sober after an arrest and mandatory drug testing. He was focused and present during the shoot in New York, seemingly in a positive state of mind. We didn't socialize much after work, but when we walked together in the morning from our hotel in SoHo to our location loft in Tribeca, he was funny and alive and sharp as a knife.

Before the shoot, Josh's dad, Bob Evans, told me, "My darling Natasha, Jimmy Toback is a good friend of mine. I called to tell him that you are like family to me, and if he lays a fucking hand on you I will kill him." I assumed Bob was just being overly protective, maybe because Josh had asked him to. Now it's common knowledge that many women have accused Toback of predatory behavior toward them, but thankfully he never stepped out of line with me.

I was nervous and excited when Fox Searchlight flew me to the Toronto International Film Festival for a press tour. *Two Girls and a Guy* and *First Love, Last Rites* were both screening at the festival. I was in a bit of a fog, uncertain of my new place. Though receiving attention for two buzzworthy films, I was still incredibly insecure, unable to enjoy the parties, the success. I was happier acting with my fellow cast and crew on set. Now that the films were in the can and the world was watching, I felt doubtful of my talent and still heavy with worries about Courtney. I knew I should be on top of the world, but often I wanted to hide in my hotel room. One night I became engaged in an interesting conversation with a writer from *Vogue*. I kissed him sweetly on the cheek when we said goodbye. The next day I was shocked and humiliated to read his review of *Two Girls and a Guy*. He wrote that I was "simply not up to the task." I was not prepared for the screenings and the reviews, which, to me, were unpleasant punctuation marks at the end of my enjoyable filmmaking experiences.

When I watch *Two Girls and a Guy* now, I can see how I could have grounded Lou more, given her a stronger dose of gravitas. I try to forgive myself for the inadequacies of my performance because, at that time, it was the bravest work I was able to do, and I was proud of it. I consoled myself with the fact that Robert—whose talent I admired—thought I was a good actress.

Next I auditioned for a film by Larry Clark, director of the controversial *Kids*. I knew who Larry was, and I loved his photography. As soon as I read the script for *Another Day in Paradise*, I fell hard for the character of Rosie, a drug addict. I knew Rosie. I knew how lonely and needy she was. I certainly saw a bit of Courtney in her. Set in the 1970s, the film is based on Eddie Little's book about a teenage meth addict who becomes a safecracker to feed his drug habit. James Woods and Melanie Griffith were cast as an older couple showing Vincent Kartheiser and me how to live a life of crime.

From day one, James Woods (Jimmy) and Larry clashed. Larry's freewheeling style didn't gel with Jimmy's focused and organized pace, and they were constantly at odds with each other. Instead of letting it unsettle me, I used the tension between them on the set to inform my character. Rosie doesn't have parents, so I created a backstory for her. I decided she was an orphan and that she felt a connection with her boyfriend and with drugs that made up for her lost childhood. I made a mixtape of songs, Rosie's blues, that I would listen to in my car driving to set and on my Walkman in between takes. Again I was using a role in a film to understand my own story, channeling my own feelings of loss into the part.

In these years of my twenties, Baba was still a presence in my life. I would call her on the phone, make a date, and then drive over to her condo on Goshen Avenue in Brentwood. Baba had always been a difficult person, and she didn't get any easier as she got older.

"People had to endure her, not enjoy her," Daddy Wagner once explained to me. "I told your mother I would always take care of Mud, so I tried to include her as often as possible." My dad continued to support Baba, buying her condo for her outright and giving her a monthly stipend. Now that I was older, I became the one to see her most regularly. If I didn't maintain a connection to Baba, no one would.

When she called me, I could tell it was her the moment I heard her drawing breath. Rapid and caught in her throat, like a hiccup, that was how excited she was to talk, to tell me what she needed. Her sputtering and humming and searching for the word she wanted to say in English sounded like the revving of an engine that doesn't quite kick over. "Emmmmmm, ummmmm, ehhhhhh, ahhhhh, Natashinka, dis is Baba, how are you, my darrrrrlink."

Baba continued to live in a world of her own invention. As a child, that had seemed delightful to me, but now it could be exhausting. We weren't able to have conversations about real things. She loved me because I was an extension of my mother. She wasn't particularly interested in who I was becoming.

When I arrived at her apartment, she would usually be putting the finishing touches on her makeup or rearranging one of her many tabletop still lifes. In her older years, Baba created miniature tableaux that she would display on glass trays: a little gold bird, a tiny birdbath, an angel. She had a way with live creatures too. I remember once she tamed two bluebirds to land on her balcony railing by feeding them nuts and seeds. Forever the romantic, she named them Romeo and Juliet and tended to them as a child tends to her dolls. Speaking in a friendly low whisper: "Good morning, Romeo, good morning, Juliet, *krosheny, belochka*, I love you. *Lyublyu tebya.*" Then she would shuffle around her house in her long dress, her feet padding the plush, white carpet.

We usually went to the Sizzler around the corner from her apartment. She loved the salad bar. Since it was not her style to ask questions about my life, we talked about her life, her fan mail, her friend Roger, whom she was usually mad at. As always, she'd be dressed like a movie star, in a jewel-toned velvet dress with lots of costume jewelry and red lipstick, her hair freshly colored chocolate brown. If a man complimented my grandmother on her dress, her voice would raise three octaves, and she would bat her eyelashes. "Oh, sirrrrr, thank you so much, you have made my dayyyyy." Why couldn't she see that the stranger was just being polite to a fragile old lady? Why was she so easily duped by false flattery, fakery?

I tried to be patient with Baba, to hide my frustration. I got used to holding my breath and clenching my stomach muscles to stay calm around her, hoping for the time to pass quickly so I could leave. Her childlike ways, her living in the past, her need to be known as Natalie Wood's mother were in stark contrast to my need to move through the world unrecognized.

Every now and again, I searched her watery blue eyes for a glimpse of my mother. *Where is my mom inside of my grandmother? Can I find her?* No, I could not. Baba was Baba and my mom was my mom and there was no similarity that I could sense, see, or feel. They smelled different, they looked different, they spoke different.

The truth is, my grandmother was a child. She was a grown-up child. My mother had mothered her, and now in my mid-twenties, I mothered her too.

At some point it became clear that my aunt Lana, her daughter Evan, and their eight cats had moved into Baba's condo. After my mom died, Lana had continued to write to my dad asking him for money and loans. While my father felt an obligation to support Baba, he didn't see why he should support Lana too, so he told her no. As soon as I turned eighteen, Lana began writing to me as well. My father advised Courtney and me to refuse these requests. In our family's opinion, it didn't seem to matter how much money we gave Lana; it would never be enough.

After Lana moved into the condo, Baba would complain to me

that her daughter and Evie needed money, which was why she turned over her Social Security checks to them every month. They had taken over the master bedroom. Baba was now in the small second bedroom. Soon, neighbors began complaining that a putrid smell was emanating from the apartment. When Liz went to investigate, she found dirty plates piled up in the sink, trash that had not been taken out for weeks, and cats and cat feces everywhere. We moved Baba out of the condo and into a one-bedroom apartment on Barrington and Wilshire in West Los Angeles. Our attorney sent a letter to Lana telling her to vacate the condo within thirty days. It took another three months to clean and disinfect the place and make it habitable.

From then on, whenever I picked Baba up, it was from her new digs on Barrington. Immediately, I noticed something about her had changed. Her lipstick was not exactly on her lips. Her hair was only partially dyed. The roots were black, but a few inches down from the roots were bands of gray, and the ends were more auburn than usual. I caught glimpses of long white hairs dangling from her chin and above her lips. Often, her beautiful velvet dresses were stained. She was forgetful, and little things seemed to confuse and overwhelm her. She was experiencing the beginnings of dementia.

We didn't go out to lunch as much anymore; instead I ran her errands. Sometimes I would take her to visit my mother in the cemetery, and then to Ralphs, where we would stock up on her favorite food, Lunchables.

One day Liz got a call from the apartment manager saying that Baba had set her apartment on fire and had been taken to the hospital. My grandmother had become certain that nefarious people were following her every move, waiting to pounce when she wasn't looking so they could steal from her. These wild, paranoid fantasies would compel her to hide pieces of her jewelry in bizarre places, then promptly forget where she'd put them. On this particular day, she seemed to remember that she had stashed her jewels under the bed, so she lit a candle and crawled under the mattress in hopes of discovering her buried treasure. It never occurred to her that she would set her bed on fire, which is exactly what she did. Once her bed was ablaze, Baba thankfully realized she was in danger and ran out into the hallway in her nightgown, yelling, "I am Natalie Wood's mother and my apartment is on fire!" Her apartment was badly damaged, and it was clear to all of us that Baba could no longer live alone.

Baba moved in with Lana in Thousand Oaks, in the northwestern suburbs of Los Angeles. I visited her at Lana's house once or twice, and then at the hospital after she was admitted with pneumonia. Toward the end, she would offer me a faint smile of recognition, but I don't think she really knew who I was. When she died from pneumonia on January 6, 1998, her last words to me were: "You have a pretty face. You ought to be in the movies."

# Chapter 15

Jill, Natasha, and R.J.
on Natasha's wedding day, 2003.

It was June 1998 and I was in Chicago, on the set of the new Stephen Frears film *High Fidelity*, based on the novel of the same name by Nick Hornby. Even though my character, Caroline, would appear in only two scenes, this was one of my biggest, most high-profile projects to date. I was almost twenty-nine. My relationship with Josh was already two years in the past. Over time, we had become more like brother and sister than boyfriend and girlfriend and decided to separate. After our breakup, I dated here and there, but mostly I focused on my career, eventually landing this small but sought-after role in the film, which starred John Cusack as Rob, a music lover with a phobia about romantic commitment.

My first day on set in Chicago, I was filled with nervous excitement. To steady myself, I was watching a scene unfold on a monitor when a man with wavy brown hair and large dark eyes approached me.

"Hi, I'm D.V.," he said. "I'm one of the writers. . . . I am so glad you're here."

I said hi and shook his hand, then we turned our attention back to the scene. We were watching an up-and-coming actor I'd known slightly at high school when he was a grade above me. "That's Jack," D.V. said, "the Scene Thief." Jack Black had been playing supporting roles in movies for a few years, but *High Fidelity* would be his big comedy breakthrough. It was obvious that he was running away with every scene. Stephen was directing his actors in a posh English accent that reminded me of my dad: "Wonderful. Again, just faster and better." When John Cusack walked over and introduced himself, I was struck by his height (six foot two, a giant next to me at five foot two).

That night the cast, director, and writers had dinner at an old Italian restaurant. D.V. sat across from me at the table. Every time I looked up, he was staring at me with his great big eyes, eyes that seemed to be trying to tell me something. When it was time to leave, D.V. and John, who were childhood friends, got into a playful tug-of-war over who would drive me home. D.V. insisted, and so there we were, alone together for the first time in his car. He asked me if I wanted to go have a drink, but it was getting late, so we postponed for another night and he dropped me off at my hotel.

My scenes with John went smoothly. The butterflies in my stomach worked well for the character, who was excited to meet John's character. Between takes, I wandered the "record store," checking out the real albums and the carefully placed set decoration. A variety of flyers and posters covered the walls. The one that drew my attention advertised an upcoming party on July 20. "How funny," I said, thinking aloud. "July twentieth is my mom's birthday." Suddenly, there was D.V. again. "That's my birthday too," he said.

I had two days left shooting in Chicago when we went for dinner, just the two of us. That night, without warning, D.V. leaned in for a kiss. I felt dizzy, elated. I wrapped my scenes on Tuesday and spent the night at D.V.'s apartment. He dropped me at my hotel seconds before the van left to take me to the airport. He lived in Los Angeles and we promised we would see one another again soon.

On the flight home, I struck up a conversation with a nice older man in the seat next to mine. He told me that he was a retired police officer whose name was—believe it or not—Krupke. By mere chance, I was seated beside Officer Krupke, just like the character the Jets sing about in my mother's film *West Side Story*. I had just been swept off my feet by a man who was born on the same day as her, and now this. Although I had long ago stopped trying to summon her spirit by holding séances in the closet, the air seemed to be alive with connections to my mother. Was she out there somewhere, pulling some mystical strings? My mom had been famous for her big brown eyes, so much like D.V.'s. His dark, wavy hair and small frame reminded me of her. When I looked at him, I could see her in his eyes. Though our time together had been brief, somehow I could envision this man I hardly knew as my soul mate. *If D.V. and I married and had a little girl*, I thought, *she would look just like my mom.*

After I returned to LA, I was scheduled to start rehearsals for a movie about Hugh Hefner's life, in which I would play Hefner's assistant Bobbie Arnstein, who had taken her own life in 1975. Aided by a 1960s and 1970s wardrobe and hairstyle, I stepped into the skin of Bobbie, a woman who fell into a deep depression after she was arrested on drug charges and sentenced to prison. Everything ended for her in a downtown motel, where she fatally overdosed. I had to re-create her lonely death, just as my mom had created suicide scenes in *The Cracker Factory* and *Splendor in the Grass*. I also had to lie in an open casket as Bobbie's corpse for the funeral scene.

After I finished filming that day, I went to meet D.V. at a preview of the movie *The Perfect Storm*, about a fishing boat ravaged by an intense storm at sea, its crew trying valiantly to avoid drowning. In retrospect, watching two hours of people fighting for their lives in the middle of the ocean may not have been the best way to unwind after lying in a coffin all day, pretending to be dead. Although I hadn't consciously realized it, placing myself inside a casket for hours had brought up long-buried memories of the last time I saw my mother, our final goodbye at the funeral home. And then the movie *The Perfect Storm* reminded me of the last moments of her life.

As soon as D.V. and I left the theater, the lights of Hollywood Boulevard started to blur. I felt woozy. Before I knew what was happening, tears were streaming down my face. I turned to this person I barely knew and told him all about the most profoundly painful wound in my life—something I did not discuss openly with most people. D.V. comforted me, his dark eyes full of empathy. That was new for me. He didn't reach for a phone and tell me to "Call Miss Malin," nor did he try to change the subject, as so many people would have done. He held me gently in his arms and silently allowed me to feel what I was feeling, to cry it all out until it passed.

Just like that, our romance moved to a deeper level. His compassion for my pain felt like a strong foundation for our relationship. D.V. was going to heal me—I knew it. I had been through so much therapy, so many tears, so much growing, but I was still a sad little girl who longed for her mother. Maybe D.V. was the missing piece of my scattered, Scotch-taped puzzle self.

Wanting deeply to connect, I saw signs everywhere. My mom and D.V. were born under Cancer, the zodiac sign that rules motherhood. Just like my mother had done, he had a way of making all the different parts of me welcome. If I were feeling anxious or sad or shy, it was all hunky-dory in his book. "Everything's going to be okay," he would say in a soothing voice. "You're safe and I love you." I began to believe D.V. was the mirror I had lost when my mom died. He made me feel whole and beautiful. He was also someone I respected and adored. If he thought I was fine, I must be fine.

We officially became a couple. D.V. folded me into his world—and what a compelling world it was. A former DJ, he lived in the burgeoning artistic community of Los Feliz and surrounded himself with musicians, painters, writers, and creators. I became friends with most of his friends. D.V. was the Golden Boy at that time. That was truly everyone's nickname for him. He had made his own way and scored coveted writing jobs, one after the other. Between D.V. and his friends and family, and my friends and extended family, and our dogs—D.V.'s Percy and Manny and my Westie, Oscar—my life was starting to resemble the abundant days of my childhood on Canon Drive. Everywhere I turned, I saw friends, family, pets, laughter, and love.

Around the time I met and fell in love with D.V., my sister Courtney discovered opiates. The pills made her feel better, stronger, and braver. One night, she took too many pills and was rushed to the hospital. Things had just taken a much more serious turn. We staged an intervention right there at the hospital—my dad; Jill; Liz; Kilky; three of Courtney's dearest friends; her boyfriend, Renn; and me. We took turns telling Courtney how much we loved her and what her addiction had done to her and to our relationship with her. I had never been so terrified of losing her as I was that day.

Courtney listened, she paused, and then she turned to the interventionist and asked him two questions.

How long had he been doing this?

And how cold was it in Minnesota, where Hazelden, the rehab hospital he was suggesting, was located?

He answered, "Ten years and very cold."

Even though Courtney really doesn't like cold weather, she agreed to go.

I went home that afternoon and slept for twenty-four hours.

While she was away in rehab, I wrote her long, supportive letters, hoping that my words on the pages would sustain her spirit and keep her afloat.

I even wrote a letter to my mom, asking for her spirit to help Courtney. "She needs you so desperately," I wrote. "You and Court and I are sort of three parts of a triangle, and maybe that's why we can't stand up straight. You are gone. But if she goes, then all I'll be is a dot. And I don't want to be that alone and insignificant. Please help. I love you. If Courtney dies, Natasha will die."

That's what I told myself and that's what I believed. My sister was my blood connection to my mother. I could not lose her. It would take me a long time to realize that addiction was a battle Courtney had to fight for herself.


D.V.'s oldest and best friend Dan owned the record label Drag City. Because of this connection, musicians and bands often stayed at D.V.'s house when they were in LA. Sometimes, D.V. would get so wrapped up in his musician friends, in the deep conversations and the long nights, that I would feel a discomfort that was almost intolerable. Was I losing him the same way I lost my mother when she went out to parties and drank too much? "I think we should break up!" I shouted at him, but I didn't mean it. At this point in our relationship, I knew I would be unable to function without D.V. Each time I got upset, he'd sit me down and softly explain, "There is nothing for you to be upset or jealous about." His soothing voice and his large eyes had a hypnotic quality, almost like he was twirling a shiny object in front of my eyes. But practically every time we went out to a party, my jealousy would rise up to the surface again. He would kiss a friend goodbye on the lips and I would think, *Why would he kiss her on the lips? I thought they were just friends.*

Once, at a party in Malibu, D.V. disappeared. The house was large and rambling, and as I wandered the grounds looking for him, I spotted some horses and went inside the stable to pet one of them. There was D.V. and a beautiful blond actress engrossed in conversation. They seemed as surprised to see me as I was to see them. We left shortly afterward and proceeded to have an argument as we twisted through Malibu Canyon.

"What the fuck were you doing in a horse stable talking to that girl for over an hour?" I asked.

"Natasha," he said with a sigh, "where is your self-confidence? Why don't you trust me?" D.V. prided himself on his strong moral compass. He had disdain for cheaters and liars. "He's cheating on his girlfriend," he would whisper to me, pointing at one of his friends at a party and shaking his head in disapproval. Now, I shrank with shame and agreed with him. Where was my self-confidence? What's the big deal if he was holed away in a stable next to a horse, standing on hay, on a dark, cold Malibu night, talking to a beautiful girl? "Seriously, Natasha, you need to call Mrs. Malin!" I told myself.

We decided to work through our trust issues. D.V. and I started going to therapy together. We were both in individual therapy: I was still with Mrs. Malin and D.V. had a therapist I'll call Ann. Under Ann's guidance, I tried to put my feelings into perspective. I always had to vie for his attention, as his life was so busy. Neighbors and friends dropped by at a moment's notice. D.V. was infectious; people were drawn to him—like they had been to my mother.

"You're reacting to your own internal feelings," Ann told me, "and not taking responsibility for them. So you project them onto D.V. and explode with jealousy when he talks to another woman."

Ann recommended a couple's therapist named Mason Sommers. D.V. and I went to the sessions together, but before long I started individual sessions with Mason too. I liked him so much I stopped seeing Mrs. Malin, who had been so wonderful—but whose guidance I felt I had grown out of. With Mason, I worked hard on myself, to be less needy, less demanding, more self-sufficient. I began to realize that the men in my life wanted a girlfriend, a lover, a woman—not a child looking to be mothered. My relationship with D.V. improved and I was proud of how far I'd come.

On the morning of my thirty-first birthday, D.V. handed me a jewelry box that appeared to hold a necklace or a bracelet. I had been hoping for a ring, but I kept my composure. When I opened the box, there was a smaller box inside, then an even smaller box—like Russian Matryoshka dolls—until the final tiny box. I opened it to find a beautiful diamond engagement ring. I screamed and burst into happy tears. D.V. got down on one knee and asked me to marry him. I said, "Yes," over and over as we hugged and kissed each other.

I took the lead planning our wedding, with D.V. only really interested in selecting the music for the party afterward. We were going to be married at my family home on Old Oak Road, surrounded by our closest friends and relatives. Both my dads were going to give me away.

I decided on a French theme, with lush velvet sofas, ornate chandeliers, oriental rugs, everything resembling turn-of-the-century Paris. My dear friend Molly Stern-Schlussel designed my wedding dress and the bridesmaid dresses. It was her first bridal gown, a fairy creation of cream silk with Chantilly lace and delicate seed pearls woven into a fitted bodice top with a separate long skirt that could be removed. After the ceremony, I was going to take the skirt off, which would transform the gown into a minidress, appropriate for hitting the dance floor.

It was a full-on family affair. My bridesmaids were Katie, Courtney, my youngest sister Poppy (Daddy Gregson and Julia's daughter), and my friends Amanda, Jessica, and Nevena (another close friend who is originally from Bulgaria). My nephew Jake (the son of my sister Sarah—Daddy Gregson's daughter from his first marriage) was the ring bearer and my niece Emma (the daughter of my sister Charlotte—Daddy Gregson's other daughter from his first marriage) was my flower girl.

Courtney was in an especially dark place in the time leading up to the wedding. She missed all the fittings for the bridesmaid dresses until the very last one, which she basically slept through. I called her and reminded her, admonishing her for not taking my wedding seriously.

A few days before the ceremony, Daddy Wagner took me to lunch. After we finished our food, he grew serious and thoughtful.

"You're about to get married," he said, "and I want you to focus on your life with D.V. You must stop allowing Courtney to take up so much of your energy. You can't control her, you can't save her—but you can save yourself."

Like a steward giving emergency instructions on a plane to attach your own air mask first before helping your child attach theirs, my dad was suggesting I prioritize my own life first and help Courtney second. I realized that we shared a strong streak of self-preservation, a special kind of resilience that keeps us going in the hardest of times. The best thing I could do for Courtney was to stay centered and build a life for myself.

The morning of the wedding, I got dressed in my gown, placing a beautiful vintage Buccellati bracelet that had belonged to my mother on my wrist. I had borrowed earrings from Amanda and had a white handkerchief embroidered with my initials in blue. Everything was covered: something old, new, borrowed, and blue.

Right before I walked down the aisle, I looked out onto the backyard, where the ceremony was being held. There were flowers and candles everywhere. We had placed wooden church pews under the giant sycamore tree of my youth, its low branches now glittering with glass chandeliers. My entire patchwork quilt of a family was waiting for my entrance. My dads' wives, Jill and Julia; my sisters; all my English siblings and their spouses and children; Katie's mom, Marion Donen, and brothers, Josh and Peter Donen; Kilky and her family; plus the whole crew from my parents' inner circle—Mart Crowley, Tom Mankiewicz, Delphine Mann—and even Helen, who had cooked for us back in the day. Ali MacGraw was there, smiling her beautiful smile, and John Cusack was D.V.'s best man.

My two dads were on either side of me, about to give me away.

They seemed subdued, clearly taking the moment very seriously. Before I started walking, I took a wobbly breath and turned to the left, where my wedding cake was waiting for the party later. The stand of the cake was decorated with a piece of the fabric from my mother's lavender checkered wedding dress from 1972. I had a piece of that fabric in my veil too. Even though she wasn't there that day, I felt her everywhere.

The singer-songwriter Will Oldham, who also goes by the name Bonnie "Prince" Billy, sang me down the aisle with Judee Sill's "The Kiss."

At the party, Daddy Wagner, looking handsome as ever, held court behind the bar, mixing drinks and regaling an audience of young actors with his tales of Hollywood in the 1950s, '60s, and '70s. I discovered what an incredible dancer Daddy Gregson was when he cut into my first dance with D.V. Daddy Wagner cut in next, then both my dads danced together, arm in arm, to Frank Sinatra. We danced and drank and partied until 2 a.m., when the neighbors called the cops.

Courtney showed up at the wedding looking beautiful and clear-eyed and seemed sober. I was filled with hope, momentarily. As soon as the vodka cocktails hit her system, however, she became a different person. On the dance floor after the ceremony, she pulled a large, heart-shaped, gold-and-pink-sapphire cocktail ring she'd designed from her finger and thrust it into my hand. "Here, Natasha. I never got you a wedding gift, so take this." At one point I saw her saunter past D.V. and grab his face seductively as if she were about to kiss him. He gently pushed her away.

Courtney's behavior that night reminded me of when she was a little girl pulling my hair and destroying my Barbie dolls. Maybe she felt it was her only recourse, to play that role. Or maybe it was her way of coping with her demons. Whatever it was, I had never felt further from her than I did on my wedding night.

After our honeymoon in Southeast Asia, D.V. and I settled back into our life together at D.V.'s house on Mulholland Drive and Woodrow Wilson, at the edge of the winding Hollywood foothills. Ours was the party house and we were the hosts, a trait I inherited from my parents, and one that came naturally to D.V. too. We hosted Thanksgiving and Christmas, midnight summer soirees, casual dinners, pool parties. Our friends were our family, and all our friends were welcome when we were in town. I had the acting career I had strived for. I was married to my dream man. Now we began talking about starting a family. For me, having a baby would complete the picture. I was ready to take the next step in my life: motherhood.

# Chapter 16

Seal tracks, Malibu, 2009.

It was June 2007, almost four years after our wedding, and I was in Vancouver, working on the supernatural TV drama *The 4400*. D.V. and I had now been together for eight years. I longed for a baby but had yet to become pregnant. On the surface, everything appeared fairly normal. It was the detective in me that sensed otherwise, the child of parents who drank too much, whose powers of perception had been honed to a razor-sharp edge. I was a master at reading the unfamiliar pauses, the off-kilter inflections, of those I loved. My senses zeroed in on the tiniest quiver.

All week, I had a daunting feeling I couldn't shake. Something in the tone of D.V.'s voice seemed off when we talked on the phone. He didn't call as regularly, didn't ask how my work was going. I told myself he was intently focused on the writing workshop he was teaching at Sundance. Also, I was in the middle of a job. When you're acting in a TV series, you have to give it your entire focus. I was playing the sister of the lead, an integral part. I loved the role and I loved the show; the challenge was being away from home, working long-distance, as they say. I told myself I'd deal with whatever was troubling D.V. when I got back to LA.

I had been reading Ian McEwan's *On Chesil Beach*, a novel about a newly married couple in 1962 discovering their differences despite their deep love for one another. When I finished, I inscribed it to D.V. with a passage from the book: "All she had needed was the certainty of his love, and his reassurance that there was no hurry when a lifetime lay ahead of them. Love and patience—if only he had had them both at once—would surely have seen them both through." Whatever problems we had were not insurmountable. If D.V. could just be patient, I knew we could work everything out. That was our plan, the reason we were spending so much time and money in couple's therapy.

After I returned from Vancouver and D.V. got back from his week in Sundance, we were going to meet up at our therapist Mason's office. Our paths hadn't crossed in two weeks, but this was a mark of pride for me. *That means we have an unbreakable bond*, I told myself. *We can withstand the separations and the storms.*

That morning it's hot out, only the beginning of summer but already in the eighties. I'm a few minutes late as I climb the stairs to Mason's office. D.V. rings my cell phone and asks impatiently, "Where are you?" I tell him I'm right outside the door. Before I can sit down, Mason, dressed in an orange T-shirt and jeans, appears at the waiting room door. This is the fastest he has ever opened the door, and I sense danger in the air. "Casual Friday?" I ask, noticing the T-shirt. We sit down in our usual spots—me on the brown leather club chair, D.V. on the green chenille sofa.

"D.V. called me last night," Mason says, cutting right to the point. "He has become aware of some feelings that he needs to share with you, Natasha."

I freeze. My heart pounds. I search Mason's face for something, any clue that might make me feel less terrified. He has never opened a session like this before. I set my coffee cup on the table beside me. I think I know what's coming and I do not want to go there.

After a moment, I turn and look at D.V., who cannot meet my gaze.

"I, uh . . ." D.V. manages to say. "I don't think I"—a pause, a deep breath—"can be . . . married anymore."

His stifled emotions escape in a sort of grunt followed by strange, uncontrolled weeping. I begin quietly, asking perfunctory questions. Is he sure, does he no longer love me? "So, you're talking about a separation, right?" I say.

D.V. shakes his head slowly before he answers, finally looking up at me. "I just don't know what a separation would do. I think I am talking about a divorce. Yes, a divorce. I want a divorce."

"A divorce," I say. I sound like an echo. But I need to say these two words, speak them out loud, feel them form on my tongue. A divorce. These are the scariest words I can imagine. And my husband of almost four years just spoke them, at 10 a.m. on a Friday morning in June. *My life will never be the same again.*

I am calm, very calm. So calm that I am momentarily unsure whether I heard him correctly. *Is this a dream?* No. This is really happening—right here, right now. *This is my life.* I am sitting across from my husband, this man I love, whom I need—my one and only for the past eight years—listening to him tell me that he wants to break up and, furthermore, that he is unhappy and has been for a long time.

"You're not happy either," he tells me.

I realize D.V. is crying and I am not. This is a role reversal. For years, I was ashamed of how often I cried in front of D.V. But Mrs. Malin felt differently. "Your tears will save your life," she told me. D.V., meanwhile, never cries. Once, after we had a particularly emotional fight, he told me, "I wish I could cry like you, Natasha."

Now my husband is crying. I want the tears to roll backward, back into his eyes. I want him to somehow take back everything he has just said in the last twenty minutes, the last two weeks, maybe the last two years. Can we please rewind the tape?

I slump down, rest my head on the cool leather arm of the chair, trying to listen. Mason is talking. D.V. is talking. I am not talking. I have no words. There is nothing to say because D.V. has said everything. All I can do is take direction from the other people in the room, who seem to have a plan.

Suddenly, I know what I need. I turn to D.V.

"Can I have Manny?"

Manny is our eight-year-old, hundred-pound black lab. I need his size, his bark, his deep brown eyes, his floppy ears. He had started out as D.V.'s dog, but as the years passed, he became my compadre, my protector.

D.V. seems surprised by my request, but all he can say in his kindliest voice is, "Of course. Of course you can have Manny. Of course," he repeats, almost to himself.

"Thank you," I reply.

Mason asks me if I need anything else, and I say, "Yes, I need Amanda. D.V., can you please call and let her know what's happening? Can you ask her to meet me at our house?" My head is so light it no longer feels attached to my body. D.V. steps outside to make the call. The moment I hear the door click closed, the familiar tears come, streaming silently down my face, staining my cheeks. D.V. returns and tells me that Amanda will meet me at our house. I schedule another appointment with Mason for the next day, and basically every day after that for the rest of the long, hot summer. A daily pilgrimage of sorts. I glance at my untouched coffee sitting on the table next to me and decide to leave it. Mason can throw it away. I leave my car in the parking lot in Beverly Hills. I can get it later or never.

D.V. drives us home from Mason's office. I curl into a ball in the passenger seat and look out the window at the landscape of my life, all of it suddenly redefined. Alien and terrifying territory that only this morning looked safe and familiar. Quietly, as a child would, I ask him questions.

"How are we going to figure this out? Why did you keep telling me you wanted to stay married if you didn't? Why did you say you were 'getting your head around' having a baby?" My questions are not angry or accusatory. They are my brain's attempts at processing the conflicting information it has received. My husband answers my questions, one by one. But I am still so very far from understanding what has just happened.

The next day I made a plan. I told D.V. that I wanted to stay in our Mulholland house for the summer. He needed to go to London for work anyway and when he returned he could rent a place. I needed a couple of months to figure out my next steps. D.V. complied, leaving me alone in the house with Manny.

Katie and her fiancé, Leif, visited me. My marriage had imploded days before their wedding at Old Oak Road. I was supposed to be a bridesmaid, D.V. a groomsman. Despite my love for Katie and Leif, I couldn't go. I could not stand under the great big sycamore tree, the one D.V. and I stood beneath only three and a half years earlier. The day was meant for their joy, not my sorrow.

After I had been living in this brave new world for a couple of weeks, Amanda and my other close friend Maya came over. They entered through my unlocked front door and perched on my bed in a shaft of afternoon sunlight. My friends did this most days, checking up on me, making sure I was okay, but even so, this particular day felt different. Amanda's chin was quivering, Maya's face a stone wall.

"What's wrong?" I asked.

"Lady, we have to tell you something, and it's not going to be easy," Amanda said through tears. They proceeded to tell me that D.V. had been cheating on me for a long time, with a lot of different people.

I absorbed the facts from Amanda and Maya, slowly, dumbly, and numbly. I didn't want to believe what they were telling me, and yet I knew what they were saying was true. On some remote, unconscious level it all made sense. Frequently during our marriage, I felt jealous or suspicious—as if some internal alarm was alerting me to danger—but when I brought these insecurities up, everyone said the same thing. D.V. was a writer, a watcher. He was funny and charming and smart. He was also devoted to me. Now I was learning otherwise.

It was the middle of the night in England, and D.V. answered the phone with a sleepy "Hello." The soothing sound of my husband's voice was a momentary comfort. I had not heard his voice in three weeks.

"D.V., it's Natasha," I said formally. "I know everything. I know about the cheating, the lying. I know about Chloe." Chloe was a younger girl whose name kept coming up. She knew he was married but sweetly referred to him as her boyfriend. They would meet for rendezvous when D.V. would spend a couple of days downtown writing at the Hotel Figueroa, telling me he was "working." All of Chloe's friends knew about "her boyfriend and his wife."

D.V. paused, took a long breath, and said nothing. I had actually hoped he would deny it, fabricate some amazing excuse, that it would be a bad dream, a terrible rumor that D.V. would fix for me. But that was not what happened next. What happened was a stream of accusations pouring forth from my mouth; raging, screaming, demanding answers: "Why did you do this? Who are you? How could you? How could you? *How could you?*"

By the time I hung up the phone, the fury inside me had been expressed. But I had not even begun to feel it all. The full force of it took weeks to sink in, and months to process.

As soon as my brain stopped spinning, I began to revisit our eight years together. The time we went to that wedding where he stayed out all night, even after I went home. The trip to Spain where D.V. eyed every pretty girl we passed in the street. The birthday party I threw for D.V. when I walked into his office, filled with people talking, smoking, listening to music, having a good time, to find D.V. seated at his desk with a pretty brunette on his lap. *Is my mind playing tricks on me? What the hell is this?* I watched D.V. spot me and shift nervously in his chair as I walked over.

"Hi, I'm Natasha," I said, the soul of composure. "I live here and you are sitting on my husband's lap."

The pretty brunette stood up, shock and embarrassment spreading across her face.

"I'm so sorry, uh, I didn't know he was married," she mumbled, and off into the night she vanished.

Later, D.V. took great pains to let me know that "she had no idea I was married!"

"Yes," I said, "but you *do* know that you're married, so why was another woman sitting on your lap?"

"Babe, it was late, we were all drunk. It's no big deal. Chill the fuck out."

*Oh right. It's me again, needing to chill the fuck out. Okay, let me keep working on that.*

Faced with cold, hard facts, I was forced to admit to myself that the whole fantasy of my life with D.V. had been just that, a lovely illusion. The fact that D.V. bore a slight physical resemblance to my mother and shared her birthday confirmed my belief that she sent him to me, that he was my destiny.

The truth was that I had chosen him all by myself. There was never going to be any baby from D.V., no daughter who looked just like my mom. I had painted a magical picture and convinced myself it was reality. When my husband was revealed to be a cheater and a liar, my rage at him branched out to include my mother too. I was angry at them both.

I would wake up in the middle of the night in tears. *The heartbreak of humility.* After the words occurred to me, the phrase wound itself around my brain, circling my head like a familiar song. I had nightmares that I was drowning in an ink-black sea filled with debris. I woke up most mornings with the shadows of my bad dreams lingering in my bedroom.

I was appalled at myself for feeling so awkward and ill-equipped to be on my own. It would have been easy to claim that this insecurity stemmed from my mother's death, but I knew it started way before that. My grandmother never left my mother alone, not even for a second. My mom grew to be a woman who simultaneously resented her mother's overprotection and craved constant company. Whenever she was not in the room with another person, she was on the phone with a friend or family member. I believe she made strides, but I'm not certain my mom ever really overcame her loneliness and dependence on other people to make her feel safe. Naturally, she passed this fear on to me. I was a sensitive child, deeply in tune with my mom. When she was ripped away from me, this terror of being alone was magnified. The gaping hole of her absence made me cling more vehemently to my dads, my friends, my sisters, my boyfriend—those I loved. Reaching, always reaching for other people. My mother had taught me that I needed her for everything. Despite all the work I had done to try to move forward, I still didn't know how to exist on my own.

In the weeks and months after my marriage collapsed, the two people who were there for me most—besides my incredible girlfriends—were Courtney and my dad. Courtney and I had been virtually estranged in the period leading up to my breakup. A new boyfriend had introduced her to heroin and she was gone.

But after D.V. left me, I needed my sister. I called Courtney and she came immediately. She slept next to me in my bed each night and brought me bubbly water in the morning when I awoke, sick to my stomach.

Then there was my dad. Around the same time I was filing for divorce, my father decided to sell the house at Old Oak Road. His daughters had moved on with their lives, and he and Jill were spending more and more time at their house in Aspen, Colorado. The only person living full-time at Old Oak Road was Kilky, and that was a big place for just one person. So my dad said farewell to the house that had been our family home for more than twenty-five years. He bought a condo in Westwood, and while it was being remodeled, Kilky stayed with Courtney, Jill went back to Aspen, and my dad moved in with me at my beach house in Malibu. He was still working as an actor, so he needed to be in LA.

It was funny living with my dad again. In the mornings, I made coffee for us before taking Manny for a walk along the wet sand. My dad hung out on the deck that overlooked the beach, waving and chatting to everyone who passed. At first I was irritated by his overly friendly ways. I was trying to keep a low profile through my divorce, trying to pretend I was invisible. The failure of my marriage was shameful and sad, and I didn't want to make it public. But the natural openness of my dad's personality drew me out of my seclusion and back into the community. We ate dinner together at the local Mexican restaurant or Italian place. Katie; her husband, Leif; and my newborn nephew, Riley, came over on Sundays and we ordered pizza and watched TV. If I stayed out late, my dad wrote me little notes and left them on the kitchen table: "I hope you had a good night. I love you." Mostly he sat with me, he listened.

At the house in Malibu in the months after my divorce, he didn't shut down or dismiss my feelings. He didn't walk away. There were times that I could still see his internal wheels turning: *What can I do to make things easier for her; how can I help her?* I could almost see the ideas forming in his mind like delicate fizzy bubbles, and then popping one by one as his thoughts returned to the here and now. He knew that there was nothing he could really do to ease my pain except to be present for me. The only way out is through.

My dad stayed about three months, until his condo was finished, then he moved out. I was sad to see him go. I stayed close to the ocean, walked along the shore with my dog, the rhythmic pounding of the surf in my ears. It was only later that I learned my mom had done this too. In the painful period following her divorce from R.J. in her early twenties, she had rented a house on the beach in Malibu, where she lived alone for the first time in her life. I was unconsciously following in my mother's footsteps.

I wanted a boyfriend, to lose myself in a new person. I had crushes and flings. I flirted and dated. But despite my efforts, I kept ending up alone. I told myself I wanted another long-term relationship, but most of the men I picked were far, far from being able to give me that. As Mason put it, "Why are you going to the hardware store to buy milk?"

On the weekends, friends would visit, and a couple of days a week, I would drive into town for various reasons, but for the most part, I was startlingly alone on the coast, at the edge of the world. Isolated, with plenty of time to sit with my ugliest fears and get to know them intimately—to offer them tea and cake, and become comfortable with them. At this time there was a writers' strike in Hollywood, so not much was happening in the way of work and auditions. Thanks to my mom's good business choices, I had the privilege of knowing that my bills would be paid. I directed my energies into acting workshops, reading, walking my dog, and soaking in hot baths.

It was a bright, blue-skied morning as I walked down the rickety wooden steps to go to the beach and saw something stirring under the house. A rather large, silvery-gray seal hissed at me as I passed. I had lived in Malibu long enough to know what to do when any marine wildlife—dead or alive—washed up on the beach. I called the Marine Mammal Stranding Network, and they arrived within the hour. "It's a baby elephant seal," they told me, "and it's molting." I was instructed not to touch or feed the seal. Signs on wooden stakes were placed in the sand around the animal, informing the public to stay at least one hundred feet away by law.

Each day I descended the old beach steps, I'd nod hello to the seal, shedding its skin, under my house. Each night as I lay in bed, I wondered if he would be there the next day. He stayed for quite a while. My constant companion under the house.

Finally, early one morning as I walked down the steps, I saw, in place of the elephant seal, a set of funny flipper tracks. The tide hadn't come up yet, so I could see the pattern he made in the sand as he wriggled all the way out to the sea, back to his rightful home.

It was time to move on.

PART 3

# Within

# Chapter 17

Natasha and Barry in Ojai, California, 2010.

The following January 2009, I found myself on a flight to New York City. My agent had called the day before to ask if I would be interested in auditioning for a play called *New Year's Eve*. The only thing was I had to be available to leave right away for NYC. I immediately said yes. I had no other obligations, so I threw some things in a bag and got on a plane. This would be my first time auditioning for a live theater production, and although I knew that getting the part was a long shot, I felt it was worth a try. My mother had been scheduled to appear in the play *Anastasia* right before she died. She had been so worried that her voice wasn't strong enough for live theater—that she wouldn't be able to project to the back of the house. But she had decided to face her fear and accept the challenge. Now I was being given that same chance.

The part I was going up for was a woman named Samantha, a soap opera star who has a close but complicated relationship with her mother, Isabel, also a famous actress, to be played by Marlo Thomas. To say that the story resonated with me would be an understatement. The play had another connection to my mother: it was by Arthur Laurents, who had written the books for the stage versions of *West Side Story* and *Gypsy*.

"You know," my godfather Mart had reminded me before I left for my audition, "Arthur did *not* want your mother to play Maria in *West Side Story* or Gypsy Rose Lee in *Gypsy*." From all accounts, it seemed that Arthur Laurents was one of the few humans in the whole wide world who did not adore my mother. Would he be unkind to me? I was curious.

As I ran my lines on the plane heading east, I realized that despite the short turnaround, I felt quietly confident. For the past couple of years, I'd been studying again with Larry Moss. After I first returned to his classes, Larry hadn't seen me in fifteen years, not since I was an unsure twenty-two-year-old with a childlike voice that didn't project beyond the front row. What would he make of me now? Right away, Larry chose a scene for me from Harold Pinter's *A Night Out*, in which I had to play a Cockney prostitute. *Whoa!* I thought. *I have to do a Cockney accent! How am I going to sound convincing?* To my surprise, the scene went pretty well.

"Natasha!" Larry boomed when I finished. "I just saw a real actress up there onstage!"

*Really?* I thought. Larry told me he saw the skillful character choices I had made, how much stronger my voice had gotten since he had seen me a decade ago. But he also told me how much I still needed to grow.

Even though I was in my late thirties, we had started off with ingenue roles. Once I had done a few of those, Larry decided it was time to tackle the more mature women found in David Hare's *Skylight* and Conor McPherson's *Shining City*. I performed scenes from David Mamet's *Boston Marriage*, Edward Albee's *The Death of Bessie Smith*,

John Guare's *Landscape of the Body*, and the movie *A Single Man*. I had worked on Irish and Southern accents. I'd played a courtesan, a nurse, a young mother with a newborn, a London schoolteacher. The disappointment of my divorce and being childless, my long-term worries about Courtney, my grief about my mother—I was able to channel all these feelings into my performances. Instead of accessing different parts of myself, as I had done in my early films, I learned to explore characters who were nothing like me.

Larry had also helped me work on the way I walked. All my years of trying to be invisible, taking tiny soft steps so that I would not bring attention to myself, meant that I floated across the stage rather than walked with purpose. He told me to take off my shoes and socks so I could walk around the stage and feel the ground beneath my feet. He instructed me to buy five-pound ankle weights so that when I walked, I walked with gravity. Slowly, my awareness began to shift from the top of my "thinking" head down through my "kishkes," as Larry would say, and to the soles of my feet. I needed to take responsibility for who I was, what I wanted, how I expressed myself.

One day Larry told me, "Natasha, you're going to be like Ruth Gordon. The best is yet to come."

Now I was on a plane heading to New York to audition for a live theater production. The thrill of performing live in Larry's classes was exhilarating, but those were just scenes in front of fellow students. If I got the part in an honest-to-goodness play for a paying audience, that would be very different. My character would be in practically every scene. Could I pull it off?

In New York, I stepped purposefully into the audition room and met the director of the play, David Saint, and Arthur, who was tiny and smiley, nothing like the grouch Mart had warned me about. The room was quiet, focused. I noticed Arthur's mouth beginning to form into a slight smile in the middle of my performance. I wore my favorite brown knee-high leather boots over dark jeans and a blue-and-black button-down oxford shirt. Not only did they like my audition, but also my outfit made such an impact that they asked me to wear it in the play. *I got the part!* My elation was undercut by a terrifying reality: *I actually have to do the play.* What did it feel like to perform onstage before four hundred strangers six nights a week plus matinees on Saturday and Sunday? I had no idea. I went to see Larry to get his help. He said, "You don't need me, you know this character, you've done the work."

Every morning I rode the subway with Arthur, who lived close to the apartment where I was staying in Manhattan. The play was being staged at the George Street Playhouse in New Brunswick, New Jersey, so at Penn Station we were picked up in a van that drove all of us across the river. (Marlo, grand and lovely, usually came separately in her personal car.) As we got to know each other, Arthur and I struck up an unlikely but fond friendship. He gave me insight into my character, Samantha, and became a trusted confidant. He had no interest in talking about my mother or revisiting the past. He only cared about me in his current play. Even with the George Street Playhouse being a relatively small theater, Arthur told me that my voice was reaching the back row. I was so pleased that I didn't have to be miked. For the next eight weeks, I knew exactly where I had to be and what I had to do every day.

When the run was over, returning to the uncertainty of my life in Los Angeles was daunting, but I felt stronger than at any point in my life since my mom died. And thanks to the months I had spent by myself at the beach house, I no longer feared being alone.

Not long after I returned to LA, I was sitting in a chair at my hair salon when I noticed a handsome guy walk in. Lea, my hairstylist, introduced him as Barry Watson. We struck up a polite conversation. He told me he was temporarily staying in Marina del Rey with his two small sons while he was waiting to move into a new house in Venice. He was easy and fun to talk to. Tall with crinkling hazel eyes. Were we flirting? I couldn't tell. It didn't matter. I learned he was an actor. I was raised by a handsome actor and had been attracted to handsome actors in the past. I told myself I didn't want to start dating another one. A couple of days later, I ran into Barry at a coffee shop.

"Hey!" I said. "Remember me?"

He did. We chatted. I learned he had played Matt Camden in the TV series *7th Heaven* (no, I hadn't watched it). This time I felt sure we were flirting, but he left that day without asking for my number.

A few weeks later Lea asked if she could give Barry my contact info, and I said yes. I knew we'd been flirting! It took another few weeks before Barry actually reached out to me. It was a Saturday night around ten o'clock and I was getting ready for bed when his text came in. "Hey, Natasha," he wrote. "It's Barry Watson. This may be kinda weird, but I wonder if you would want to go out and get a cup of coffee?"

The text conveyed a vulnerability that I found endearing, but I didn't let myself rush to any conclusions. I had become much more circumspect since my divorce. I was no princess. My castle had been crushed, and Prince Charming existed only in fairy tales. I realized now that there was more to a relationship than chemistry. I didn't trust myself to pick the right guy anymore.

I was so tired of pretending, so exhausted from showing only the parts of myself I deemed acceptable to others, that by the time I arrived at the restaurant Capo for our first date, I was early and unapologetically myself. Barry arrived wearing dark jeans and a gray oxford. He smiled easily, comfortable in his own skin. He sat right next to me and told me I looked pretty. I felt pretty in his steady gaze. We bonded over reading the menu—we both love good food and wine.

I learned that Barry had been diagnosed with Hodgkin's lymphoma at age twenty-eight. He recovered from that, then, at thirty, he'd met the woman who became the mother of his two sons. We talked about the breakdown of our relationships, which had been devastating for both of us. When we exited into the late-summer night, neither one of us was ready for our date to end, so we crossed the street to a bar and kept on talking. Just before closing time, when we stood up to finally leave, Barry kissed me, sweetly and knowingly.

The morning after our first date, I woke up to a text from Barry: "Good morning, sunshine."

We started seeing one another. It turned out that we were both looking for the same kind of life. Like me, he didn't want to go to Hollywood parties; he wanted to stay home. He was committed to his kids; he loved going hiking, cooking. Barry can be shy and watchful, yet he is the most open and honest person I have ever known.

As we grew closer, we slowly integrated me into the lives of his two young sons, Oliver and Felix. At first the boys thought of me as their friend, a kind of grown-up playmate. Like my mom, I had always felt comfortable around kids and babies, so I would come to Barry's house and play hide-and-seek, build Legos, take the boys on walks to the neighborhood treehouse, and read them stories. Oliver called me "Batasha," which was funny and sweet. One day he looked right at me and asked, "Batasha, don't you ever need to go home to your own parents?"

"Oliver," Barry said, "Natasha is a grown-up like Daddy."

Oliver looked confused. "You are? I thought my dad brought you here to play with me and Felix."

I told him that, although I loved playing with him, I was also a good friend of his dad's. Sensing his hesitation, I asked, "Are you ready for me to go home, Oliver?" Barry had his setup with his boys and I had my space.

He thought about it for a second, then replied with a nod and a decisive "Yeah."

Barry and I were falling in love and wanted to be together all the time, but we were sensitive to the boys, so we stayed "just friends" in front of them for the first year. One October day, on a drive home from the pumpkin patch, Oliver asked me directly if I was his dad's girlfriend. I paused for a moment. Barry took the lead, answering "yes." Oliver said he thought it was "kinda weird," but he guessed it was "probably okay." We had jumped the first hurdle smoothly enough.

Once Oliver realized I was the girlfriend, we had some tough moments.

"You can sleep in my bed," he told me once. "I'm going to sleep in my dad's bed!"

I had to be patient and strong because I knew Barry had his hands full with his boys; he didn't have time for my every concern and worry.

We agreed to stay living separately for the time being.

"Being a stepmother can be amazing," Julia said when I told her about Barry, Oliver, and Felix. "But most of the time, you will feel like the least important person in the room." I was surprised to hear her say this, because Julia is the most magical person, loved and adored by all, especially her stepchildren. But the truth is, no matter how much love and respect there is, a stepparent is always one step removed from a real parent. You are not a friend, you are not a babysitter, and yet you are not a parent. It's a complicated and humbling position. My compassion for Jill grew during this time, as I saw the world from a stepmother's perspective—a whole new experience for me.

Another hurdle was my deep desire to have a child of my own. From the time I was a little girl, I had always known I wanted children. My mom had always wanted to have children, too, it was just a natural thread in her life and in mine. I turned thirty-nine the same year I met Barry. All of a sudden, forty was on the horizon. I had spent my thirties throwing baby showers for all my girlfriends, being with them at the hospital as they were having their babies, buying baby clothes for their tiny sons and daughters. I wondered when it was going to be my turn. Barry is three and a half years younger than me and already had two children. He knew that I really wanted to be a mom, but he also knew that he had his hands full with Oliver and Felix, so a baby wasn't exactly the first item on his wish list.

I didn't know what would happen. I was trying to be sensitive to his situation while also balancing it with my needs—and Barry was doing the same. After D.V. and I broke up, I froze embryos. (A good friend offered to donate sperm without any other involvement.) This helped me feel secure in the knowledge that, when the time was right for me, I could become a mother, with or without a man.

Barry and I had been seeing one another for a little over a year and a half and I was a few days shy of my forty-first birthday when I realized I might be pregnant. I had Amanda on the phone when I took the home pregnancy test. Together, we held our breath for the designated three minutes. "Oh my God, lady!" I screamed when I saw that tell-tale pink plus sign. "Oh my God, lady!" she echoed. "Oh my God oh my God oh my God." She told me to take one more test before bed that night and a third one when I woke up the next morning. "If all three tests are plus pink, then you can tell Barry." They were.

I waited until he dropped the boys off at school on a rainy Monday morning. Barry stood in the garage smoking one of the last cigarettes he would ever smoke when I told him I was pregnant, the words edging their way cautiously out of my mouth. He slid down to the ground and sat there for a minute or two. He took a long puff of his cigarette, sizing up our newly colliding worlds. Though he was clearly in shock, he pulled me close and hugged me for a long time.

When I got back to my apartment, the rain had stopped, the sun was shining, and there right in front of me, just like in the movies, was a double rainbow. Baptized by the rain, solidified by the three pink plus sticks, I was practically walking on air. I had a tiny seed of an embryo growing inside of me. I was in love with a good and decent man.

But I knew this was a big step for him, and for us, and so a few days later, I sat him down and said: "Barry, I am completely okay if you do not want to participate in my life with our baby. I understand this was not something that we planned. But I am going to have this baby. You can take some time to decide to what extent you want to be involved."

I asked him not to call me until he knew what he wanted to do.

Because I was in my forties, I decided to have a chorionic villus sampling test to make sure the pregnancy was viable. Amanda took me to my appointment. Just before they were about to begin the procedure, Amanda whispered in my ear, "Barry is in the waiting room. He's going to take you home." I closed my eyes and exhaled. This just might work out.

I was back at the hair salon where I first met Barry when the doctor called to tell me that my baby was a healthy little girl. I received this information silently, reverently, soft tears forming in my eyes. A baby girl.

I walked in the door of Barry's Venice bungalow and clued him in on two important facts. "We are having a healthy baby girl, and we are naming her Clover."

Years ago I had dreamed about being pregnant and calling my baby Clover. Around the same time, a friend gave me a book on Zen Buddhism called *The Mind of Clover*. In it, the author explains that clover enriches the earth and helps the environment as it grows and that our minds can be as nurturing as clover. I loved every word of the book, bringing it with me everywhere I went. Also, I knew how much my mother's film *Inside Daisy Clover* meant to her. My mom fought to make it; she asked the producers to cast her friend Robert Redford and my godmother Ruth Gordon in it. Even our dog Penny was in the film. The movie tells the story of a young woman who wants to be an actress and singer in Hollywood. She and her mother have a complicated relationship. My mother had lived Daisy Clover's life and come out the other side. When Daisy blows up her house at the end of the movie, making the choice to live, she walks out onto the beach in Malibu. A passerby asks her what is going on and she exclaims, "Someone just declared war!" That's how I thought of my mom—triumphant, courageous, a survivor.

Above all, I wanted to name my daughter Clover because I felt so lucky. Lucky to have found Barry. Lucky to have my two dads. Lucky to have gotten pregnant at forty-one. My friends said I was "forty-wonderful" and that was so true. I had an easy early pregnancy and loved every minute of it. I ate everything and more. I felt sexy and happy and grown-up. Barry waited until I was really showing to tell the boys. He was afraid they might be upset, but instead, they were excited, with Oliver immediately asking us to name the baby Olive. Although Barry and I were still living separately, we started to talk about moving in together. Both my dads were over the moon. They knew how long I had waited to be a mom and they adored Barry.

It had been almost thirty years since my mom's death, and I was finally about to become a mother.

# Chapter 18

Natalie Wood, c. 1965.

It's November 2011, I'm still in my first trimester of pregnancy, all is well.

Then it hits.

I wake up one morning at Barry's house in Venice to a salvo of voice mails, emails, and texts from friends, family, people I have not heard from in years.

"What is going on?"

"Is everything okay?"

"Is your dad okay?"

Daddy Gregson leaves a voice mail.

"Darling, we've just read the paper," he says. "Is there anything we can do?"

This is how I learn that the Sheriff's department have reopened the case of my mother's death.

I find out that my aunt Lana has given an interview to TMZ saying that she never believed my dad's version of events, that my dad wasn't honest with the police when they interviewed him about my mom's death. Lana tells the reporter that she's "never bought" the story that my mom was trying to secure a dinghy and fell overboard. According to Lana, Natalie was afraid of the water and wouldn't even go near her own swimming pool. She says that detectives have interviewed her about the case and they have asked her if the relationship between Natalie and Robert was "volatile." She doesn't say how she answered but I can only imagine.

I am in shock. Is my dad going to be arrested? I feel my heart quickening. I'm nauseous. I need to calm down. There are two of us now. I don't want Clover to absorb my fear, that metal taste in my mouth. I take a couple of breaths. I tell Barry what's happening.

I'm not going to call my dad just yet. I want to figure out exactly what's going on first.

Before I speak to anyone else, I need information.

I call our family publicist Alan Nierob.

"Oh, this is just a bunch of total bullshit," Alan tells me. "Don't worry, Natasha."

"But, Alan, is he going to be arrested?"

"Are you crazy? Absolutely not," Alan says in his no-nonsense way. "This is all a media frenzy because it's the thirty-year anniversary of your mother's death."

He's going to find out exactly why the case has been reopened.

I breathe. Okay, I've been through this before. Ever since my mother's death, I have learned to block out the fake headlines in the trash magazines, the salacious sound bites of an upcoming "new development" just before a commercial break.

I decide to take a shower to steady my nerves before I call my dad.

The soothing warm water hits me but I am not soothed. I am outraged.

*How dare she?*

Why has my aunt decided on this moment to suddenly make her accusations? In 1984, she published a book about my mother. Around the same time, Lana did a TV interview where she was asked if she thought there was anything mysterious about my mother's death. Lana replied, "Absolutely not!" Why didn't she accuse my dad then? Why did she wait more than twenty-five years to "speak her truth"?

Lana is seemingly angry at my dad for refusing to send her money. And now she has created a scandalous story and given it to TMZ.

I will call Liz and Katie when I get out of the shower. I will get Lana's number and I will call her and let her know that this time she has gone too far.

I have a plan. I feel better. I hold Barry's computer in my hands and it tumbles down the stairs.

He starts to yell and then thinks better of it. He realizes that I am rattled. More so than I am letting on.

I am seething. My phone rings.

I hear Courtney's voice on the other end.

"Natasha, what the hell is going on?"

I have not spoken to my sister in a couple of months, not since she left her most recent rehab in Pasadena. She is angry at me for not speaking to her, and I'm resigned to the fact that I cannot help her. Yet in this moment she calls me anyway. The news has broken through her haze.

"Everything is okay. It's just the press and Lana making a circus out of Mommie's thirty-year anniversary."

"Is Daddy okay?"

"I think he's fine. Don't worry. Are you okay, Court?"

"Yes, I'm okay. I love you, sweets."

"I love you too. I promise I'll keep you posted."

I call my dad.

"Daddy, are you okay?"

"Hi, Natooshie. Jesus, I'm so sorry you have to go through this."

My dad, thinking about me instead of himself.

"I'm so sorry you have to relive that night again," he says. "You know none of us heard her. . . ."

"I know, Daddy," I say. "Of course. I know."

I'm worried about him. He is eighty-one. I am worried he will have a heart attack or a stroke from the stress.

I start to cry.

"Daddy, I love you so much. Don't worry about me. I'm worried about you."

We comfort each other. We will wait for the storm to pass.

But the accusations come thick and fast. The former deckhand on our boat the *Splendour*, Dennis Davern, appears on national TV. Dennis was the only other person on the boat that night along with my dad and Christopher Walken. Dennis now says he lied to investigators when he gave his statement at the time of my mother's death. That he wants to tell his "real story."

Dennis tells the interviewer that he was part of an attempt to cover up Natalie Wood's murder, orchestrated by Robert Wagner. He suggests that my dad deliberately failed to help my mom when she was drowning, and this is why she died.

How can Dennis say these things?

I remember Dennis from my childhood, being on the boat and at our house. He was kind and helpful. I thought he appreciated my family and enjoyed being around us. When my parents first met him in the mid-1970s, he had been down on his luck. He was working in Florida for the *Splendour*'s previous owner, and had brought the boat from there to Long Beach because its former owner wanted to sell it. My dad felt sorry for Dennis, who was about to be out of a job, and so he kept him on as the boat's deckhand. In those days, if Dennis didn't have enough money for child support or alimony, as happened often, my mom and dad helped him out.

Dennis must have fallen on hard times again because now he has decided to use the fact that he was on the boat the night my mom died to sell a book about "the truth about Natalie Wood," cowritten with his childhood friend, a woman named Marti Rulli. In the book and on TV, Dennis has completely changed his statement from the one he told original investigators in 1981. Instead, he claims that the fight between my parents culminated in my dad yelling at my mom to "get off the boat."

He says he was afraid of my dad after my mother died, and that my father was holding him hostage at our house. That's why he didn't tell the police at the time. I was living in that same house then and I think I would have noticed if Dennis was being held in my home against his will. More importantly, I would have noticed if my dad was the kind of man to hold another man against his will in the first place! I have known Robert Wagner since before I was two years old. Abusive men leave traces as they move through their lives. Where is the history of my dad's abuse? There is none. Why would my dad suddenly become secretly abusive and threatening toward his wife and others in 1981, at age fifty-one?

My dad was kind to Dennis. He helped him. After he donated the *Splendour* to the Sea Scouts, he couldn't give Dennis back his job on the boat, and so instead, he got Dennis a job as an extra in television and movies and a union card so he could find work more easily. But Dennis had a tough time making a go of it and eventually moved to Florida. We lost touch.

Now, nearly twenty years later, Dennis is using the thirtieth anniversary of my mom's death to parade this story.

We soon learn why the investigation may have been reopened. An online petition spearheaded by Dennis's cowriter on his book, Marti Rulli, has demanded that the Los Angeles County Sheriff's Department look at the case again. The petition draws eight hundred signatures. Marti also presents witness reports that she has gathered, primarily from Dennis. My mother has been dead for thirty years and the investigation into her death is reopened. My family is thrown back into the most traumatic time in our lives.

These people claim to care about my mother. They say they want "justice for Natalie." But Dennis was on the boat the night my mom died. If he cared about my mom as much as he claims, why didn't *he* try to save her? My parents' boat wasn't that big. If my dad could hear my mom's cries and ignored them, wouldn't this mean Dennis was doing the same?

Another witness comes forward, Marilyn Wayne. She claims she was on her boat, the *Capricorn*, when she heard a woman calling for help the night of Natalie Wood's death. Like everyone else, Marilyn seems to have changed her story. On December 3, 1981, Marilyn Wayne told the *Los Angeles Times* that she heard a woman crying for help that night and indicated that her boat was approximately three hundred feet away from the *Splendour*. In 2011, she declared in an official signed statement to the police that her boat was fifty feet away. Somehow, over the course of thirty years, her boat miraculously moved 250 feet closer to the one belonging to my parents.

Our publicist advises our family not to comment, not to give any credence to the accusations and allegations. He puts out a statement saying that our family welcomes the investigation of Natalie Wood's death if the information comes from "a credible source or sources other than those simply trying to profit from the 30-year anniversary of her tragic death."

Lana's and Dennis's accusations ignite a media frenzy. Thirty years after my mom's death I am back at the grocery checkout averting my eyes from headlines claiming that she was murdered by my dad in a jealous rage, or that she was supposedly sleeping with Christopher Walken, or that her cries for help were ignored.

The press needs to interview someone and Lana is more than willing. My aunt tells reporters that her sister hated water. That a fortune-teller told my grandmother her daughter would die by dark water, that she was afraid of it, that she wouldn't even go into her own swimming pool at home. But my mother loved the water! She was always drawn to water, whether swimming pools or the ocean. She fell in love with boating at eighteen when she and R.J. were first dating, and even after they divorced she went boating on the weekends with her friends and spent a year living on the beach. When she remarried R.J. in 1972, they held the ceremony aboard a yacht at sea. Our family albums are filled with pictures of my mom in pools, in lakes, on beaches, and on boats. My mom did have an aversion to immersing herself in water that was dark enough to be opaque, because she was not a strong swimmer and didn't like being in the ocean out of her depth.

In the wake of the new investigation, Duane Rasure, the sheriff assigned to Mom's case in 1981, goes on CBS News to defend his original findings. He confirms that if there had been *any* evidence that my dad was involved in any foul play, he would have arrested him personally. That my mother's drowning was an accident. He also reminds people that Dennis Davern has a strong motive for stirring up the story again.

"I think Dennis Davern is exaggerating this whole incident to sell his book."

Hardly anyone else seems to notice that the only accusations against my dad have been drummed up by Dennis, Lana, Marti, and others who appear to benefit financially from making my dad look bad.

In early 2012, it is reported that the reopened investigation has uncovered no new evidence. But the sheriff's department presses on. Around this same time, my dad is identified as a "person of interest" in the case. As our lawyers quickly explain to me, anyone within the vicinity of the boat that day would be a person of interest, including Dennis and Chris Walken. "Person of interest" doesn't mean someone is a suspect, it simply means they were there. The sheriff's department asks my dad to come in for questioning. He refuses, making it clear that he has said everything he has to say. Chris Walken also refuses, for the same reason.

Because the case has been reopened, the Los Angeles County chief coroner is obliged to look at my mother's death certificate again. He must also apply newer regulations within the coroner's office that weren't in effect when my mother died. Under these new standards, he must alter the wording on the death certificate, changing the cause of her death from "accidental drowning" to "drowning and other undetermined factors."

In a document, the coroner also states that the circumstances of exactly how Natalie Wood ended up in the water "could not be clearly established." In January 2013, the same coroner's office issues another statement explaining that my mother may have sustained some of the bruises on her body before she got into the water but that it could not be definitively determined. According to one forensic pathologist, she would have been particularly susceptible to bruising because of a medication she was taking.

For the first time in my life, I examine closely the details of that weekend. I turn them around in my mind. I reexamine them. I talk to my therapist, my dad, Liz, Katie, and my mom's friends. I discover that although decades have passed and the investigation has been reopened, there is no new evidence and my understanding of events remains the same.

After my one last hug with my mom in her soft angora sweater, she drove with my dad and Chris Walken to the boat. That first night, my dad was not able to secure a mooring inside the harbor, and so he had to drop anchor outside the breakwater. The boat was rocking up and down and my mom was getting seasick, so she decided to go ashore to Catalina Island to stay in a hotel for the night. Dennis, our deckhand, went with her. (This is where she had called me at my friend Tracey's house to see if I was okay.)

The next morning, she came back to the boat, and my dad set off on course for the Isthmus, the strip of land connecting the two parts of Catalina Island. Here, they tied up. At this point, my dad took a nap because he was tired from the rough night before. When he woke up, Natalie and Chris had taken the dinghy and gone ashore. My dad called for a shore boat—a local vessel that you can radio to come and pick you up—so he could join my mom and Chris at a local bar. The three of them had dinner together, drank some wine, and then came back to the boat and opened another bottle of wine. My mom and Chris kept talking and talking about their work on the film *Brainstorm*. At some point, my dad says Chris told him what a great actress my mom was, how much he enjoyed working with her, and how important it was that she continue to work as an actress. My dad remembers feeling irritated by this statement—after all, my mom had three kids to take care of on top of her work—and so he told Chris, "I think it's important you stay out of her life!"

Before long my mom had had enough of the conversation and decided to go to bed, going down below to the stateroom where my parents slept. My dad stayed in the salon with Chris and the conversation continued, getting more and more heated. Again, my dad told Chris, "Stay out of her life!" even smashing a bottle of wine on the table to make sure his point had been made. Chris left the room and my dad followed him out onto the deck.

To this day, my dad knows that his anger wasn't justified. He had been drinking and he hadn't slept well the night before. Out on the deck, in the cool sea air, he quickly calmed down, and the two men returned to the salon and talked for a while. Then Chris went to his cabin and my dad and Dennis cleared up the glass from the floor. Soon enough, my dad went below to go to bed.

Right away, he realized my mom wasn't in their stateroom where he expected to find her. He looked in the bathroom, she wasn't there. He went out onto the deck. Where was she? He saw that the dinghy was gone. He went to find Dennis, saying, "Natalie's not here!" Had she taken the dinghy to shore? That didn't seem possible as the *Splendour* was only sixty feet long and anyone on it would have heard her starting up the dinghy as she left. But what other explanation could there be?

My dad radioed for another shore boat, and went to Catalina to look for my mom. The restaurant where they'd eaten dinner that night was closed and there was no sign of Natalie or the dinghy in the dock. He came back to the *Splendour*. By now it was about 1:30 a.m. and he was frantic with worry. He called the Coast Guard, and they came out to the boat and looked over every inch of it. Then they started their search-and-rescue mission, the Coast Guard helicopters strafing the ocean with searchlights. My dad remembers waiting for what seemed like an eternity. Eventually, at around five thirty that morning, the Coast Guard found the dinghy in a cove near Blue Cavern Point on Catalina Island with the key in the off position, the gear in neutral, and the oars at its sides. Clearly my mom did not take out the dinghy; it had floated there. Two hours later, my mother's body was found, wearing only her nightgown, red parka, and socks, in the ocean off the Catalina coastline.

When my dad heard the news, he remembers feeling as if "every-thing just went out . . . went away from me." His first thought was for his children. How was he going to tell us? Mart picked up my dad and Chris, and together they drove to my dad's therapist, Dr. Arthur Malin, so my dad could ask him for guidance. Dr. Malin told him that he shouldn't minimize what had happened, that he needed to tell us straight and then reassure us that we would always be a family. And then he came home.

After my mom's body was found, the coroner, Thomas Noguchi, and Sheriff Duane Rasure, along with a team of investigators and experts, analyzed all the evidence and reached the conclusion that Natalie Wood drowned accidentally. Our boat had a swim step that led down to the dinghy, made of teakwood. When it got wet, it was incredibly slippery. Everyone on the boat had been drinking for the better part of the day. My mother was petite; it didn't take more than a glass or two of wine to make her tipsy. The coroner said her blood alcohol was at 0.14 (at a time when the legal limit for driving was 0.10). My mom had likely gone down to the dinghy to fasten it more securely so it wouldn't bang against the side of the boat, disturbing her while she was trying to sleep. She must have lost her footing on the swim step as she bent down to retie the dinghy, hitting her head and falling into the water. This is what everyone assigned to the case in 1981 believed happened. The original detective on the case, Duane Rasure, had never changed his assessment once in thirty years.

For me, the wording on her death certificate may have changed, but my understanding of what happened to my mom remains the same. I have always understood that my mother slipped and fell, bruising her body and possibly ending up unconscious before she entered the water—but we can never know with complete certainty. The circumstances of exactly how Natalie Wood ended up in the water will never be clearly established because she was alone when she died. And so I focus on the things I do know, that as certain as I am that the earth is round, my father would never have harmed my mother or failed to save her if he knew she was in danger. I focus on my love for my mom, for my dad, for my family. I cultivate a mind of clover.

# Chapter 19

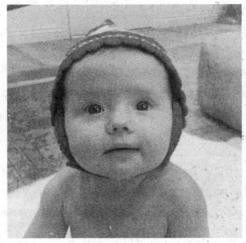

Clover, Venice, California, 2013.

When I was around three and a half months pregnant, Barry and I went to visit my dad at his condo in Westwood, a few days before Christmas, to have a drink with him and Jill. R.J. was in his early eighties then. He had let his dark hair turn gray. His blue eyes remained crystal clear. Despite the recent accusations, my dad was full of happiness for Barry and me, so delighted that he was going to be a grandparent again. Jill still had her bright red hair and gorgeous figure. The two of us have grown closer over the years, establishing a real friendship. Like my dad, she was deeply happy for me. I remember I was wearing a long red-and-white-striped dress, and I had a little bump on my tummy where Clover was growing.

My dad told me he had a gift for me. He handed me a small box. In it was a necklace with a large gold charm in the shape of a clover. Along with the clover was a gold rectangular charm that said "Clover" on one side and "Love Grandad" on the other. Engraved on the back of the clover were the words: "R.J., you are lucky for me. Love Wat. 1955." My dad's dear friend Watson Webb had given him this clover charm in 1955.

Clover's last name was going to be Watson. Maybe some things are meant to be.

My pregnancy was my golden time and I knew it. More than once, I pulled out a letter from my mom to my first godmother, the actress Norma Crane, written just after my birth. The letter was five pages long, dated October 8, 1970, the stationery embossed with my mother's name at the time, "Natalie Gregson."

My mom and Norma first met in 1957, when Norma was auditioning for a role in *Marjorie Morningstar*. Although Norma didn't get the part, the two of them clicked, becoming close friends from that moment until Norma's death—tragically young from breast cancer— just a day before my third birthday in 1973. Before she passed away, Norma stipulated in her will that when I turned eighteen, I would inherit the letter my mom had written to her about my birth, which is how it came into my possession.

My mom wrote the letter in hot-pink ink, in large, excited, loop- ing handwriting, detailing the entire experience of giving birth to me.

*Dearest Norma,*

*. . . I do wish you could see this darling, adorable, tender little incredibly beautiful sweetheart sleeping like a little angel on my bed as I write this. There really is no way to describe the intense joy I feel. I feel also newborn and naked—all emotion and no cover—it's lovely and scary and happy and anxious and terrific! Yay! YAY! . . .*

*. . . I watched her make her appearance into the world—it is such a profound moment, I don't know what I said or did. I*

*think I was speechless and awed. . . . Natasha is steady and alert and bright-eyed. The moment that they bring her to you—about twelve hours later—that is the ultimate. I know I will never know anything like it again . . .*

She went on to observe that I had my Daddy Gregson's legs and a combination of both of their noses.

*And she does have Richard's dimple. And she has this smile— it just knocks me out. She actually smiles and grins and shows her dimple—Natasha of the smile. She was so aware and alert the minute she came out screaming and wailing. Good strong lungs— strong little body. A small, tender toughie.*

Her only complaint about my birth (told with her characteristic humor) was about being expected to sign autographs in the recovery room.

*When you're in a hospital having a baby, it's better not to be a celebrity. That's only good for getting a table in a restaurant.*

Whenever I read my mother's words, I could hear her voice: her throaty laugh, the wobble in her voice when she was emotional, her delight in the retelling of a good story. Somehow, Norma had foreseen that one day I was going to need these five pages. Norma had no way of guessing that she and my mom would both die young. Had my mother lived, the letter Norma left me would have been a touching memento. Without my mother here to share my pregnancy with me, it reconnected me to her in a way I could have never imagined.

In the second trimester, I began to feel the first stirrings of Clover's kicks and wriggles inside me. My mom's letter to Norma kept playing itself out in my head. I heard her words—*Yay! YAY!*—in bright pink cursive in my brain. *Natasha of the smile,* or *a small, tender toughie,* or *thank God she has Richard's legs.* Her words echoed in my heart, reverberated in my body.

Mother's Day was a few weeks before Clover's due date. Barry and I had a simple lunch in Venice. This was the first Mother's Day since my mother's death when my focus was not on me being motherless. I was mother-full—a brand-new feeling. Instead of being consumed by lack, I felt expanded. I was keeping my baby alive inside my body. My heartbeat and her heartbeat were in sync. I could feel her squirming, making her presence known. I felt certain I knew how to be a mom. I knew how to give the good love. The good, safe, solid, golden love that my mom had given me. I could give this love to Clover and I could not wait. I would love her more than love.

Clover was due on May 31, a couple of days after Memorial Day. The day of the holiday, I felt sure I was ready. I woke around four the following morning with mild contractions. The next afternoon, we checked into the hospital. I had told my OB that I wanted a natural birth if possible. After a long night of contractions without enough dilation, they broke my water and gave me Pitocin to induce labor. With Amanda and Barry by my side, I pushed, grunted, screamed, and swore for hours and hours. My OB and his nurses turned me around, they put a rebozo sling underneath me, and hung me in it from a metal bar overhead. Everyone was hoping I could have my baby naturally, but no matter what we tried, Clover refused to make her exit.

After five hours of serious pushing, I begged the doctor for a C-section.

He agreed and the medical team started prepping me for surgery. Barry was standing next to me on the table. I was awake but felt incredibly woozy and strange from the drugs in my system. They put a curtain up so I couldn't see what was going on. Everything happened so quickly.

"Oh," the doctor said as he made the initial incision, "no wonder you couldn't push her out. She's tucked up tight in there. All right, here she comes!"

I heard Barry react first. "Natasha, she looks like a mini-you!"

Barry laid her on my chest. Clover was crying and swollen and her hair was blood-soaked. *A small, tender toughie.* She immediately found my breast and started feeding. *How does she know how to do that?* She fed a little. They took her away to clean her up, then they gave her back to me. I gazed at her. Blondish hair, elfin nose, Barry's gorgeous mouth. I felt overwhelmed with humility and gratitude. At seven pounds, two ounces, Clover was ready to begin our journey together.

They wheeled us into another room, where my dad and Jill and my godmother Delphine were waiting for us. The date was May 30. That was the date in 1969 that my mom and Daddy Gregson were married.

The early days with Clover were spent in a bubble of contentment. First we were at my place in Malibu and then at Barry's house in Venice. Clover slept in our room in a Moses basket right next to my side of the bed, her sweet baby smell perfuming the air around us. Her soft grunts and gurgles were the soundtrack of my dreams.

After Clover's birth, I read my mom's letter to Norma again. Her words held new meaning now. That feeling of cradling your child in your arms. The love! It just *knocks you out*! Looking at my beautiful, perfect baby, all I felt was yay! YAY! How did I get to be her mother?

The Japanese have a method of repairing broken pottery called *kintsugi.* Instead of trying to disguise the fractures and cracks, they highlight them with a special gold glue that makes the repaired piece more beautiful than the original. The scars from breakage add glorious new patterns. Rather than throwing away a broken vase or dish, they make it more valuable than ever by emphasizing its flaws. I had been a motherless daughter since age eleven. I was broken and jagged. Clover was my golden glue.

Early motherhood was not without its challenges, however. One afternoon in Malibu, Barry went to change Clover's diaper. From the corner of my eye, it seemed to me that he was doing it sloppily (never mind that he had been through this twice before with his sons). I raced over, literally shoving my body in front of his. Elbowing him in the chest, I planted myself in front of her changing table, forming a firm barrier between him and Clover. Some kind of feral vigilance had swept over me. My body and I were keeping this human alive. If I failed, she failed. I had never been so vital to another human's existence. Barry was shocked and hurt. I wasn't usually this fierce with him.

We hired a baby nurse for the first month, but I had a hard time allowing her to care for Clover so that I could take a break. I stopped sleeping. What if I fell asleep and Clover needed me, but I wasn't there for her? I became exhausted, short-tempered. Honestly, I wanted everyone to leave me alone so that I could focus on Clover. Barry, the boys, the nurse—they were all in the way. The boys were loud, they were hungry, they wanted to play, they wanted to hold the new baby, they had a million questions. They wanted mothering too, and I felt guilty that I was unable to meet their needs. Suddenly, a wedge had formed between us: me and Clover versus Barry and the boys. I got angry when Barry sided with Oliver and Felix. My nerves were on edge; a ribbon of stress and fear rippled through me every day. Clover didn't like a bottle, so I was the only one who could feed her. I had a painful C-section scar to deal with. My body was a mess, my house was a mess, my relationships were a mess.

When Clover was six weeks old, Barry had to go to New York for the summer for a job. I was actually relieved. The boys stayed with their mother. I hired a nanny named Susan to help out, but I was excited to have Clover all to myself. I craved quiet time with her. We went on walks through the neighborhood. She was all smiles for me, mischief in her eyes. We were a pair.

My need for Clover and only Clover was initially so strong, I was seriously considering parting ways with Barry and raising our child on my own, just like my mother had split up with Daddy Gregson when I was a baby. After Barry returned from working in New York, and Clover was four months old, we took a trip to Michigan, where

Barry was born. Barry let me know he was completely committed to me and to our child. I realized I loved him, that he was a great dad. I remember thinking: *I am going to lose this man if I don't make an effort to reconnect with him.* It seemed as if I were waking up from a dream. I realized that I wanted a life with him, I wanted to be a stepmother to the boys, and I wanted Clover to have a life with her dad and her brothers. So I began making a conscious effort to share Clover with her father, to make time for the boys. It wasn't hard to do. Julia always says that a baby is like a fire, everyone gathers around. I had been keeping Clover away from Barry and the boys, and as soon as I let them in, she drew them to her.

My psychopharmacologist recommended a specialist in post-partum depression. At our first session, the doctor instructed me to turn my phone off.

"There is no way I am going to do that," I said. "You don't understand. What if Clover needs me? I have to be reachable at all times."

I felt as if thin gossamer strands connected me to my baby. I could almost see them. They pulled me back to her, making it nearly impossible for me to even go to the gas station on the corner or to run to pick up groceries. When I took a shower, I would bring Clover into the bathroom, wrapped in towels and propped comfortably on the heated floor, rather than leaving her with Barry or the nanny. I told the doctor about the anxiety I felt, the overpowering responsibility to keep her alive, the familiar feelings of panic and hypervigilance that would take over. These overly protective and dark emotions took me by surprise. They felt extreme and scary to me.

When I spoke to Daddy Gregson, he remembered my mother's similar, almost obsessive concern for me as a baby. He was in the delivery room to witness the moment when we came face-to-face for the first time. He remembered that day I slid into the world. He was the one who had described my mother as "a panther, ready to spring if anyone said anything about you which she didn't like."

When I was about a year old, my mom and I were alone in the house on North Bentley Avenue. My mom was divorcing my dad and was taking care of me by herself. I tried to push open a big sliding glass door and it slammed on my thumb. A typical childhood injury, but my mother didn't just call the doctor—she also called the paramedics and the fire department.

How much of my mother's obsession with me was fueled by Baba's obsession with her? Baba's devotion to my mom was overprotective to the point of paranoia. She couldn't stand to let her little girl out of her sight for a moment, terrified of kidnappers, attackers, and other imagined threats to her safety. When fire engines would wail past their house, Maria would run to check on Natasha, even if she was only playing in the next room. On at least one occasion, Baba even called to check on my mother when she was grown and married because she heard a siren in the night.

I had become possessive of Clover to the point of ignoring her father, and anyone else who tried to come between us, just as my own mother had, and probably her mother before her.

I got back on Prozac. I had taken the drug off and on since my twenties, but I had come off it during my last trimester on the recommendation of my doctor. After Clover was born, I had tried to manage without medication, but clearly I needed it. Slowly, I came out of the fog of postpartum depression. My symptoms had been my hypervigilance, my fixation on the idea that no one could take care of Clover except for me. I started leaving Clover with her dad, with our nanny. I could handle this. I could do it. Clover would be okay. Barry and I would be okay. At six months old, my daughter seemed sturdier, less like an egg that might break. Sometimes, as I held her, it was as if my mom were holding me. Maybe I was enough of a mother for both of us; maybe there was enough mother love to go around.

Clover hated her car seat and would always cry on our drives. The teacher at our toddler group told me I should sing to Clover when we were driving in the car. It worked instantly. I found I had no shortage of songs. Songs I had forgotten I knew, all the songs my mom used to sing to me: "Bayushki Bayu," "Fried Ham," "Frère Jacques," "My Favorite Things." I started to hear my mom's voice in mine as I sang

and spoke to Clover. I was Natooshie, and she was Clovie-girl. My voice rose an octave, a blend of singsong and talking—just like my mother's. My focus landed squarely on Clover as I remembered my mother's on mine. I knew how to love this kid.

To this day, I still struggle with my desire to overmother and overprotect Clover. I constantly resist the urge to obsess over her whereabouts every second of the day, to nag Barry about what to put in her lunch, what to feed her for dinner, the temperature of her bathwater, and on and on and on. For better or worse, I am my mother's daughter and Baba's granddaughter. At the same time, the intimacy of motherhood comes so easily to me. The mechanics of bathing, feeding, and putting my child to sleep. I love the schedule, the routine, the closeness, the affection. I have my mom and Baba to thank for this too.


Clover celebrated her first birthday on May 30, at Whitebrook Farm in Wales, and took her first steps the very next day on Daddy Gregson's front lawn. Now that our little girl was a toddler, Barry sold his tiny bungalow in Venice. I sold my little beach house in Malibu. Together we bought a house in Venice. Its backyard, shaded by oak and sycamore trees, reminded me of Old Oak Road the minute I set foot on the soft green grass. Everyone could have their own bedroom; toys could be stored neatly away. The boys lived with us half the time, and the other half with their mom.

That year, I turned forty-three, the same age as my mother when she died. I was acutely aware that I would outlive her now, that I would grow older than she ever got to be. I was aware of time marching forward, moving faster and faster. I missed her in a different way now. I longed to talk to her about motherhood, about being in your forties, about how it feels to look in the mirror and notice the lines around your eyes.

On the afternoon of Barry's fortieth birthday, just before Clover turned two, he knelt down on one knee in the middle of our living

room and proposed. The boys had just gotten home from school and were playing rambunctiously. Clover was occupying herself with her toys. The chaos of our life was in full swing. This was not an intricately planned romantic fantasy, but a gesture that reflected the daily life that we were living. The kids gathered around the coffee table and joined us as I agreed to be Barry's wife.

Our wedding took place on December 21, 2014, in the backyard of our new house. My Daddy Wagner and Barry's dad, Mike, married us (they both became ordained for the occasion). My Daddy Gregson had been diagnosed with Parkinson's and sadly was too frail to make the long trip to Los Angeles. Barry's son Oliver read a poem; Clover brought us our wedding rings. We had invited a small group of thirty guests to an "engagement party" in hopes of keeping the atmosphere relaxed. Instead of white, this time, my dress was pale pink jersey, cut on the bias with a flowing skirt and a pink-and-green lace top. Barry wore a green plaid tuxedo. We ate and drank and made toasts until we were filled to the brim with happiness.

# Chapter 20

Clover, Natasha, Barry, Felix, and Oliver
on Natasha and Barry's wedding day,
December 21, 2014.

As my daughter Clover grew from a baby to a toddler, I began to think more carefully about my mother's legacy. For so many years I had kept her memory at arm's length, worried that if I looked too closely, it would be impossible to forge my own identity. Now I began to feel a newfound desire to protect and reclaim my mother. What version of her grandmother's life would Clover inherit? Would it be rumors and hearsay about Natalie Wood's so-called tragic death and difficult life? Or would Clover be able to learn about the mother I knew, the complex woman and actor who was devoted to her craft, who was a warm and loving wife, parent, and friend? As I reached my mid-forties, I started to wonder if I might play some part in telling my mom's story.

It was 2015 when I agreed to help put together a book of photographs about my mother. Around the same time, I launched a fragrance, Natalie, based on the gardenia perfume that my mom always wore. People at the auction house Bonhams had been asking Daddy Wagner and me if they could auction some of our mother's items. We had always resisted in the past. Now we thought it might be a way to create buzz for the coffee-table book. We knew we couldn't keep all her things forever, so we decided to select a few items that we felt we could part with to go up for auction in LA and New York. We wanted to present items we thought might most interest her fans and film scholars: her scripts, the certificate for her Academy Award nomination for *Splendor in the Grass*, the Golden Globe for *From Here to Eternity*.

And so I found myself back at the storage unit where her possessions were kept to look for photos and objects. The first time I had visited the storage unit I was barely out of my teens. All I could do then was grab a few items and run away. I wasn't ready to spend time in the past, to immerse myself in the world of Canon Drive. This time was different. I was a forty-six-year-old woman now, a mother. And I had a job to do.

I returned to the storage unit with a sense of purpose, treading the concrete floors with a mightier foot. Enough time had passed. I was ready to reconnect with my mother. I truly felt that she wanted me to begin this deep dive, that almost thirty-five years after her death, she was ready to be seen again. I went back to the unit over and over, spending countless hours amid her possessions. I dug through boxes, reached up into every shelf and container, and cracked the spines on old albums that hadn't been opened in decades. I found scrapbooks put together by Baba. A bound copy of the original script for *Miracle on 34th Street*. A folder of letters from my fourth-grade class thanking her for taking us on a field trip to Olvera Street, Los Angeles' historic Mexican district. This was the same year she was our room mother. In my letter, I wrote: "You're just wonderful as a room mother, person, actress, mother, and everything else. I love you so much. Tell Daddy I love him too. You both are just terrific."

A friend helped to convert the old home movies and film reels we discovered, and I found myself transported back in time to the 1970s through grainy, sun-bleached Super-8. Us in the pool at Daddy Wagner's house in Palm Springs. My naked body squirming and splashing while my dad holds me, securely guiding me through my first splashes in the pool. He is suntanned and handsome and can't stop smiling. My mom, long hair pigtailed, wearing a yellow bikini, mugging for the camera, jumping off the diving board, holding her nose in a mock "I hate the water" pose.

One day I was at the storage unit with my collaborator on the coffee-table book, Manoah Bowman. We had already been here for a couple of hours and I was beginning to feel woozy with information, my eyes glazing over from so much searching. On the floor, we stumbled upon an unremarkable brown box. Manoah opened it and pulled out some ¾-inch tapes. Beneath them was a small leather book, its binding stripped and worn with age. I turned the book over and there in gold lettering was my mom's name: "NATALIE WOOD WAGNER."

I opened the book and found a note inscribed on the inside: "to Nat from Nick." The book was actually a journal, a birthday gift to my mom from Nick Adams, her costar and friend from *Rebel Without a Cause*. The date was 1958.

". . . it is a rare love that you both have for each other, and it is a rare love that I have for you and RJ . . ." Nick wrote. "Perhaps you can use this book to keep the many memories of your beautiful and wonderful life with RJ."

In 1958, my mom had just married R.J. for the first time. I flipped through the pages. Inside, my mom had placed love notes to her from my dad. There were dried roses flattened in pages. Many of the journal entries described the love my mom felt for R.J., his kindnesses to her. How he brought her a "single white rose because we were separated for 10 hours."

Letters and notes were taped on different pages. One fell out, catching my eye because it was written on pale blue airmail paper. Light as air.

The front of the note said "Natalie Wood" but I recognized the writing that said "personal" immediately. That was Daddy Wagner's unmistakable handwriting, all caps, long, well-formed letters. The letter was dated March 6, 1962.

I started reading the letter out loud to Manoah. R.J. began by telling my mother how proud he was that she had been nominated for an Oscar for *Splendor in the Grass*. He told her "you've got my vote."

Then he mentioned that his lawyer Andy had spoken with him. Andy had said that my mom was willing to go through with the divorce action. My dad then thanked her for the Christmas gifts that my mother had sent his sister Mary's children. He also told her that his "Mother and Dad appreciated your thoughtfulness . . . they think you are a marvelous girl."

He went on, "you look marvelous as Gypsy, hope all is going well on the film."

As I reached the end of the letter, my eyes filled with tears.

"My thoughts will be with and for you on Oscar night and believe me Nat, I hope with all my heart that when they open up the envelope that it's you."

This letter was from the period of my parents' divorce. My dad could have been angry, lashing out at my mom. Instead he wished her well, hoped she would win her Oscar, wanted the best for her. So much has been written about my parents and their "tempestuous marriage." So much has been made of the fact that they divorced when they were young and fought on the night of my mom's death. But in many ways, the relationship I knew, that I grew up around, was marked by a kind of old-fashioned decorum, a courteousness rooted in kindness and mutual respect.

The letter validated everything I knew about my parents, that they loved each other with a deep and rare love. Yes, they had their disagreements, but above all, they adored and appreciated one another. It was as simple as that. I cried for the elegance that existed between them—even as they separated. These were the people who raised me. This was the love that I had witnessed. This relationship of theirs was what made me. This love was the same love I was sharing with my own husband and passing down to my daughter.

At that storage unit in Glendale, I was able to meet my mother over and over again, in photographs, in albums and home movies, through the objects that she kept and loved, the gifts she had been given. I also began to discover her in her own words. My mom was such a compulsive communicator, always jotting things down in her datebooks, sending letters and notes, drawing little pictures of sweet faces with big smiles and curly hair at the bottom of the letters she wrote to Courtney and me. There were letters that she had written to my dad in her journal, letters to directors that she planned to send, stern letters to Daddy Gregson telling him what would or wouldn't fly when it came to parenting me. I got the sense that my mother wrote these letters first for herself, to clarify her thoughts on paper. Then she transcribed them onto her stationery once they were ready to send.

I felt I was meeting my mother eye to eye, at her own level, instead of seeing her through the filter of her film roles or other people and their perceptions of her. One day, while looking for photos, I was rifling through yet another brown cardboard carton that looked as if it hadn't been touched in decades. At the bottom was a plain white notebook. I pulled it out. As I opened it up, I found fifty pages of writing. Some pages were typewritten, some were handwritten; some of the typewritten pages had notes on them in my mother's handwriting. They were dated 1966, with the title "Public Property / Private Person."

I did the math. In 1966, she was between her first two marriages. She was twenty-eight years old. She had gotten divorced from R.J.

but had yet to marry Richard Gregson. This was before she had me, written while she was making the movie *Penelope*.

I began reading. The article was a kind of memoir of her life to that date. It seems my mom had been writing an article for *Ladies' Home Journal* and these were her drafts and notes.

"Hollywood is where I live," read the first sentence.

*It is the only home I have ever known. I have been making a living here since I was a child. I have performed in forty films, and before I reach the age of thirty I will be eligible for a twenty-five-year pension. Looking at it from the outside it must appear to be a very pleasant way to make a living (as indeed it is)—hanging on to your childhood, playing at make-believe, being Cinderella, meeting Prince Charming . . . all the while being paid quite well. But like most things, there is another way of looking at it too—from the inside. This is a tough and hotly competitive business, and it is particularly hard on women. Your ego is constantly on the line when your every mood, pound, and inch is scrutinized by experts every day. Part of the bargain is being exploited, misunderstood, and occasionally misled.*

I finished the first paragraph and closed the notebook. I didn't want to read it all at once and so when I left that afternoon, I took the pages with me. It was a long article, about the length of a novella. In the morning, I sat in my bedroom in Venice after dropping Clover at school and began reading. I didn't want the article to end so I stretched out the process, reading a few paragraphs at a time, over the course of three or four days. Cross-legged on the wooden floor or propped up in my bed with a cup of coffee next to me. If the phone rang, the call went unanswered—I was too busy visiting with my twenty-eight-year-old mother. The drafts included many handwritten notes from my mom with instructions to her editor—"this page out!" There were letters from the editor of *Ladies' Home Journal* and her responses. Always her lawyer Paul Ziffren copied on everything.

As I read, I realized that when she wrote these words, my mother had been in the public eye for more than twenty years. In the article, she wanted to remind people that she had a private side, that she was so much more than the painted version of herself they saw on the screen and in the movie magazines. My mother explains in the article:

*It's a strange feeling to see people watching you in a film. And it brings with it a barrage of mixed feelings. You remember all the crises associated with a certain scene, or . . . how good you felt when you were able to make a particular moment work. It may have been months since the film was completed, and by now, you are deeply immersed in another. . . . It's always seemed bizarre to me that all those months of work, the crises, the turmoil, the decisions, finally get compacted into one hundred minutes of film. . . . Sometimes you wish you could say to the audience, "Would you please forget that last scene? I wasn't feeling well that day." But you can't run up and down the aisles, and you can't try to do it better the next night. Once it flashes on the screen, it is there. It no longer belongs to you. That part of me is public property. But there is a private person behind the image. Her name is Natasha Gurdin.*

My mom talked at length about her childhood, growing up on bustling soundstages and sets, completing homework to the sound of a banging hammer. She writes about how, when she was twelve, my grandfather suffered the first of a series of heart attacks and could no longer work.

"This meant my acting was the sole economic support of my family, and therefore getting jobs became a tremendous responsibility," she recalled. "It felt like heartbreak time whenever I heard a casting director say: 'She's too skinny—too short—too tall—in the awkward stage.' The worst one was 'Not pretty enough.' When I lost a job, I always felt Nature had played a dirty trick on me."

My mother describes how she began driving the family Chevy at twelve because her father was too ill and her mother too anxious. Driving a car and earning the money to keep her family at the age of twelve! She was so petite she could barely have been able to see above the steering wheel. . . . I felt such a pang for her, a feeling of wanting to reach back through the years to wrap my arms around her and to comfort her.

She didn't focus only on her childhood; she reckoned with the collapse of her marriage to R.J. too. My mother was someone who always seemed so in control. To read about her remorse about their breakup, her feelings of failure, how palpably she still missed R.J. and hoped to reconcile with him, really shook me. At the core of their problems, she explained, was their inability to push aside illusion and deal with reality. My mom wrote:

*We were aware that we had problems but tried to avoid the real conflicts. We maintained a superficially happy relationship and hoped that by pretending there was nothing wrong, the problem would go away. It was extremely difficult for us to really face serious flaws in the relationship when everything looked so ideal on the surface. Looking at it from the outside we must have seemed like the American dream. We were both attractive and successful, so what could possibly be wrong? We not only worked at illusion, we lived in it. How do you separate reality from illusion when you have been steeped in make-believe your whole life? Marriage requires patience and work, as well as the capacity to accept another human being, flaws and all, without cloaking him in a smothering mantle of perfection. It was unfair to heap all my dreams on one man's shoulders.*

And yet despite this, or perhaps because of it, my mom was determined to find her way through, to stop sweeping her childhood problems "under a rug labeled Marriage," as she put it, and to face the hard truths.

*Since the collapse of my marriage in 1961 I have been consciously trying to examine and unravel the real cause and effect of all my behavior. I think it takes a long time—years—to realize what it means when your marriage fails; all the promises to love forever, the faith, and the belief in another person and yourself. I started psychoanalysis at this crisis in my life. . . . I had been on a merry-go-round since I was four, and perhaps it was beginning to need some repairs. Because I felt I had so few inner resources, I was extremely dependent on other people and their reactions towards me. It was as if I were the sum total of all the parts I had played and I had no idea who I really was. . . . I always did as I was told as a child and on the set. These superficial props were no longer satisfying, dependable, or appropriate to my age. For the first time in my life, I considered, in horror, the possibility that I might join that sad parade of famous movie ladies who wind up desperately lonely, with nothing more substantial to sustain them than their scrapbooks and old photos, and memories of romances and divorces. I could no longer expect a magical Prince Charming or even a good doctor to wave a wand and make the pain go away. Nor would I find the answer in work, travel, or material things. Something was wrong and I wanted desperately to put it right. I knew the answer lay within myself.*

Toward the end of the article, my mother writes about her new-found desire to educate herself, not only by spending time on her therapist's couch, where she had grown so much, but by reading and studying too. At the time, she was taking an English literature class at UCLA.

"The course helped me to realize that my feelings are not as unique as I once supposed; in fact, they are so common they are universal," she pointed out.

*People have always had to fight the feelings of loneliness, emptiness, and estrangement from other human beings. Everyone deals with these feelings in a personal way. I don't want to forget the painful memories. It is from remembering that pain of failure and trying to overcome it that one can possibly begin to grow. . . . I was once asked if my goal in life was to be a good actress, and at one time perhaps it was. But now I know that, most of all, my hope is that I will be totally committed to another human being and that that union will bring children and happiness.*

When she wrote her piece for *Ladies' Home Journal* my mom of course had no idea that she would marry my dad, become a mother to me, remarry R.J., and have Courtney.

It wasn't hard for me to relate to the young woman I found in the writings, struggling in her relationships, searching for herself, on a quest to find a deeper value and meaning away from the gaze of the public and the camera, someone who was still waiting to find her life partner and to have children. These had been my struggles too, the struggles of so many women. I recognized the seeking, insightful, articulate author of the article, lost in the confusion of her twenties, trying to make sense of the past. I felt protective of her and compassionate toward her. And at the same time, I felt such a deep pride and happiness for the young woman that my beloved mom had been and all that she hoped for herself.

The *Ladies' Home Journal* article was never published. We don't know why. I wonder if my mother finished it and then thought better of her decision to expose herself to the world. Manoah and I decided to publish an excerpt from it in the coffee-table book, alongside beautiful black-and-white photographs of my mother at the age she had been when she'd written the words.

The year of the auction, my aunt Lana decided to write a letter to Christopher Walken, begging him to "tell what really happened" that night, which she published on Radar Online, the celebrity gossip website. In the age of Internet clickbait journalism, Lana had found an outlet eager to feature her theories about my mom's death. A year later, my father was on a trip to Palm Springs with Jill and was sitting having dinner when a waiter came to the table with a note from Lana, asking him to speak with her. My dad went out to the lobby, where Lana was waiting for him. My aunt proceeded to plead with him to speak about "what happened" that night. What my dad didn't know was that Lana had brought with her a TV crew from Radar Online. In the video—which ended up all over YouTube—my eighty-six-year-old dad looks surprised but does his best to remain calm as Lana barrages him with questions and accusations. It takes him a moment to notice the cameras, to see that he has been ambushed.

Three years later, the most recent media blitz about my mom's death hit, with Lana at the center. It was the summer of 2018, and I was in the Midwest, at the hundred-year-old cabin Barry and I had just purchased. The house sits on a beautiful calm bay. Serene and cool blue, the lake sparkles and shimmers when the sun dances on its surface. They call it "unsalted and shark free." I like this saying. It means we can swim in the water safely, see the sand at the bottom, know that nothing is coming to get us. Behind our cabin is a forest. Trees—some bent and broken, leaning on each other for support, others growing tall and proud, reaching for the sun—surround us. Ash and cedar, maple and birch. Evergreens everywhere.

Early one June morning shortly after we arrived, Clover and I took a golf-cart ride through the woods. Out of the corner of our eyes, we both caught a flash of brown. It was a mama deer, her baby fawn just behind her. Together they darted across the road.

"Mama, did you see them?" Clover asked, thrilled at our close brush with wildlife.

"I sure did."

A few days later we were in the car. Off to the right of the highway, we spotted a dead deer, its body still intact. "Could that be the mama deer we saw in the woods?" Clover wondered. It might have been. As we passed, we noticed five or six vultures feasting on her, tearing out her flesh, her blood. They were hungry and she was their meal.

When our family's publicist Alan called to let me know that a podcast series had come out about my mother's death, I immediately thought of the mama deer. In the coming days, it seemed like every time I looked at a newspaper or magazine there was a plug or mention of the podcast. There was a trend for "true crime" podcasts at the time and my mother's story had somehow been morphed into a murder mystery, with my dad as the prime suspect, even though he has never been charged with any kind of crime. They had even used my mother's words from her *Ladies' Home Journal* draft in the series, claiming that it was a "never-before-seen-or-heard memoir" even though the words had already been published in our coffee-table book. The podcast went straight to the top of the iTunes charts. Suddenly we were thrown back into the tornado of supposition and speculation.

I made the decision not to listen to the podcast, but close friends did, and they filled me in. The usual people were interviewed for the series, pointing their fingers at my dad. Lana. Dennis Davern, the skipper. Marti Rulli, his cowriter. These were the same people who had campaigned for the LA County Sheriff's Department to reopen the case of my mother's death. For the podcast, however, Lana, Dennis, and Marti went one step further than they had in 2011. Apparently they now said that my dad had committed premeditated murder, planning to kill my mom, deliberately engineering events that weekend to execute his plan and cover it up afterward. Lana, Dennis, and Marti had no new evidence to support their claims. They had simply decided to say the words out loud. It was as if over the years, they had told their story so many times that they had completely convinced themselves of my dad's guilt.

Throughout the podcast, the "facts" of my mom's case were apparently presented without any journalistic due diligence. The producers seemed to be much more interested in proving my dad's guilt than they were in telling a balanced and impartial account. Basic information that could have been easily fact-checked by the production team was blatantly wrong. My parents didn't get married the second time on the *Splendour*. They didn't even own the boat then—they got married on the *Ramblin' Rose*. Laurence Olivier, Fred Astaire, and Rock Hudson didn't carry her casket at her funeral. They were "honorary pallbearers," and Laurence Olivier wasn't even there. We soon learned that the host of the podcast was a longtime tabloid journalist, part of an entire industry that profits from celebrity scandal, blowing up clouds of smoke where there isn't a fire.

Lana's testimony for the podcast was apparently emotional and heartfelt, filled with claims of devotion to her sister while outright accusing Natalie's beloved husband of murder. To this day I feel sorry for my aunt. She lost her sister in 1981 and her only child, my cousin Evan, to a heart attack in 2017 after a long battle with Hodgkin's lymphoma. I am sorry for all of that. I am sorry for the frustration Lana feels over not being able to point her finger at a bad guy responsible for my mom's death. But sometimes there are no bad guys. Sometimes accidents happen.

The original detective on my mother's case, Duane Rasure, passed away in 2014 and could no longer dispute the claims made in the series. Without the lead investigator around to defend his own work, the producers were able to discredit his decades-old investigation. But the fact remains that Rasure and his team were *there*. None of the people making the podcast were part of the investigation in 1981. Do they know more about the accident than those who examined the case at the time? It is impossible for me to believe that they do.

I have lived with the confusion and controversy of the night my mother died for most of my life. I knew immediately at age eleven that we would never know exactly what happened that night because my mom was alone when she died. I had to make my peace with not knowing. I wish others could do the same. But it seems that when there are no details available about a death and no witnesses, this creates a fertile ground for speculation. The imagination can fill in the blanks. When that person is a celebrity—and a beautiful female celebrity who is gone too soon—the temptation to elaborate and invent is irresistible. My mother's death, and the absence of information about what happened to her, has become a Rorschach test for people. What you see depends on who you are.

Our family is not close with Chris Walken, the other man on the boat that night, and I have never spoken to him about my mother.

Walken did give one interview to *Playboy* in 1997, where he talked about what happened that night and his words resonate with my own understanding of why people remain so fixated on revisiting the night of her death.

"What happened that night only she knows, because she was alone," Walken said in the interview. "She had gone to bed before us, and her room was at the back. A dinghy was bouncing against the side of the boat, and I think she went out to move it. There was a ski ramp that was partially in the water. It was slippery—I had walked on it myself. . . .

"You hear about things happening to people," Walken went on. "They slip in the bathtub, fall down the stairs, step off the curb in London because they think that the cars come the other way—and they die. You feel you want to die making an effort at something; you don't want to die in some unnecessary way."

Back in the early years after my mother's death, Walken made one of his only other statements on my mother's death, saying, "The people who are convinced that there was something more to it than what came out in the investigation will never be satisfied with the truth. Because the truth is, there was nothing more to it. It was an accident."

My mother no longer has a voice of her own, but I do, and this is what I know to be true. My mother was not a tragic, doomed person. She was vibrant. Her life was devoted to her art, her children, her husband, and her heart. This is how she would want to be remembered, not as someone who is defined by her death, but by her life.

# Epilogue

As soon as she was old enough, Clover and I began to watch my mother's movies together. Just as my mom had watched me watching her in *Miracle on 34th Street*, I watched Clover watching my mother in the same film.

My five-year-old daughter sat in front of the TV, observing closely as tiny Susan Walker pulled skeptically on Santa's beard.

"Mama, she's my grandma?"

"Yes, Clover. That's her as a little girl," I tell her.

"She kind of looks like me," Clover replies.

Clover takes after Barry in that she is tall for her age. She has pale blond hair and green eyes. But she has a nose and profile that are 100 percent my mom and me.

Clover loves to watch Grandma Natalie's films, especially *West Side Story*. Her favorite part is the "I Feel Pretty" number, although she calls it "Maria and her friends." She knows all the words to the song. Clover also loves *The Green Promise*, a picture my mother made when she was ten, the same film where she fell from the bridge and got the bump on her wrist. In the film, my mother plays a rural tomboy who loves animals, just as she did in real life. Clover loves animals too, so she really connects with seeing her grandmother on a farm surrounded by lambs and cows and horses.

When I watch my mother's movies now, I'm filled with pride and the deep desire to protect her. *What is this feeling?* It didn't take me long to recognize it as maternal love. When I see my mom on-screen, I feel like I'm her parent and she's my daughter, and not the other way around.

My love for my mom these days is a lot like my love for Clover; I want to do right by them both. The mother-daughter cycle continues, and sometimes the barriers blur again, as they did when I was a child. Who is the mother, and who is the daughter? We are still entwined, mother and child. Except that I am her protector now. I did not know that I would feel this way.

I study my mom on the screen like an anthropologist, searching her face for clues about who she was, who she might have been today. In *Gypsy*, I see both aspects of her personality: the regular person backstage and the charismatic entertainer onstage. That's just how I remember her. In a split second, she could switch from being my Mommie to a glamorous movie star. She could be intimate and cozy, cooing, "Natooshie, do you want a glass of Ovaltine?" and giving me a warm hug. Then suddenly the cameras would click and she was Natalie Wood, the ravishing beauty with the dark, soulful eyes.

My daughter knows all about her grandmother, who she was, when she died, and how much we miss her. I want the two most important people in my life, my mother and my daughter, to have a relationship.

And Clover! How I wish my mom could meet this daughter of mine, her granddaughter. I marvel at Clover's beauty, her light, her humor. This child was born a happy girl. As she grew, her personality emerged, determined and strong-willed like her grandma.

Clover is a Gemini, ruled by Mercury, the planet of communication. From the moment she was born, she was intent on expressing herself. She communicated with sounds and body language and her eyes before she had words. When we began to read books to her, words became her thing. She couldn't get enough of them. She spoke clearly and with intent from a young age. At three and a half she told me, politely but firmly, to please take the purple rug out of her room and all the dresses out of her closet. She likes pants and sneakers, basketball and skateboarding. Clover has a crystal-clear conviction about who she is.

My sister Courtney is a big part of Clover's life. Courtney is in a good place these days; she has been clean for four and a half years at the time of this writing. She finally realized she loved her life and her family more than she loved drugs. Not long after Courtney turned the corner with her addiction, Kilky had a heart attack on her ninetieth birthday. She always said she wanted to live to be ninety. Our beloved Kilky made her exit peacefully, surrounded by all her family and ours: Katie, my dad, Courtney, me.

Now my sister takes things day by day. She lives in Nashville with her best friend Alex and her dog Winnie. Since Courtney has come back into our lives, she has forged her own connection with Clover—one that has nothing to do with me, and everything to do with their shared love of music and mischief. Courtney still has a childlike way about her that entrances Clover.

"When is Courtney coming over, Mama? Can Courtney have a sleepover soon?"

Courtney is allowed to brush the tangles out of Clover's hair (they share the same blond locks). Unlike me at that age, Clover doesn't seem to mind. Courtney gave Clover her first pair of roller skates. Courtney and Clover are the ones in the kitchen eating Popsicles on a hot summer day, whispering funny stories in each other's ears.

Courtney and I often talk about our mom when Clover is around. Last year, on the evening before Mother's Day, I was giving Clover her nightly bath. That weekend, Courtney was staying over and so she came into the bathroom to sit with us. Clover was five at the time.

The conversation turned easily to Grandma Natalie. Courtney and I began to speculate on how different our lives might have been had our mom lived.

"I just can't imagine what it would have been like to have a champion all these years," Courtney said. "She could have helped us to figure out what we were going to do with our lives, babysat Clover, made fun of Daddy."

"I know she would have loved email and cell phones . . . Instagram," I point out. "She was such a great letter writer and communicator. I'm sure she would have written her own book by now."

What would the world be like if my mom were still in it? Would she have continued to work as an actor as she matured? Some of her best acting performances may have been ahead of her for all we know. Before she died she was veering into writing, directing, and producing. Would she have put her acting career on pause as she moved behind the camera? If she were alive today, would she have lent her voice to the moment? Would she have come out in support of the Me Too movement, speaking honestly about her brushes with powerful, lascivious men when she was a young girl in Hollywood? I know she would have been at the forefront of demanding equal pay for women as she was throughout her life.

What about the little things? Would Courtney and I have a standing yoga or Pilates class that we would take with her? Would we meet at La Scala for chopped salads? Would we hike together in the Santa Monica Canyon? How much mother-daughter therapy would we have had? How would she have evolved as she aged? Would she have let her hair go gray and embraced her wrinkles, or had Botox or even a face-lift? Would she still paint her eyes chocolate brown?

Would my parents live on Canon Drive or would they have moved to the East Coast? My mom loved the city, with its theaters, museums, and glittering lights. She thought the combination of New York City and a place in upstate New York would have been a good fit for our family. My parents always said New York was a lucky city for them.

Would my mom and R.J. have worked out any wrinkles in their relationship and gone the distance? As I write this, my dad is on the verge of turning ninety. He lives most of the year in Aspen now. His voice is as robust and commanding as ever. He walks a little more slowly, but his mind is still open and seeking. We speak on the phone daily. We talk about my sisters, what animals he may have seen that day on his drive into town—a herd of buffalo, deer, maybe a fox. My dad has always loved nature and animals and he is happiest living among them. If I have a question about my mom, a certain period of time, a funny story I heard about her, he is there to clarify, or just to reminisce. Not long ago, I sent him the latest round of home movies that we had transferred to digital, including their windswept wedding on the *Ramblin' Rose*, my dad looking so dapper in a white turtleneck and navy jacket, my mom a vision of femininity in her lavender wedding dress.

"Jesus, Natasha, what a long time ago all that was," he says. "What a great life we had, huh? Nat was so beautiful—and look at the way she looked at you. God, she loved you."

Time has not dulled the pain in his eyes or his voice when he talks about losing our mom. It is not an exaggeration or a cliché to say that a part of him died along with her that night. "If it hadn't been for you and Courtney and Katie, I wouldn't have made it," he has said to me. I am grateful every day he found love again with Jill. They are a team, they take care of each other, they protect one another.

How would my mom's friendship with Daddy Gregson have deepened as they both aged? My darling dad was diagnosed with Parkinson's disease in his eighties and passed away in August 2019, after a brave battle with the illness. Despite his frail and compromised health in his final years, his mind remained sharp, his noble humor intact. For my entire life he had always been just a phone call or a flight away. Each time I called him, his voice would rise up an octave—"Hello, darling! Hello, Natasha!"—sounding so delighted to hear from me. I miss his crinkly eyes that laughed and cried at the same time, the stories around his dinner table, his gameness for fatherhood and life.

How would Courtney and I be different if our mom had lived? Would we have grown into young women who were confident in our abilities to travel far from home, graduate from college, pursue challenging careers and stable relationships? Would Courtney have skipped over her addictions and jumped right to being the grounded person she has become? Would I have felt that I needed to follow my mother into a career as an actor? I might have stayed in college and studied literature or art, perhaps even lived in Europe. Would all of life's hills and valleys have been easier for us to navigate? I have to believe that my mother's strengths would have made an immeasurable impact on all of us as we matured—me, my dad, Courtney, Katie,

Mart, and our whole extended family. Our lives would have stayed intact, instead of being smashed into a million pieces and scattered in the wind. My dad's life would not be marred by trumped-up scandals and accusations.

In the early hours of Mother's Day 2017, I dreamed that my mother returned to me. Someone told me that she was in the next room. I was nervous to see her. I was a grown-up now—so different from when she last saw me. Would she remember me; would she like me?

There was my mom, looking beautiful in a pale purple 1970s ensemble. She wore her gold Elsa Peretti heart-shaped hoop earrings and a scarf tied around her head. Her eyes were made up with her signature dark eyeliner. She smiled her familiar smile, but she was timid and slightly reserved with me. Our conversation was polite. I wanted her approval and to feel our mother-daughter bond. She seemed distant. There were so many questions I wanted to ask her, so much to say. "Mommie, you can't believe how many times Daddy and Jill made Courtney and me go to the UK in the eighties!" She laughed her sweet maternal laugh. "Oh, Natooshie," she said, and folded me in her arms. In the dream, there were no goodbyes, just a feeling of connection.

Sometimes, on a rainy morning, I can still hear her voice talking to my dad. I close my eyes and we are back on Canon Drive. The sky is dark and gray; fat drops of rain make tracks down the windows. My mom sits on her bed in her white flannel nightie. My dad is walking in and out of the room, to and from his closet down the hall, getting dressed to go to work on *Hart to Hart*.

"R.J., it's raining so hard," she says. "Don't you think the girls should stay home from school today?"

"Whatever you think, Nat." He would often readily agree with anything she said.

What was it about the rain that made her afraid for us to go to school? Was she worried that we would catch a cold? That our feet would get wet at recess? Was it the drive that seemed dangerous?

I will never know the answers to these and a million other questions.

Not a day has gone by since I lost her that I haven't wished she were back, even if just for a few minutes. I will never again feel her warmth, her hugs, her hands gently stroking my hair. To resume my life as if I hadn't lost the most important person in it would have been to live an impossible lie. But these are the pieces of my life and this is how I have arranged them.

Last November Barry, Clover, and I were in the backyard as the last rays of late-afternoon sun began to fade. Clover was playing with her Legos; Barry and I were having a glass of wine and listening to country music.

"This music reminds me of Thanksgiving," Clover said, now six years old.

"Really?" I wondered what she meant. "In a good way?"

"Yes. It makes me think of Grandma Natalie. I miss her."

"What do you miss, honey?" I asked her gently.

"I just see so many pictures of her, but I don't know her."

Her eyes searched my face for clues.

"What's her last name?"

"Wood. Her last name is Wood," I say.

# Acknowledgments

Thank you to my alphabet soup of a family.

My sisters, Sarah and Charlotte Gregson, Katie Wagner, Courtney Wagner, and Poppy Wall. My fearless protectors, thank you for your support while I wrote this book and for always picking up the phone when I needed to go over "one more detail . . ."

For your friendship and love: Leif Lewis and Riley Wagner Lewis; Jake Gregson and Emma Webster; Joshua Donen and Nikki Donen; Aunt Mary Scott and Lesley Scott Carr.

My two belle-mères, Julia Gregson and Jill Wagner, both of whom read early drafts and offered guidance and remembrances. I am grateful for your love.

My sister-in-law, Christi Watson. My sweet boys Oliver and Felix Watson. My mother-in-law, Karen Watson.

Unending love and thank-yous to my Daddy Gregson and my Daddy Wagner. I lost Daddy Gregson in the course of writing this book; however, Julia was able to read an early draft of the book to him and he liked what he heard.

I would also like to thank Bernie, Dimitri, and Cara Viripaeff for graciously sharing their memories of my grandmother Baba and my aunt Olga.

Susan Crespo and Blanca Caceres.

Friends who are family: Mart Crowley, Peggy Griffen, Stephana Stander Kamer, Delphine Mann, Alan Nierob, Liz Applegate.

To the dear ones we've lost: Hugo Gregson, Peter Donen, Howard Jeffrey, Ruth Gordon, Norma Crane, George Kirvay, Roddy McDowell, and Willie Mae Worthen (aka Kilky).

My constellation of girlfriends. You are my sisters, my mothers, my confidantes, and I cherish you: Amanda Anka, Nancy Banks, Leah Bernthal, Nevena Borrisova, Stephanie Danan, Dana Delany, Naomi Despres, Heather Heraeus, Tory Johnson, Jessica Kruse, Alexia Landeau, Jane Mass, Michelle McGrath, Maya McLaughlin, Yifat Oren, Jennifer Parsons, Whitney Rosenson, Eve Somer, Molly Stern Schlussel, Lena Wald, Maggie Ward, and Susan Woods.

Lea Journo: thank you, cupid.

Jesse Peretz for taking the time to find "the photo!"

Russell Francis and Elisabeth Wegman for keeping four eyes out for me.

Merritt Loughran, Robin LeMesurier, Michael Cutler, Marc Rona, PDR fulfillment house, and everyone at Natalie Fragrance.

To my teachers and guides: The Sunshine School, Curtis School, Hedgerow School, Crossroads School for the Arts & Sciences, Larry Moss, Tanda Tashjian, Laurie Turner, Mitra Rahbar, Naomi Malin, Mason Sommers, Rami Aizic, Gayle Spitz, Chad Hamrim. Thank you for lighting the way.

Janis Hansen and Tracey Mikolas. Your home was my home. Thank you for holding me close on that awful Sunday and in all the days that followed.

To Sloan DeForest, thank you for your insight and early research.

Thank you to Manoah Bowman for your devotion to my mother and your guidance in rediscovering her. For your stunning archives and your time and generosity in letting me access them.

And to Matt Tunia for transcribing those dusty Super 8s and 16 mms into a veritable wonderland of memories.

To Ali MacGraw, my friend. I love you.

And to Josh Evans for teaching me so much when I was sometimes too young to understand.

To Jeff Briggs for being wise, calm, steady.

To Oscar, Manny, FouFou, Buster, John Wayne, and Willy.

And gratitude to Alexander Friedman for translating my mother's baby book into English.

## ACKNOWLEDGMENTS

To Laurent Bouzereau and Markus Keith for the journey of our documentary, *Natalie Wood: What Remains Behind*, and the friendship we made along the way.

To Hope Edelman and *Motherless Daughters* for naming the thing that I am.

To Pema Chodron, who taught me how to make friends with my suffering.

To Andy Young, excavator extraordinaire.

Lynn Nesbit, extraordinary agent. Grand person. Thank you for your steely guidance and brilliant clarity.

Eve Claxton. Queen of the written word. My friend. Thank you for your invaluable help shaping this story.

Valerie Steiker, my editor, for your tenacity, sensitivity, and insight.

Nan Graham, publisher extraordinaire, and the entire team at Scribner: Colin Harrison, Roz Lippel, Brian Belfiglio, Kate Lloyd, Ashley Gilliam, Sally Howe, Jaya Miceli, Kristen Haff, Erich Hobbing, Kathleen Rizzo, and Stephanie Evans.

Clover, my dearest darling, I love you beyond the beyond.

To Barry, thank you for showing me the good, golden love. Without it this book could not have been written.

Thank you to my mama. Your love made me and saved me.

# Photograph Credits

Interior

Pages 13, 27, 47, 67, 95, 105, 117, 131, 143, 157, 171, 223, 235, 257: Wood-Wagner Private Collection

Page 79: Photo courtesy of Michael Childers

Page 183: October Films, 1997. Courtesy of MPTV

Page 197: Strand releasing, 1998. Photo courtesy of Jesse Peretz

Page 211: Photo by Lara Porzak. Wood-Wagner Private Collection

Page 245: Photo by John Engstead. Courtesy of MPTV

Page 267: Photo by David Schlussel. Wood-Wagner Private Collection

Insert

Page 1: top, Wood-Wagner Private Collection; bottom, courtesy of MPTV

Page 2: top left and bottom, courtesy of MPTV; top right, Wood-Wagner Private Collection

Page 3: top left and right, Wood-Wagner Private Collection; middle and bottom, courtesy of MPTV

Page 4: Wood-Wagner Private Collection

Page 5: Wood-Wagner Private Collection

Page 6: Wood-Wagner Private Collection

Page 7: Wood-Wagner Private Collection, except bottom right, photograph by Jane Mass

Page 8: top, Wood-Wagner Private Collection; bottom, photograph by Clover's father and my husband, Barry Watson

# About the Author

Natasha Gregson Wagner has acted in such films as *Another Day in Paradise, High Fidelity, Two Girls and a Guy*, and David Lynch's *Lost Highway*, and in the television shows *Ally McBeal, House M.D.*, and *Chicago Hope*. In 2016, she coauthored a coffee-table book titled *Natalie Wood: Reflections on a Legendary Life*. She is one of the producers of the HBO documentary about her mother's life: *Natalie Wood: What Remains Behind*. Wagner lives in Los Angeles with her family.